Empires of the Mind

Empires of the Mind

I. A. RICHARDS

AND BASIC ENGLISH

IN CHINA, 1929-1979

Rodney Koeneke

STANFORD UNIVERSITY PRESS
STANFORD, CALIFORNIA

Stanford University Press
Stanford, California
© 2004 by the Board of Trustees of the
Leland Stanford Junior University
Printed in the United States of America

Library of Congress Cataloging-in-Publication Data
Koeneke, Rodney B.

Empires of the mind : I. A. Richards and Basic English in China,
1929–1979 / Rodney B. Koeneke.
   p. cm.
   Includes bibliographical references and index.
   ISBN 0-8047-4822-5 (alk. paper)
   1. Richards, I. A. (Ivor Armstrong), 1893——Knowledge—Language and
languages. 2. Richards, I. A. (Ivor Armstrong), 1893——Knowledge—
China. 3. Richards, I. A. (Ivor Armstrong), 1893——Journeys—China.
4. Richards, I. A. (Ivor Armstrong), 1893——Influence. 5. English
language—Study and teaching—Chinese speakers. 6. English
philology—Study and teaching (Higher)—China. 7. British—China—
History—20th century. 8. Educators—Great Britain—Biography.
9. Critics—Great Britain—Biography. 10. Language and culture—
China. 11. Communication, International. 12. English language—
China. 13. China—Languages. 14. Basic English. I. Title.
PR6035.I337 Z76   2004
828'.91209—dc21   2003011521

This book is printed on acid-free, archival-quality paper

Original printing 2004

Last figure below indicates year of this printing:
13   12   11   10   09   08   07   06   05   04

Designed and typeset at Stanford University Press in 10/13 Palatino

Acknowledgments

In undertaking this study I have had the help of several people. I would like to thank Dr. Richard Luckett for his generous access to the Richards Collection at Magdalene College, Cambridge and for his helpfulness in answering my many inquiries. John Paul Russo offered invaluable encouragement in reading the final manuscript. Michael Jameson kindly shared memories and materials about his father, R. D. Jameson, while John Haffenden allowed me to read portions of his manuscript relating to Empson's period in China. I am also indebted to Thomas Rosenbaum at the Rockefeller Archive Center in North Tarrytown, New York, for his assistance in explaining the Rockefeller Foundation's interests in the Far East.

A Stanford University Fellowship as well as funding from the Harris, Weter and Mellon Fellowship Programs at Stanford helped to make a challenging process considerably less stressful.

Finally, my greatest debt is to Professors Paul Robinson, Paul Seaver and Peter Stansky for their constant encouragement, stimulation and support. It is difficult to imagine three more complementary models of the historian's craft, and I owe a great deal to each one. Working under Peter Stansky's benign guidance in particular has been an education in how to reconcile scholarly rigor with grace.

Contents

Empires of the Mind

1 ⌒ Introduction

I

On February 9, 1950, noted educator and literary critic I. A. Richards boarded a U.S. liner bound for China. He was departing at a particularly inauspicious time. The Communists had recently ousted the Kuomintang, China's ruling party of the last twenty years, leaving the nation's affairs in a state of violent disorder. Hong Kong, Richards's first port-of-call, swarmed with refugees arriving daily from the mainland. Entry permits into China for foreigners were being denied with no official explanation. Reports of famine, civil uprising and revolt in the Chinese countryside filtered to the West from the exodus of residents displaced by the new regime. In Washington, officials fretted over the consequences of a hostile Communist China; five months later, the United States would be at war with North Korea and threatening to use the atomic bomb if the Chinese interfered.

Richards spent the voyage preparing lectures on Homer's *Iliad*. He wrote them in English, as he spoke almost no Chinese, for an audience of Western-language students at Yenching University, just outside Peking. To accompany the lectures he brought copies of the *Iliad* translated into Basic English, a simplified form of the language that he had been working on in China since his first stay over twenty years before. On the face of it, Richards's response seems odd. That the *Iliad*, that most fundamental of Western texts, could have practical value for the Chinese at such a time appears somewhat eccentric, even sinister. It implies an assumption of cultural superiority, evokes a familiar pattern of dominance and interference in Europe's encounters with other cultures. Yet Richards saw his actions in a very different light. The vision informing his lectures on the *Iliad*, and his involvement with China generally, was one of cultural pluralism and communication on a global scale. This study is a history of that vision and the consequences of its application.

I. A. Richards was the leading English literary critic of his time. As a founder of the "Cambridge School" of English in the 1920's, he pioneered a rigorous, analytic approach to literature that sought to ground its principles on a systematic, "scientific" basis. His work in this area is widely considered to be the foundation of modern literary studies. Richards was also one of the first critics to champion literary modernism in Britain: his early advocacy of T. S. Eliot led to a life-long friendship. But his criticism in the Twenties addressed a whole range of postwar concerns. The cultural climate in Britain immediately following the First World War was exceptionally turbulent. For many intellectuals, the world described by Einstein, Freud and Eliot seemed radically different from the one they had known before the war. At the same time, a growing consumer and entertainment industry raised "highbrow" concerns about the direction of contemporary culture.[1] Richards was deeply involved with these issues and debates. His new "science" of criticism was fundamentally an attempt to reconcile the modernist sensibility with an older humanistic tradition—to update Matthew Arnold for a skeptical and scientific age. Borrowing elements from contemporary psychology, linguistics and philosophy, Richards argued for the continued value of poetry primarily as a highly complex form of communication. Readers who are able to respond fully to a poem, he reasoned, learn to perform the kind of intricate mental operations required for dealing with the new "information overload" of modern life. This in turn became for Richards part of a solution to the challenges of modernity that he believed could have global applications.

In 1929 Richards accepted a visiting professorship at Tsing Hua University in Peking. The trip was a watershed in his career. Richards's interests by this time had turned from criticism increasingly to theories of pedagogy. Teaching English literature to Chinese students offered the chance to test the validity of his ideas about reader reception and communication. The misunderstandings Richards encountered at Tsing Hua in the transmission of texts, even among advanced students and professors of English, convinced him that miscommunication was not merely a symptom of debased cultural life in Britain, but a severe world problem. He returned to Cambridge the next year with a new orientation. Over the next fifty years China would occupy a significant place in his work and thought.

While Richards's literary and critical influence has been carefully studied, most accounts of his life tend to neglect the Far Eastern aspect of his career. His impact in Britain in the Twenties is seen as a pinnacle, the growing interests in China and pedagogy as a footnote to his critical work. As one critic describes it, "from the commanding heights, the very center of the cultural debate, [Richards] gradually wandered away—first to China and then to Harvard to work on primary education and linguistics."[2] Less dismissive assessments confirm this opinion in their thin treatment of Richards's period in the East. In an otherwise exhaustive treatment of his intellectual life and work, John Paul Russo's recent biography of Richards devotes just thirty-three pages of its nearly seven hundred to the years in China.[3] The single volume of Richards's letters published in 1990 also includes scant reference to China in a correspondence spanning nearly seventy years.[4] Even *I. A. Richards: Essays in His Honor*, a festschrift assembled in Richards's own lifetime and including valuable reminiscences and interviews, pays virtually no attention to his engagement with the Far East. At best, these sources treat Richards's experience in China as a spur to his thinking about language; more often, as an interlude or diversion in a primarily literary career.

One reason for this oversight is surely that on the surface, Richards's years in the East seem to have been a failure. The *Iliad* did not turn the tide in 1950; some months later, China was firmly Communist and closed to the Western democracies. Over the next decades, a period of radical change in China erased many marks of the pre-war years. At Richards's death in 1979, there seemed little to show for his time there. But given how bright the prospects had once been, and the intimate place that China occupied in his life and thought, the neglect of this period is harder to understand. Richards spent a total of nearly five years in the Far East, most of them concentrated in the 1930's. For the most part he was there in support of Basic English, a streamlined version of the language containing 850 words, including a mere 18 verbs, invented by his close friend and collaborator C. K. Ogden. Basic was intended primarily as an instructional tool for non-native speakers, though Richards and Ogden hoped it would also be of use to English speakers in purifying their language of unnecessary rhetoric and cant. Rooted in the conviction that the First World War was the consequence of a gross breakdown in rational communication, Basic was designed as a logical medium for fostering better understanding between different cultures, while at the same time making scientific and technological knowledge more accessible to other nations. Its ambition and scope epitomized several aspects of Richards's thought. Most important among these was the conviction that language, any language, carries with it sophisticated philosophical propositions embedded in even its simplest words and statements. This made the teaching of English to the Chinese a very high-stakes game. Given the language skills to understand a text like the *Iliad*, even in an attenuated Basic form, Richards believed that the Chinese would have access to a whole range of Western ideas and values. This in turn was to help China in its scramble to modernize and enter an emergent global, industrial economy as an independent player.

Richards's invitation to teach English Literature at a Chinese university in 1929 came at a crucial moment in China's history. The offer itself was a sign of the larger transformations taking place within the country at that time. A century of invasion and imperial maltreatment had convinced many Chinese that major reforms were needed to stop the process of Western exploitation. Toward the end of the nineteenth century, serious efforts began in China to free the country from foreign influence. The Boxer Uprising of 1898–1901 starkly demonstrated the depth of hostility felt toward the Western powers in China, while highlighting the instability of its current regime. In 1911 revolution ousted the centuries-old Ching dynasty and began the tangled process of establishing a national government for China. The end of the First World War sparked further protests across the nation, particularly among students and intellectuals who felt deeply betrayed by Western concessions to Japan at the Paris Peace Conference. One result of these movements was a growing conviction on the part of many Chinese officials and intellectuals that development along Western lines offered the best defense against the humiliation of foreign encroachment.[5] A university like Tsing Hua, founded in 1924, reflected this outlook in its secular curriculum—a significant fact, given Christian missionaries' traditional control of Western education in China—and in its stress on sciences and Western languages. In inviting a literary scholar of Richards's stature, Tsing Hua was making a gesture toward the West that was in turn part of a larger strategy to secure an independent future for China. Given these conditions, an idea like Basic English seemed to many Chinese an ideal solution to their country's problems.

Throughout the 1930's, the period of Richards's greatest activity in China, his hopes for Basic English appeared to be well founded. In 1936 he returned to Peking on a grant from the Rockefeller Foundation, then in the process of extending its own program of economic modernization in China. Enlisting the help of both Chinese and resident Western scholars, Richards established the Orthological Institute of China. Fundamentally an organ for Basic English, the Institute set to work researching language-teaching techniques at both the secondary school and university levels. The Chinese educational system left much of the responsibility for language instruction with the universities, where students were also expected to be reading advanced English texts. Richards felt that structured English teaching should begin much earlier. He began preparing a series of Basic English primers for use in Chinese secondary schools and widening his contacts in the university circles of Peking. When Richards left to teach at Harvard at the end of the year, the Institute was well on the way to developing a comprehensive program of teaching materials for students and instructors.

Back in Peking on a renewed grant from the Rockefeller in 1937–38, Richards and several of his Chinese colleagues were invited to take part in the Nationalist Government's newly formed Committee on Secondary Education. Meeting in the capital at Nanking and including educators from around the country, the Committee was asked to reform the national curriculum for the secondary schools of China. In May 1937, the Nationalist Ministry of Education agreed to adopt Basic English in schools across the country, appointing the Orthological Institute to develop a workable program. This was the culmination of Richards's hopes for Basic in China, and promised to be the beginning of a series of triumphs for Basic internationally. It was also the last and greatest success Basic English was to win.

On July 26, 1937, the Japanese invaded Peking. Richards and his wife Dorothea watched as the trenches were dug in the streets and Japanese planes bombed the city by night. They witnessed the columns of Japanese troops pass in triumph through the city gates, staying in Peking through the initial stages of occupation. The situation for Basic English in wartime China looked nearly hopeless. Low on resources and badly disorganized, the Nationalist government was in no position to make language instruction a priority. But Richards managed to keep the Orthological Institute in operation during the war. In 1938 the combined universities of Peking, under the pressure of Japanese occupation, fled for unoccupied territory in Yunnan, a rural Chinese province over 3,000 miles south-east of Peking and out of range for the moment from Japanese bombs. Here, in the city of Kunming, Richards regrouped the Orthological Institute and, with further support from the Rockefeller Foundation, ensured that its work would continue. Richards himself returned to the United States to take a position at Harvard, where he felt that his efforts on behalf of Basic and the British cause would be more effective. He remained at Harvard for the duration of the war, keeping in contact with the Kunming institute as closely as conditions allowed. In spite of wartime hardships and the worsening fortunes of the Nationalist resistance, reports from the Institute sounded hopeful. The governor of Yunnan was supportive of the Institute's work and promised to adopt Basic in schools across the province in peacetime. With the Nationalist government now based in Yunnan, it seemed possible for Basic to become a model, or "seedbed" as Richards called it, for language instruction in peacetime China.

Peace, however, proved to be elusive. Immediately after the Allied defeat of Japan, civil war broke out in China between the Communists and the Nationalist government. Although the Rockefeller Foundation continued its support for the Orthological Institute, its presence by now was virtually symbolic. Richards shifted his attention to other areas, working on projects for Basic in Latin America and designing a humanities curriculum for Harvard. By 1950 the Communist victory was certain. The nature of the new regime, however, was still unclear. Though the Communists were committed to a program of economic modernization and reform, whether they would look to the Western democracies or to Russia for aid was still an open question, given China's tangled relations with both. In this highly charged political atmosphere, language became a vitally important issue in determining China's position among the Cold War powers. What languages would schools teach under the new government? Would Russian or English become the medium of technical instruction? Were Western languages to fall out of favor at the universities? These issues involved the entire status of China's future relations with the West.

In the spring of 1950, the Western Languages Department of Yenching University invited Richards to Peking to give a series of lectures on English literature and language instruction. Given the uncertain political environment, the gesture was a pointed one. The precise status of universities under the Communists was still in doubt; in spite of talk about trimming foreign languages and increasing the focus on science and engineering, no official changes had yet been made. Inviting Richards to speak was a way of registering approval for continued links with the West. Meanwhile, China's diplomatic relations with the United States and Europe were rapidly deteriorating. In Hong Kong Richards found many Western acquaintances who had been forced to leave the country at the Communist accession. In spite of the offer from Yenching, Richards's own chances of getting an entry permit to the mainland looked slim. After nearly a month of official delays, however, the government suddenly relented and allowed Richards entry, one of the first Westerners permitted to do so for some time.

This fourth stay in China lasted six months. Richards gave courses to English-language students on Communication Theory, Literary Criticism and Shakespeare. The experience was not a particularly encouraging one. Nearly fifteen years of continual war had badly decimated the student body, and Richards found the quality of those who remained sadly low. But he saw his lecturing as a serious chance to turn the tide in the ongoing government deliberations over a new university curriculum. Basic, he felt, might play a valuable role in keeping the channels of cultural exchange open between a Communist China and the Western democracies. This seemed particularly important to Richards given the promising changes he saw taking place under the new regime. After witnessing the corruption and inefficiency of the Nationalist government in the 1930's Richards, like other Western observers, found the Communists a remarkable improvement. Better housing, power and sanitation facilities were in the process of replacing the earlier squalor of Peking. The army, police and other civic officials seemed to function with a new competence and vigor. And most impressive to Richards, former opponents of the Communists were being given generous opportunities to renounce their former "errors" in non-coercive group meetings and re-treats. Although he saw many troubling aspects in the process of transformation, on the whole Richards found the changes encouraging: changes of the kind that he had always hoped Basic English could help the Chinese to make. Compared to Chiang Kai-shek's brutal purges of the universities during the war, in which many of Richards's acquaintances were ousted or killed, the Communists seemed a more humane alternative. Richards left China deeply impressed with their energy, orderliness and apparent preference for persuasion to force. "If the Empires of the future are the empires of the mind," he wrote home jubilantly, "I know who's going to win through."[6]

The cause for Richards's hopes began to evaporate almost before he left. In July 1950, toward the end of his stay, the United States entered into war with North Korea. Richards saw first-hand the panic and hatred that the U.S. intervention inspired in the Chinese; it seemed to verify all the anti-Western propaganda that he had found so objectionable in the new regime. On returning to Harvard in August, he began lecturing for greater tolerance and understanding of the Chinese situation in the face of what he saw as the blind stupidity of U.S. policy. But the political realities of the Cold War soon shut off any opportunities to maintain his contacts with China. Meanwhile, Basic English itself foundered internationally. Following the Second World War, its intentions became suspect to Americans and non-Westerners alike as a vestige of British imperialism, an impression which the sudden enthusiasm of Winston Churchill for Basic in 1943 did nothing to dispel. Ogden also grew increasingly jealous of his creation throughout the 1950's and came to see Richards's efforts on its behalf as a threat to his control of the venture. By the 1960's, the moment for Basic had clearly passed: perhaps nowhere more so than in China, now facing the massive disruption of the Cultural Revolution.

The coda to Richards's involvement in China was an invitation from the Chinese government to undertake a lecture tour in 1979. The offer was a gesture of rapprochement with the West after the tumultuous years of the Cultural Revolution. Richards was 86; against the advice of his doctors, he elected to go. The Chinese treated Richards with great respect and dignity, with old friends and delegations from the universities greeting him at each stop. Again he lectured on methods of English instruction, this time advocating English Through Pictures, a refinement of Basic developed over the years at Harvard.

Within two weeks of his arrival, however, Richards fell seriously ill and had to be hospitalized. On July 15, ten weeks after his arrival, it was decided that he should return to England for treatment. He was immediately flown back to Cambridge, where he died some weeks later. Promoting English in China had been the last undertaking of Richards's career.

II

Given the earlier scope of Richards's ambitions in China and the fate of Basic English generally, it is easy to see why his biographer, John Paul Russo, feels that "China had given Basic its first real defeat, and had given Richards his first defeat along with it."[7] But this rather summary assessment leaves some of the most crucial questions about his involvement in the Far East unasked. What are the factors that condition this kind of judgment? How did China become a field for Richards's ambitions to begin with? What were the historical circumstances that made the Basic project even possible? I would suggest that Richards's experience in China is best understood as an instance of cultural imperialism. For the Basic project was, quite clearly, a product of empire. The circumstances that brought a Cambridge don into a position of influence with Chinese educators and officials depended upon a complex history of colonialism and imperial resistance. It would not have been possible if Britain had not held an empire, or if China had not been forced to react to that empire. The very choice of English as a universal language highlights the historical situation against which Richards's thinking took shape. Perhaps less obviously, the Basic experiment was also dependent upon the cultural milieu that nourished a sensibility like Richards's and a concept like Basic English.

But what makes Richards's career particularly instructive in this regard is that he saw his own cultural project as fundamentally anti-imperial. Basic English, like so much of his thought, was inspired by an international, even "multi-cultural" perspective that bears little resemblance to the familiar imperial mind-set. The First World War had convinced Richards that notions of cultural or national superiority were inimical to world peace, and the years in China deepened his sense of the need for methods of thought that take a variety of perspectives into account. Moreover, many of Richards's insights resemble the theoretical tools used by the most committed postcolonial critics working today. Edward Said, for one, has lauded Richards's theory of Multiple Definition, developed largely through his encounter with China, as "a genuine type of pluralism."[8]

And yet he brings the *Iliad* to China; sets out to modernize the "backward" Chinese; institutes the English language and literary canon in the name of progress—the familiar assumptions of empire. The central question of this study is how someone like Richards could involve himself in a project that looks so suspiciously "imperial" to contemporary eyes. What was it about the period that made the work in China look like the right thing for a committed intellectual such as Richards to do? What were the historical factors, the cultural contexts that shaped his sense of the world situation and made language seem the solution to its problems? What accounts for the initial promise of Basic English in China, and what led to its eclipse? Asking these questions will add to the complexity and depth of our current understanding of the intricate relationship between the intertwining realms of culture and empire.

To frame Richards's story in these terms, it is important to understand the semantic freight they carry today. In his recent study *Culture and Imperialism*, Edward Said summarizes some of the major shifts in the meaning of these two concepts over the last twenty years. Said argues that culture, far from being the disinterested repository of "the best which has been thought and said" that Matthew Arnold so famously imagined, in fact reflected and constituted the ideological assumptions sustaining imperial power. By creating the sense of a unique and essential European identity through novels, travelogues, operas, surveys, scientific investigations and other narrative forms, culture in fact *enabled* empire. Said reasons that "the will, self-confidence, even arrogance necessary to maintain such a state of affairs [as empire] . . . are at least as significant as the number of people in the army or civil service, or the millions of pounds England derived from India."[9] He shows that the assumptions sustaining empire were more widespread than many scholars have supposed, finding in novels like Charles Dickens's *Great Expectations* or Jane Austen's *Mansfield Park*, works that seem to have little explicit concern with matters of empire, a subtle but pervasive engagement with Britain's imperial identity. It is here, in narrative, that Said locates the constellation of attitudes linking cultural productions and imperial behaviors. "The power to narrate," he writes, "or to block other narratives from forming and emerging is very important to culture and imperialism, and constitutes one of the main connections between them."[10]

For the purposes of understanding Richards's encounter with China, three notions of the linkage between culture and empire are particularly relevant. One is the power of language to shape cultural representations. This type of approach is that now familiar to historians as the "linguistic turn." Broadly speaking, this kind of interpretation replaces the Marxist view of history, with its fundamental reliance on material causation, and more traditional forms of cultural/intellectual history, emphasizing the transformative power of ideas, with a model that stresses the primacy of representations. To take one current example from British studies, the notion of "Englishness": a historian of the linguistic turn asks not what English culture or identity *is*—its causes, its essential features, its reality prior to the act of interpretation—but rather *how* the notion of what it means to be English has been represented at different stages in time. In the context of colonial history, this representational understanding of culture radically alters the picture of the imperial enterprise. It shifts the focus of empire from its more traditional sites in barracks, colonial outposts and government offices to surveys, primers, maps, studies, narratives. It centers largely on the *linguistic* domination imperialism exercised in the incessant naming, mapping and legislating of foreign territories and peoples; in the colonizers' insistent control over the means of translation, both of language and of the meanings that languages authorize.

In *Orientalism*, Said's ground-breaking study of Europe's engagement with the Near East, representation through language is the very engine of the imperial process. Claiming that the notion of the East owed less to factual observation than to a set of internally consistent ideas about the "Orient," he shows how Western colonizers were able to produce certain types of knowledge by representing the Near East as essentially different from or "other" than Europe. Seemingly disinterested fields of study—linguistics, history, philology, anthropology—consistently figured the Orient as a passive subject for European discovery and endeavor, a figuring that in turn sanctioned its colonization. The power of these disciplines to represent the East, along with the interlocking web of institutions which sustain them, are part of the process Said calls Orientalism: "a Western style for dominating, restructuring and having authority over the Orient."[11]

The Orientalist process implies another development that bears upon Richards's experience in China: a consciousness of the interests that inform representation. The understanding of culture as a system that perpetuates certain relationships of power brings a corresponding awareness of the voices and interests which that system obstructs. Said defines cultures as "humanly made structures of both authority and participation, benevolent in what they include, incorporate and validate, less benevolent in what they exclude and demote."[12] The focus on differences and particularities that those structures erase informs a great deal of recent work in the humanities. Historians are increasingly sensitive to the divisions of region, class, religion, race and gender that are effaced in negotiating cultural identities such as "Englishness." In the colonial situation, the process is more brutally explicit. Here the silence of the colonized is a precondition of the imperial enterprise. What sanctions Western representations of subject cultures is the assumption that these cultures cannot represent themselves. "Without significant exception," writes Said, "the universalizing discourses of modern Europe and the United States assume the silence, willing or otherwise, of the non-European world. There is incorporation; there is inclusion; there is direct rule; there is coercion. But there is only infrequently an acknowledgment that the colonized people should be heard from, their ideas known."[13] In its exclusive control of representation through cultural forms such as language, narrative, laws and institutions lies the power of the colonizer to subject and maintain empire.

This notion of exclusion leads some critics to take the enforced silence of the colonial subject as a starting point for their recovery of native voices. Homi Bhabha and Gayatri Spivak, for example, look to the gaps, obfuscations, contradictions and breaks in the written records *of* empire for traces of resistance *to* empire. In the "problems" and ellipses of imperial narratives these scholars find the signs of those groups systematically excluded from the authorized cultural narrative, worrying the record by their presence and defiance. In Bhabha's work on the Indian Mutiny, for instance, the "mystery" of circulating chapati bread carried between villages—a phenomenon that the official chronicles of the Mutiny are unable to account for— becomes the key to unlocking an entire pattern of peasant solidarity and resistance.[14] A similar spirit informs the practice of the Subaltern Studies group, which reads the history of peasants or the "lower orders" in the colonial situation from the disjunctions and omissions of the authorized sources.[15]

The notion of subjects left outside or at the margins of culturally authorized narratives constitutes a third crucial aspect of the relationship between culture and imperialism: the necessity of imagined opposites. On this view, identity requires the representation of an opposite against which to define itself. To return to the case of England, Linda Colley has shown how being "English" by the eighteenth century was largely a matter of not being Catholic; an exclusionary definition that subsumed other differences of dialect, region, class or sect within the polarity of religion. In the Orientalist example, Said holds that "the insistence upon the essential opposition of Orient and Occident" bolstered the European project there, a project by which "Europe gained in strength and identity by setting itself off against the Orient as a sort of surrogate and even underground self."[16] What sanctions imperial behavior in this case is the cultural narratives that systematically represent willed or constructed categories such as East and West, colonizer and colonized, as essential, unchanging binary oppositions. In reaction, postcolonial scholarship tries to circumvent dialectical modes of thinking with a notion of cultural hybridity. "[W]e have never been as aware as we are now," Said writes, "of how oddly hybrid historical and cultural experiences are, of how they partake of many often contradictory experiences and domains, cross national boundaries, defy the police action of simple dogma and loud patriotism."[17] Homi Bhabha's recent volume of essays takes up the same point to argue that hybrid forms of identity, in refusing to conform to any one of the binary and essentializing terms through which cultural power operates, are a means of resisting the power of such categories.[18] The insistence upon the mixed or hybrid nature of cultural identities in these scholars is a response to a long experience of Western pronouncements about the "true" nature of subject peoples and territories, and is part of an attempt to break the circuit of cultural and imperial power.

These elements of the culture/empire equation—language, the silenced and the oppositional other—are relevant to Richards's story because his project in China intimately involved each one, though in ways that postcolonial scholarship may not be able to fully account for. As a theorist of language, he was exceptionally alert to its power in creating our categories of thought. Richards saw the First World War as a tragic consequence of mistaking artificial divisions for essential ones, an error produced by a crucial misunderstanding of language. From his first book, *The Meaning of Meaning*, published in 1923, to his last lectures in China, he insisted upon the instrumental nature of language, its status as a human tool for structuring perception. Like many intellectuals today, he hoped this insight would lead to a questioning of the limits that language imposes. These linguistic ideas carried over to his project in the Far East. If imperialism depends upon the silence of the colonial subject, Richards's promotion of English was certainly intended to give the silenced a language to speak. He believed that bringing the *Iliad* to China would give access to Western categories of thought manifest in its language. This in turn would allow the Chinese to represent themselves in a Western humanistic discourse from which their culture had been previously excluded. Richards saw this as opening a process of interaction from which Europe and the United States would benefit as well. In *Mencius on the Mind*, the book that resulted from his first trip to China, he discussed techniques for bringing Eastern modes of interpretation to bear on the problems of traditional Western philosophy. Finally, Richards went to China with no notion of an "essential" Orient, different from and inferior to the West. In fact, as we will see, his refusal to acknowledge any fundamental differences in Chinese ways of thinking blinded him to many of the very real cultural and political realities that separated China from Europe. His insistence upon the artificial nature of oppositions such as East and West was in marked contrast to the essentialist divisions that drive the imperial process. Richards's later ideas about the interdependence of categories that present themselves as opposites, partly inspired by his experience in China, in fact has a strong affinity with the postcolonial notion of the hybrid.

And yet his China was to a large extent an imagined East. Richards was not a sinologist, and his efforts to learn Chinese were never more than dilettantish. The elements he found most appealing in the culture—its pacifism, its civility, its taste—bore the distinct marks of Cambridge in the Twenties. It also represented to some degree an escape from intellectual pressures in England. Richards's cultural criticism of the West deeply informed his picture of China; his praise of its culture and people often betrayed a frustration with developments in Europe and the United States. The sheer size of the country was an attraction, appealing to Richards as a vast field for the application of his linguistic ideas. It seemed a place where modernization might be done "right," with forethought and conscious planning, avoiding the pitfalls that had bedeviled the West. Although the kind of East Richards imagined differed widely from the imperial model, it was to some extent a product of his own desires and interests, and as such it reflects the culture of its time.

The point of this study is not to bring Richards to trial before the bench of contemporary theory. Rather, I want to argue that his ambiguous role in the imperial enterprise complicates our notions of the interaction between culture and empire. What seems to be at stake in the work of postcolonial scholars like Said, Spivak and Bhabha is the possibility of getting outside of oneself, of gaining some critical distance from the patterns of thought by which culture and history shape the individual. As Said writes in *Orientalism*:

> If it is true that no production of knowledge in the human sciences can ever ignore or disclaim its author's involvement as a human subject in his own circumstances, then it must also be true that for a European or American studying the Orient there can be no disclaiming the main circumstances of his actuality: that he comes up against the Orient as a European or American first, as an individual second. And to be a European or American in such a situation is by no means an inert fact. It meant and means being aware, however dimly, that one belongs to a power with definite interests in the Orient, and more important, that one belongs to a part of the earth with a definite history of involvement with the Orient almost since the time of Homer.[19]

If this is true, it leaves little possibility for change. It implies that an enterprise like Richards's, whatever his intentions, was in a sense doomed in advance by a structure of cultural and imperial domination. And yet there must be some way to account for the fact that a figure like Richards was able to see himself as an opponent of imperialism with just as much certainty as a Said or a Bhabha does today. Richards's time in China involves the question whether a critical stance outside a given structure of power or interests is possible for an individual within that culture. The contradictions of his project may thus point to a contradiction in the postcolonial agenda generally, its theories about the power that culture wields outstripping its desire for change. Was Richards then an imperialist or a champion of cultural hybridity? The answer—an appropriately hybrid one—is both, and in examining his experience in China I hope to show the limits and possibilities that his historical situation provided.

Ultimately, the purpose of this study is not simply to fit Richards to a convenient moral rubric, its points fixed in advance. On the contrary, I began it with the desire to restore some of the nuance and complexity of Britain's imperial relations, a complexity that at times runs the risk of being lost as our understanding of imperialism continues to expand. One consequence of the new appreciation of the role that knowledge and information play in a larger system of colonialist control is that it has become easier to make *a priori* judgments about historical players' perspectives and intentions. As the emphasis in historical studies shifts from individuals to the linguistic and cultural structures that condition them, it becomes tempting to use the wealth of new theoretical models at our disposal as ever more elaborate ways to identify the "bad guys." At its most extreme, the move from intentions to structures can hamper the ability to distinguish in any meaningful sense between, say, an I. A. Richards and a Cecil Rhodes: both ultimately become products (and beneficiaries) of a particular field of power relations in which the key moves are determined in advance of their actions or intentions. I was concerned to see the definition of imperialism grow so broad that *any* attempt to promote one's ideals or reform an apparent injustice might automatically be labeled an act of imperial control, foreclosing a deeper analysis of their actual content. Teaching the British Empire at Stanford confirmed my sense that the current direction in imperial studies, sophisticated as it is at the scholarly level, can translate to students as a license to tar anyone on the British side of the colonial divide with the identical brush. I began to wonder if, armed with our powerful twenty-first-century theoretical tools, useful as they are, we might also be liable to a certain imperialism of our own: a colonization of the past that erases the very real differences in values, identity and belief structures that stand between ourselves and the inhabitants of Britain's imperial centuries. As British studies, particularly in North America, weds itself more closely to the larger story of the empire, it seemed vital to me that story should become infinitely more, not less, complex.

Richards seemed an ideal candidate for testing the limits of contemporary orthodoxies about Britain and its empire. A Cambridge pacifist and intellectual democrat whose theories depended upon a belief in the liberating powers of individual reason, funded by an American foundation at a time when the United States was stoutly opposed to Britain's imperial ambitions, Richards was worlds away from the kind of jingoistic empire-builders that one generally associates with the colonialist enterprise. Yet as I discussed my research with friends and colleagues, I could see the flags go up when I described Richards's project. Richards's ambitions in China had all the markings of a scheme to reform the world in Britain's linguistic image; my attempts to explain that his enterprise was more intricate and conflicted than it looked from the face of it did little to ally their suspicions. It seemed increasingly important and challenging to understand Richards's ideals from his own point of view as an interested historical actor. Framing the study in this way would not mean forgoing the kind of rigorous critical analysis that historians bring to their sources, but rather applying it to the China that Richards actually saw, or believed he was seeing, rather than the one we might want him to have seen. In this way, I hoped to make sense of some of the apparent contradictions of his project. How did Richards square a desire for world peace with a plan for world English? How could he see himself simultaneously as an apostle of progress and a harbinger of the dangers of Western science? Balance the need he perceived for reform in China with his respect for its cultural splendors? The best answer to these questions seemed to lie in an attentiveness to Richards's own version of his observations, convictions and motives. Accounting for the complexities and obvious tensions inherent in the Basic English "moment" meant recovering the particular angle of vision out of which Richards's hopes for it grew.

To a large extent, the decision to reconstruct the dramatic transformations which occurred in China and the West during the years of Richards's Basic enterprise from the evidence of his diaries, letters and published writings reflects the kind of questions I asked about the way we narrate the history of British imperialism. It also reflects my own limitations. British historians of the future will no doubt read a number of languages in addition to English (many already do) as the history of Britain is increasingly folded into that of the empire which for so long gave it its meaning. I read no Chinese, and speak about as much as my subject did. As a consequence, the enormously important story of Chinese reactions to Richards's efforts, as well as to those of the Rockefeller Foundation and other Western institutions in China during the tumultuous years between the Ching Dynasty and Mao's Revolution, can only be hinted at here. The excellent work done by scholars like John Israel or Jonathan Spence, both of whose interpretations tremendously enriched my own, offer an account of many of the same events from a Chinese perspective with more depth and expertise than I can provide in this monograph.[20] It is my hope that the present study will contribute to a more complete history of the cross-cultural encounters between China and the West during the modern period.

One great advantage of considering Richards's own construction of events in China is that it helps us to reconstruct an important aspect of Britain's dealings with other cultures, one that holds true across the entire spectrum of imperial relations. Richards's work in China reminds us how easy a matter it was for a Briton in his position to live comfortably within his own conceptions of the East, even when the realities of Chinese life seemed to challenge his ideals. Writers like George Orwell and E. M. Forster have brilliantly exposed the hermetic world of the British club in parts of the empire like Burma and India, an institution whose dull routines and strategic exclusions served to separate the British—physically, socially and, wherever possible, sexually—from the peoples they ruled. The club imposed distance in the face of a potentially dangerous proximity; for Forster and Orwell, it enforced the social cohesion necessary to maintain the divide between sovereign and subject. By analogy, Richards's experience reminds us that the club could exist as a state of mind as well. Richards's distance from some of his colleagues and rivals, judging from the record he left in his diaries and correspondence, was at times remarkable. In part, his remoteness from the realities that threatened Basic's success in China was temperamental. Richards's idealism was unrelenting throughout his career, and he always regarded Basic's fortunes in China as just one part of his wider global vision. As a result, he could be surprisingly indifferent to the personal situation of his various colleagues, both Western and Chinese, often measuring their value in relation to the work they contributed to his Orthological Institute. Victor Purcell, head of the British Protectorate of Chinese in Malaya who traveled with the Richardses during their flight from Peking to Yunnanfu, remembered Richards's unusual aloofness in the face of crisis, rivaled only by that of his student

William Empson, who did math problems to kill time during Japanese bombings along the way.[21]

But Richards's distance also conforms to a broader (and not exclusively British) pattern of removal from regional exigencies that might preclude desired reforms. His experience in China reminds us that the "empire of the mind" was in part a mind-*set* which, however well intentioned, often made it difficult to appreciate local obstacles. Objections to Basic tended to be dismissed as wrongheaded, doubts as inefficiencies, hesitations as a symptom of bureaucratic inertia. While Richards's comments on individual Chinese are remarkably free of cultural stereotyping, and his harshest criticisms of Chinese culture as a whole were most often the result of pique, he also showed little interest in penetrating more deeply into local conditions where doing so threatened to slow his work. I have tried to recapture this particular aspect of his encounter with China by giving to certain colleagues and competitors the narrative weight that Richards accorded them, just as I have retained Richards's spelling of Chinese names. In doing so I hoped to convey something of the air of privileged aloofness which Richards enjoyed as an Englishman abroad.

A word on the sources. Much of the surviving correspondence we owe to Richards's wife, Dorothea. A fascinating figure in her own right who deserves a separate study, she recorded in the pages of the common diary she shared with her husband Ivor invaluable records of meetings, conversations and impressions along with those passages from their letters she felt were of special importance. Where the original document doesn't survive, Dorothea's historical instincts saved many key exchanges for posterity; several of Richards's letters cited here exist in her own writing on the back covers of the diaries and reflect her sense of what was worth remembering. Her editorial hand is a distinct if not always immediate presence in the history that follows.

Richards's story begins at Cambridge University. The inspiration for an international form of English first came to him and Ogden on Armistice Day 1918, as medical students looted Ogden's shop for his outspoken criticism of the war. The First World War and its effect on Britain's cultural life form the context for Richards's thinking about language and culture. Chapter 2 details the importance of this period in shaping the ideas that he later brought to China. Richards's literary theory and cultural critique during his time at Cambridge deeply informed his project in the East, while earlier Cambridge commentators on China such as Bertrand Russell and Goldsworthy Lowes Dickinson influenced his own sense of the possibilities for China's future. Chapter 3 examines Richards's first year at Tsing Hua, analyzing the reasons for his attraction to life in China and considering some of the difficulties in communication he encountered there. Chapter 4 provides an account of Basic English and Richards's growing hopes for its application in China. He returned to Peking in 1936 with the support of the Rockefeller Foundation. The activities and agenda of this institution, and its motives for funding a Basic English program in China, is crucial to understanding Richards's successes in the following year. Chapter 5 describes the events leading to the foundation of the Orthological Institute of China in 1936, the main organ of the Basic movement, and outlines its initial reception in China, culminating in the Chinese Ministry of Education's offer to help draft a revised national curriculum that would include Basic English.

Chapter 6 concerns the fate of the Orthological Institute during the war years. Despite the Japanese invasion, Richards and his colleagues continued their work in China under increasingly difficult circumstances with the hope that Basic would be useful in peacetime. I chart the changing fortune of Basic through the vicissitudes of war, exile and political unrest, tracing the local events and broader historical circumstances that gave it shape. The growing politicization of English in China during the final years of the war changed the nature of Richards's project and pointed the way for the obstacles Basic would encounter during the Cold War. Richards's penultimate visit to China in 1950 forms the subject of Chapter 7. Following the recent Communist victory over the Nationalists, his three-month stay in Peking allowed him to assess the relative merits of the new regime and its prospects for the nation's future. It was on this visit that he witnessed the Chinese reaction to the outbreak of the Korean War, and began to realize the obstacles that the Cold War would present to an international project like Basic. Chapter 8 offers a brief account of Richards's last visit to China in 1979 and a final assessment of his Far Eastern career.

The story of Richards's time in Asia involves some of the major developments of the twentieth century. The period of his engagement with China was a volatile one in both Europe and the Far East. When Richards first arrived in Peking, northern warlords were fighting in territorial skirmishes reminiscent of Confucius's time. Fifty years later, he came at the invitation of a Communist government to signal the re-opening of relations with the West after the Cultural Revolution. In the years between, through war, occupation and political instability, China made the first crucial steps from a traditional agrarian society to a major world power. Britain's role also changed dramatically over this period. Before the First World War, the British held an empire and still dominated an increasingly competitive world economy. By 1950, the year of Richards's voyage to Communist China, Britain had relinquished much of its former empire and ceded economic preeminence to the United States. Richards's career involved him to varying degrees in the affairs of China, Britain and the United States, and the account of his experience in the Far East includes the history of this global transformation as well. Aside from the published works of Richards and his colleagues, my primary sources are Richards's diaries and correspondence, located at Magdalene College, Cambridge University, and the reports and correspondence available at the Rockefeller Foundation archives in North Tarrytown, New York. Because of Richards's distaste for biography, this study is among the first to make a thorough use of Richards's diaries in accounting for his motives and activities in China.

"If the Empires of the future are the empires of the Mind, I know who's going to win through." Richards's assessment of the Communist regime applies to his own project as well. It captures something of the ambivalent nature of his work in China, expressing his belief in pacifism and the powers of persuasion, the necessity of communicating and convincing, but also his desire to influence, change minds, institute the ideals and values of his culture. If Basic in the end didn't "win through," Richards was surely right in seeing the empire of the future as one of minds, growing exponentially as new information technologies expand the parameters of cultural influence and exchange. The study of Richards's time in China is thus a rich starting-point for understanding the postcolonial complexities of our own.

2   ☞ The Cambridge Background

I

I. A. Richards was arguably the most influential literary critic of the 1920's. Along with T. S. Eliot, whose critical essays began to appear in the same decade, Richards's writings helped to define a new sensibility in the years following the First World War. In his memoir *Lions and Shadows*, Christopher Isherwood gives a vivid picture of Richards's impact on the age. Describing the effect of his lectures upon students like himself at Cambridge in 1926, Isherwood writes:

> To us, he was infinitely more than a brilliant new literary critic: he was our guide, our evangelist, who revealed to us, in a succession of astounding lighting flashes, the entire expanse of the Modern World. Up to this moment, we had been . . . romantic conservatives, devil-worshippers, votaries of "Beauty" and "Vice," Manicheans, would-be Kropotkin anarchists, who refused to read T. S. Eliot . . . or the newspapers, or Freud. Now, in a moment, all was changed. Poets, ordered Mr. Richards, were to reflect aspects of the World-Picture. Poetry wasn't a flame, a fire-bird from the moon; it was a group of interrelated stimuli acting upon the oracular nerves, the semi-circular canals, the brain, the solar plexus, the digestive and sexual organs. It did you medically demonstrable good, like a dose of strychnine or salts. We became behaviourists, materialists, atheists. In our conversation, we substituted the word "emotive" for the word beautiful; we learnt to condemn inferior work as a "failure in communication"; or more crushing still, as "a private poem." We talked excitedly about the "phantom aesthetic state."
>
> But if Mr. Richards enormously stimulated us, he plunged us, also, into the profoundest gloom. It seemed to us that everything we had valued would have to be scrapped. . . . We were banished from that world forever.[1]

Isherwood's account highlights some of the more salient qualities of Richards's work in the 1920's: its anti-aestheticism, its emphasis on art as communication, its recourse to scientific, even physiological, explanations of artistic response. Above all, Isherwood captures the almost missionary fervor of Richards's essays at the time. His brand of Modernism seemed more than a new aesthetic; it involved a kind of ethical conversion, a rejection of traditional literary terms and values in favor of a world-view in which poetry played an active, therapeutic role. This chapter will examine how Richards's style of literary criticism, developed in the atmosphere of interwar Cambridge, led to the enterprise in China.

Richards's thought has been closely evaluated and criticized in several other studies.[2] How his poetics connect with his work in China has been less carefully considered. In a 1990 review in the Times Literary Supplement, Jonathan Culler observed: "There are thus, in Richards's career, two stories: the account of what he achieved in literary studies, which calls for critical evaluation, and the tale of the activities that took him away from literary criticism."[3] The problem with Culler's assessment is that it overlooks the ties between Richards's literary ideas and his Far Eastern experience. By separating his criticism from his Basic work, Culler's division ignores the underlying relationship between Richards's literary, cultural and international activities. To what extent did Richards's poetics inspire his work in China? Why did his linguistic interests lead to a program for global English? How did his literary theories evolve into concerns with modernization abroad? In short, what are the connections between Richards's literary and political activities?

In approaching these questions, this chapter examines three aspects of Richards's experience at Cambridge in the 1920's. The first section considers his ideas about language and literature from the publication of *The Meaning of Meaning* in 1922 to *Practical Criticism* in 1929—the last book he wrote before his first extended visit to China. A close examination of Richards's writings over this period indicates that his interest in the Far East did not represent a break with his critical career, but rather formed a logical extension of his literary theories. In its stress on communication, readers' responses and the salvific effects of literature, his work in the 1920's anticipates his later concerns with the teaching of English in China.

The second section describes the historical context of Richards's criticism, charting the impact of the First World War and the cultural changes that followed in its wake upon his unique understanding of the relationship between language, literature and culture. Linking Richards's views on modernity to his work in China is his ambivalence about a rising consumer culture and the growing prestige of science. China came to represent for Richards an alternative to the excesses of Western "progress" that he identified in his critical writings of the Twenties, and these concerns strongly colored his perception of the East.

Finally, Richards's picture of China was deeply informed by the particular ideals and values current at Cambridge during his time there. To describe the importance of this background to his understanding of the Far East, the final section examines two other influential Cambridge figures whose interests in China anticipated Richards's own. Goldsworthy Lowes Dickinson, whose writings were a strong influence on Richards as an undergraduate, had a lifelong fascination with China. His *Letters from John Chinaman*, written in 1900 before Lowes Dickinson had visited the country, was a critique of the West written from the perspective of a Chinese observer. In it he expressed many of the values that shaped Richards's own cultural criticism and contributed to his picture of China. Bertrand Russell, a member with Richards of the Cambridge Moral Sciences Club and a friend with the inventor of Basic English, C. K. Ogden, also wrote famously about China following his year-long stay in the country in 1920. Russell's analysis of the virtues and defects of Chinese society in *The Problem of China*, published in 1922, reveals many of the assumptions that Richards would bring to his later interpretation of the East. Lowes Dickinson's and Russell's pacifism, aestheticism and faith in progress defined a distinctly Cambridge-inflected vision of China. An appreciation of this background is crucial for understanding how Richards's literary work at Cambridge relates to his later engagement with China. The transition from Isherwood's Modern "evangelist" to a prophet of English in China was thus in no way an abandonment of Richards's earlier literary concerns, but rather their extension into the realm of global politics. As such, his career represents one of the most significant attempts in the twentieth century to bridge the gap between literature and action, to transform the politics of theory into a pragmatic theory of political action.

II

I. A. Richards was not the first to address wider social and cultural concerns through literary criticism. In rejecting the formalist aesthetic of his day, he was returning to the tradition of Victorian critics like John Ruskin and Matthew Arnold whose writings embraced a wide range of moral and political issues. In fact, it is more often with these Victorian critics than with his Modernist contemporaries that Richards is now identified. As John Paul Russo points out, "the fact that Richards invents his own system and language to convey certain mid-Victorian values should not conceal his deep indebtedness [to those values]."[4] Pamela McCallum credits Richards, along with T. S. Eliot and F. R. Leavis, with "the reinvention of Arnoldian intellectual and moral dimension within literary criticism."[5] More recently, Steven Heath finds Richards "directly echoing Matthew Arnold" in his notion of literature as a modern substitute for religion.[6] But if Richards echoed the substance of Arnold's criticism, he applied it to the concerns of a distinctly different age. In responding to the particular cultural environment of interwar Britain, he developed a theory of literary value that would inform his Basic work in the Far East over the next decades.

In evaluating Richards's work in the Twenties, three themes stand out as particularly relevant to his later activities in China. The first is his insistence upon poetry as, above all, a means of communication. In approaching literature as an instrument for transmitting emotions rather than an occasion for aesthetic rapture, Richards was responding to the emergent linguistic philosophy at Cambridge pioneered by G. E. Moore, a significant influence upon his Bloomsbury contemporaries as well. Richards's emphasis on literature as communication, developed in part through his contact with Moore, forms a bridge between his literary and Basic work. A second theme in his early criticism is the stress upon poetry as everyday experience. Breaking with Paterian ideas of an elevated aesthetic state, Richards reclaimed poetry as a psychological event that, in Isherwood's phrase, "did you demonstrably medical good." This insistence upon poetry's relevance to contemporary social and technological transformations helps to explain Richards's eagerness to put his critical ideas at the service of a more concrete form of action in the Far East. Finally, Richards conceived of poetry as a type of mental training that could equip its readers for the increasingly complex stimuli of modern life. His argument for the necessity of poetry in a scientific age led directly to the conviction that English studies would be useful to a developing modern nation like China. Each of these concerns in Richards's critical work of the Twenties thus answered to the contemporary milieu in ways that anticipate his later ambitions in the Far East.

Although known today primarily as a literary critic, Richards first came to public attention with a work of semiotics. *The Meaning of Meaning*, written in collaboration with C. K. Ogden, contains the essential ideas about language and communication that underpin his writings throughout the Twenties. Umberto Eco has called attention to the "broad interdisciplinary awareness" of Richards and Ogden, whose interests range from Saussurian linguistics and anthropology to the philosophy of Frege, Russell and Wittgenstein.[7] This wide, even eccentric array of influences was deployed toward a coherent theoretical program that deeply informed Richards's subsequent "scientific" approach to literary studies, and eventually to his hopes for a global language.

Central to the book's argument is its authors' case for an instrumental view of language. "Words," they assert, "'mean' nothing by themselves. . . . It is only when a thinker makes use of them that they stand for anything, or, in one sense, have 'meaning'. They are instruments."[8] On this view, words have no innate connection with the things they describe. Richards and Ogden dismiss this age-old notion of the relationship between sign and signified as "Word Magic," an important term in their vocabulary to describe a "verbal superstition" that leads us to attribute false powers to language. Instead, they argue that words acquire meanings through association. Just as the notion that matches cause fire follows from the repeated observation of striking matches, so a word evokes the context in which it is habitually used. By replacing "Word Magic" with a contextual theory of meaning, the authors reduce philosophical disputes to arguments about *words* rather than things. Debates about abstract notions such as Beauty or Truth say less about the nature of reality than they do about the different interpretive habits and associations of the contending parties. Language is ultimately an instrument of human interpretation; a convenient shorthand for evoking a particular experiential context, but not an objective representation of the world.

Tending to obscure this recognition, Ogden and Richards argue, is the fact that we use the same words for a variety of ends. A term like "Good," for instance, can be used to discuss ethics or to describe the weather. To clear up this confusion, Richards and Ogden separate linguistic usage into two distinct categories: the Emotive and the Symbolic. All uses of language, they contend, fall along a scale between these two poles of meaning. They define the distinction as follows:

> The symbolic use of words is statement; the recording, the support, the organization of references. The emotive use of words is a more simple matter, it is the use of words to express or excite feelings or attitudes.[9]

At the extreme end of the symbolic scale they place mathematics, a purely referential language with no evocative content whatsoever. On the other, emotive, extreme they locate poetry, which is concerned exclusively with conveying emotional experiences, or "attitudes," rather than strictly accurate referential truths. Failure to distinguish between these separate but equal linguistic functions accounts for most of the traditional controversies of aesthetics and philosophy. In their view,

> All such terms as Intuition, Intellect, Emotion, Freedom, Logic, Immediacy, are already famous for their power to confuse and frustrate discussion. In general, any term or phrase, 'elan vital,' 'purely logical analysis' . . . which is capable of being used either as a banner or a bludgeon, or as both needs, if it is to be handled without disaster, a constant and conscious understanding of these two functions of language.[10]

The instrumental view of language avoids such confusion by shifting attention from the things that words describe to the end or purpose for which words are used. What is the speaker trying to communicate? What mental associations does he or she want to evoke in the listener? Are words being used with Symbolic or Emotive intent? By seeing language as instrumental rather than descriptive, Richards and Ogden believed they could recast all philosophical error as instances of miscommunication.

In shifting the focus of language theory from the meanings of words to their communicative intent, Richards was responding in part to the influence of G. E. Moore, under whom he had studied at Cambridge. Describing the influence of Moore's insistence upon a microscopically exact discrimination of terms in philosophical debate, Richards later recalled:

> [Moore] shaped me in a thousand ways—*negatively*. I spent seven years
> studying under him and have ever since been reacting to his influence. I
> feel like an obverse of him. . . . He could hardly ever believe that people
> could mean what they said; I've come to think they can hardly ever say
> what they mean.[11]

The contrast with Moore reveals the orientation of Richards's
critical approach throughout his writings of the Twenties. His tendency to see disputes as semantic misunderstandings rather than errors about the nature of reality gave his criticism a strongly utilitarian
slant. What prevents people from being understood, from being able
to "say what they mean"? How can we improve our understanding
of language to avoid such failures of communication? The same questions that motivated Richards's literary inquiry guided his later experiments with English in China.

This interest in the problems of communication resurfaces throughout Richards's critical work in the Twenties. In the *Principles of Literary Criticism*, published a year after *The Meaning of Meaning*, he asserts that "the arts are the supreme form of communicative ability,"[12]
attributing to this quality their power of inducing "a balanced poise,
stable through its power of inclusion."[13] The unique value of poetry
for Richards lies precisely in its ability to transfer emotional states
from artist to audience through the medium of language. A poem, although "a strictly limited piece of experience," is distinguished from
everyday occurrences because "it is communicable. . . . It differs from
many other experiences, whose value is very similar, in this very
communicability."[14] Already Richards was incorporating linguistic
concerns familiar from *The Meaning of Meaning* into his literary criticism. By the time of *Practical Criticism*, published just prior to his departure for China in 1929, he had come to see literature primarily in
terms of his communicative theory. "Poetry itself is a mode of communication," he asserts in the Introduction. "What it communicates
and how it does so and the worth of what is communicated forms the
subject matter of criticism."[15] What follows in the text is an analysis of
student survey responses to various poems which Richards had been
gathering from his lecture classes since the mid-1920's. The protocols
reveal gross misunderstandings and insensitivities to a group of thirteen poems that Richards examines in great detail, ranging in quality
and difficulty from John Donne to Henry Wadsworth Longfellow.
His experiment had a profound influence upon the teaching of poetry

in both Britain and America, where Richards's dissection of a poem in terms of Tone, Feeling, Attitude and Intention dominated the New Criticism for decades. Its significance to the work in China, however, is the way that it shifted the focus of literary criticism from poems to readers, from questions of literary quality to problems of reader comprehension. From here it was a short step to the issues of pedagogy and language training that would absorb Richards in China the following year. The difficulties he encountered among sophisticated readers at Cambridge—"the majority undergraduates reading English with a view to an Honours Degree"—encouraged him to generalize his ideas about communication to include more fundamental questions about language and reader reception.[16] By the time of his trip to China in 1929, Richards's literary work had already led him to many of the concerns that would occupy him during the Basic English years.

A second feature of Richards's literary criticism is his repeated attack upon the prevailing aesthetic formalism in fashion at the time. In defending the value of poetry, Richards discredits Walter Pater's familiar defense of art as "elevated experience," stressing instead its practical uses in a modern, technological society. In the *Principles of Literary Criticism*, he traces a lineage for the "aesthetic" approach to art leading from Kant through Pater to contemporary critics such as Vernon Lee and Clive Bell. The assumption these critics all share, according to Richards, is that aesthetic experiences are distinct from and more elevated than our everyday states of consciousness. He cites Clive Bell's claim in *Art* (1914) that "to appreciate a work of art we need bring with us nothing from life, no knowledge of its ideas and affairs, no familiarity with its emotions" as a "recent extreme statement of the Aesthetic Hypothesis."[17] Richards condemns this "phantom aesthetic state" on the grounds that it separates art from common moral and social concerns. This segregation of art from life is, in his view, all the more dangerous in the face of the accelerated rate of technological change. "Human conditions and possibilities," he writes

> have altered more in a hundred years than they had in the previous ten thousand, and the next fifty may overwhelm us, unless we can devise a more adaptable morality. The view that what we need in this tempestuous turmoil of change is a Rock to shelter under or cling to, rather than an efficient aeroplane in which to ride, is comprehensible but mistaken.[18]

Against this aesthetic escapism, with its notion of an empyrean, unchanging realm of Beauty, Richards provides a more utilitarian defense of literature that borrows heavily from recent science.

In his search for a more scientific basis for literary criticism, Richards makes use of a model of the mind developed by the Cambridge-trained biologist C. S. Sherrington.[19] Sherrington had maintained that the mind is essentially an agglomeration of neurological impulses. He explained human psychological responses in terms of the need for this complex mental system to achieve an equilibrium among competing disturbances. Applying Sherrington's psychology to literary studies, Richards developed what he called a "psychological theory of value" to explain the importance of artistic experiences. At the heart of his psychological approach is the Sherringtonian notion that emotions are primarily *physiological* responses to outward stimuli. "Stimulating situations," he writes in the *Principles of Literary Criticism*, "give rise to widespread ordered repercussions throughout the body, felt as clearly marked colourings of consciousness. These patterns in organic response are fear, grief, joy, anger and other emotional states."[20] In contrast to the aesthetic separation of art from life, he insists that the stimuli a poem presents to our nervous systems are no different in kind from those we meet in everyday experience. If Richards ultimately attributes to art an importance similar to that of his aesthetic opponents, he does so on strictly psychological grounds. Artistic experiences, he maintains,

> are the most formative experiences, because in them the development and systematisation of our impulses goes to the furthest lengths. In ordinary life a thousand considerations prohibit . . . any complete working out of our response. . . . But in the 'imaginative experience' these obstacles are removed. . . . As a chemist's balance to a grocer's scales, so is the mind in the imaginative moment to the mind engaged in ordinary intercourse of practical affairs.[21]

Successful poems are therefore models of how to balance the tangle of stimuli arising from complex experience. The "aesthetic state" as Richards understands it thus has a practical, even therapeutic, utility. Rather than elevating us from the mundane, poetry prepares the mind for the increasingly chaotic impressions of modern life.

Richards returns to the practical effects of poetry elsewhere in his writings of the Twenties. In *Science and Poetry*, first published in 1926, he laments:

> Far more life is wasted through muddled mental organization than through lack of opportunity. Conflicts between different impulses are the greatest evils which afflict mankind. The best life then that we can wish for our friend will be one in which as much as possible of himself is engaged (as many of his impulses as possible). And this with as little conflict, as little mutual interference between different sub-systems of his activities as there can be. . . . And if it is asked, what does such a life feel like, how is it to live through? the answer is that it feels like and is the experience of poetry.[22]

The aim of poetry, then, is to produce "a permanent alteration of our possibilities as responsive individuals in good or bad adjustment to an all but overwhelming concourse of stimulations."[23] As an instrument of equilibrium, aesthetic experience offers a model of how the mind ought to function in the face of complex, varied stimuli. Reading a poem induces attitudes or feelings that guide its audience to a more nuanced approach to everyday experience. Better reading is, quite literally for Richards, an essential step toward better living. The ethical implications of his psychological theory of value are spelled out most clearly in *Practical Criticism*. Significantly, in a closing chapter he describes poetry's effects in terms of Confucius's doctrine of "self-completion" in the *Chung Yung*. Casting Chinese ethics in the language of contemporary psychology, he asserts that human development

> seems to be predominantly in the direction of greater complexity and finer differentiation of response. . . . It is but a step further to conceive of it as also tending to relieve internal strains due to these developments imposed from without. And a reordering of its impulses so as to reduce their interferences with one another to a minimum would be the most successful—and the 'natural'—direction which this tendency would take.

Such a re-ordering would be a partial self-completion.[24]

The closing chapters of *Practical Criticism* indicate how far Richards had pushed the borders of literary criticism in the Twenties. Rather than limiting himself to judgments of aesthetic or literary value, he expanded his concerns over the course of the decade to include elements of psychology, linguistics, reader reception and Chinese ethics. Uniting these interests is a constant preoccupation with the practical value of poetry. In a 1972 interview with John Paul Russo, Richards summarized his critical agenda in the following terms:

> Sooner or later enough discussion of language . . . should mean improvements. What worries me about so much of these discussions is that

they're not practically oriented. My own peculiar slant on language, I think, is that I regard studies in language as, for me, preludes to linguistic engineering.[25]

The orientation of his criticism throughout the Twenties, from the instrumental view of language in *The Meaning of Meaning* to the student protocols of 1929, thus points toward the experiment in "linguistic engineering" he would undertake in China. His departure for Peking in 1929, immediately following the publication of *Practical Criticism*, in no way signaled an abandonment of his literary concerns. Rather, China helped to galvanize the practical imperatives implicit in his criticism since *The Meaning of Meaning*. Far from diverting his critical career, the experience in China would show Richards a way to realize his most deeply held ideas about literature and its value.

III

A final component of Richards's work in the Twenties is his cultural criticism. If Richards's attraction to China was due in part to his literary theory, his account of literary value in turn took shape from the cultural atmosphere of interwar England. The period immediately following the First World War was a time of radical innovation at Cambridge. The influx of returning soldiers swelled the student body from a low ebb of 235 undergraduates in 1916 to 2, 635 by January 1919, a number that would grow to 3, 844 by May.[26] These new students brought a spirit of intellectual enthusiasm to the university that contributed a great deal to the substance and tone of Richards's criticism. "They were just too good to be true," Richards remembered of these incoming veterans. "It was a joy to deal with those people; those who got back to Cambridge from all that slaughter and were back *for reasons*."[27] In the scramble to accommodate the growing student body, some traditional aspects of Cambridge life were forced to change. In 1919 Richards was invited to become a lecturer in the newly created department of English studies, giving courses on the principles of literary criticism as well as the contemporary novel, until then not considered a suitable object of academic study. Richards initially lectured "on approval," receiving fifteen shillings for any student who came to his class at least three times.[28] His courses were soon among the most popular at the University, attracting students eager to learn about the latest developments in modern literature.

Over the next decade Richards took an active part in shaping the relatively young program of English studies at Cambridge, becoming one of the gifted amateurs who set the tone for the "Cambridge School" of literary criticism.[29]

In addition to changes within the university, developments in the wider culture also claimed Richards's attention and were reflected in his criticism. A concern with the accelerated growth of mass culture, aided by technological "advances" such as cinema and radio, along with doubts about the rising prestige of science at the expense of literature, appear throughout his writings of the decade. Richards's perception of these developments strongly colored his interpretation of China, where changes of the same kind were eagerly (and, to Richards's mind, often thoughtlessly) underway. When Richards later insisted that the West had much to learn from China, he had in mind the cultural ills that occupied his attention in the Twenties. Insofar as Richards's was an "imagined" East, it took shape as an alternative to the excesses he identified in interwar England. To understand Richards's later ideas about China, it is crucial to examine the cultural context in Britain, and specifically Cambridge, during his years there.

English studies had its origins at Cambridge in the introduction of the Modern Languages Tripos in 1878. The examination included an English option that required students to trace the development of the language from its Anglo-Saxon roots to the present. In the same year the first Cambridge professorship in Anglo-Saxon was inaugurated. As at Oxford, the approach to English was largely philological, focussing on the historical evolution of the language from its early medieval antecedents. In 1910 literary studies at Cambridge assumed a more modern cast when Harold Harmsworth, Viscount Rothermere, founded the King Edward VII Chair of English Literature. The first appointment to the post was Sir Arthur Quiller-Couch, or "Q," an appropriately Edwardian choice. Advancing a decidedly *belle-lettrist* approach to literary appreciation, Q's open university lectures were among the first to address recent literature and were exceptionally well received.[30] Though many dons were reluctant to establish literary studies as an academic subject (F. M. Cornford argued that it "would ruin the spontaneous appreciation of the fine things in English Literature"),[31] by 1917 a group of scholars led by A. C. Benson and Mansfield Forbes had succeeded in developing a separate English Tripos. The examination was to include a philological along with a literary component, with an unprecedented amount of attention devoted to English literature since Shakespeare. The first English Tripos was officially offered in 1919, the same year that Richards began lecturing at Cambridge, with F. R. Leavis among the examinees.

According to E. M. W. Tillyard, the impetus behind the adoption of an English Tripos at Cambridge was rooted in a spirit of internationalism that resembles Richards's later global concerns. The earlier, philological approach to English studies had been closely tied to racial notions of English history that formed a convenient prop to late-Victorian nationalism.[32] The new Tripos, developed in the midst of the First World War, reacted against "old pre-war Romantic Teutonism" by encouraging a more analytic, ahistorical concentration upon individual poems.[33] In its preference for rational analysis and a willingness to consider more recent texts, English studies at Cambridge embraced a distinctly "anti-isolationist" idea of literary studies. By the time Richards joined the faculty in 1919, some of the fundamental features of Cambridge English—"an instinctive reaching after practical criticism, a dislike of the expansive and the florid in critical method, and a distrust of mystical theories of literature"—were already largely in place.[34]

English studies at Cambridge took its shape from the First World War in other ways as well. The first generation of students to benefit from the new English Tripos was that of the returning veterans. After the attenuated student body of the war years, the new influx of undergraduates brought with them an optimism and energy that influenced the forward-looking direction of Richards's own criticism. Although in many ways insulated against Continental thought—"of the major corrosives of the century," remembered Basil Willey, "of Marx and Freud, for example, hardly more than a *soupcon* had as yet trickled into our fool's paradise"—the enthusiasm of the postwar student generation contributed to the spirit of experimentation apparent in Richards's writings.[35] "There was an atmosphere, such a dream, such a hope," Richards recalled of the postwar spirit at Cambridge.[36] Richards soon found himself involved in designing a program of study for which there was little precedent. Along with a relatively young group of colleagues including Forbes and Tillyard, Richards was given a free hand in developing courses and setting student examinations. According to Basil Willey, the "pre-1914" English lecturers were unable to adapt themselves to the influx of new students, finding "there was just no tradition capable of helping."[37] As a result, a younger generation of "gifted amateurs"—some of whom, like Richards, had no formal training in literary studies—assumed the work of developing the English course. His role in shaping English studies in its nascent stage gave Richards a long-lasting influence over the tenor of Cambridge English; Basil Willey, F. R. Leavis, T. R. Henn and G. H. W. Rylands were all products of the new English Tripos in the Twenties who came under his direction. This practical, and highly successful, experience of institution-building would contribute greatly to Richards's skill and confidence in establishing the Orthological Institute of China.

While the atmosphere of postwar Cambridge contributed positively to the sense of mission apparent in Richards's criticism, his impression of developments in the wider culture was less sanguine. Already as an undergraduate he had informed his tutor, Frank Salter, that he wanted to read for something other than History because he "didn't think History ought to have happened."[38] The First World War confirmed Richards's catastrophic view of the past. He attributed the War to a massive breakdown in international communication, and his sense of its futility fueled much of his critical agenda in the Twenties. The irreverent treatment of traditional language theories in *The Meaning of Meaning*, in which the authors breezily dismiss a line of authorities stretching from Plato to Russell as practitioners of "Word Magic," reflects in part the hostility toward accepted conventions that both Richards and Ogden, a committed pacifist, ranked among the primary causes of the war. "In war-time," they write, "words become a normal part of the mechanism of deceit."[39] Nor are Richards and Ogden optimistic about the society emerging in the wake of the First World War. "The twentieth century," they argue,

> suffers more grievously than any previous age from the ravages of such verbal superstitions. . . . Influences making for its wide diffusion are the baffling complexity of the symbolic apparatus now at our disposal; the possession by journalists and men of letters of an immense semi-technical vocabulary and their lack of opportunity, or unwillingness, to inquire into its proper use; the success of analytic thinkers in fields bordering on mathematics, where the divorce between symbol and reality is most pronounced and the tendency to hypostatization most alluring; the extension of a knowledge of the cruder forms of symbolic conventions (the three R's), combined with a widening of the gulf between the public and the scientific thought of the age; and finally the exploitation, for po-

litical and commercial purposes, of the printing press by the dissemination and reiteration of clichés.[40]

These points form the basis of Richards's cultural diagnosis throughout the Twenties. The fragmentation of linguistic communities, the growing authority of science, the rise of an uncultivated consumer public and a powerful mass media to supply it are themes he constantly returns to in his literary criticism of the period. For Richards, the First World War and its social consequences laid bare the hazards of modernity. His later advocacy of Basic English was meant to save China from the pitfalls he saw corroding his own culture in its transformation into a mass society.

Richards's suspicion of the past is taken up again in *Science and Poetry*, published in 1925. The book opens with the claim that

> outside the sciences, we think very much as our ancestors thought a hundred or two hundred generations ago. Certainly this is so as regards official views about poetry. Is it not possible that these are wrong, as wrong as most ideas of an equally hoary antiquity?[41]

The tendency to equate antiquity with error is familiar from *The Meaning of Meaning*. Richards's insistence on the obsolescence of old ideas and the irrelevance of tradition to the problems of modernity marks his criticism as a product of the First World War, part of the cultural anomie shared by contemporaries like T. S. Eliot and Ezra Pound. Like them, Richards takes the debacle of the war as evidence of an outmoded system of values. "None of the afflictions of humanity," he writes in the *Principles of Literary Criticism*, "are worse than its obsolete moral principles." Citing the "obsolete virtues of nationalism under modern conditions," he alludes to the First World War in arguing the need for a more international perspective.[42] Pursuing the same theme *in Science and Poetry*, Richards makes use of the war itself as a metaphor for modern decline. "In the past," he writes,

> Tradition, a kind of Treaty of Versailles assigning frontiers and spheres of influence to the different interests, and based chiefly upon conquest, ordered our lives in a moderately satisfactory manner. But Tradition is weakening. Moral authorities are not as well backed by beliefs as they were; their sanctions are declining in force. We are in need of something to take the place of the old order. Not in need of a new balance of power, a new arrangement of conquests, but of a League of Nations for the moral ordering of the impulses; a new order based on conciliation not on attempted suppression.[43]

Richards's conviction that the war had irrevocably dissolved the old order of "Tradition" connects to his work in China in several important respects. First, it contributed to his relative neglect of China's differing historical circumstances in his prescriptions about its future. Assuming that the process of modernization in China was different only in degree from that of the West, he tended to read the immediate Western past into China's current situation, often neglecting the particularities of local history and circumstance that made its predicament unique. The same assumption also encouraged Richards to see China as a place where modernization might be done properly, without the violence and cultural disruption that had attended its progress in the West. Finally, while Richards was committed to China's future, his sense of rupture with the past occasioned by the First World War deepened his admiration for a society that seemed to preserve a living contact with its traditions. His enthusiasm for China's prospects was inspired in part by what he saw as its deep connection to its past, a relationship that the West had lost in the aftermath of the First World War.

Accompanying Richards's catastrophic view of the war was a marked suspicion of technology. Despite his embrace of science as a model for literary criticism, Richards cited the increasingly technological nature of modern life as a factor in creating the disorientation that he believed poetry could help to correct. For if poetry is the best means for ordering the impulses, Richards argued that technology is a prime cause of the increasing chaos modern minds have to negotiate. "We have not yet fathomed the more sinister potentialities of the cinema and the loudspeaker," he claims in *Principles of Literary Criticism*, a metonymy that illustrates his tendency to see modernity in technological rather than political or economic terms.[44] "The Cinema," he laments elsewhere in the text, ". . . tends to develop stock attitudes and stereotyped ideas, the attitudes and ideas of producers: attitudes and ideas which can be 'put across' quickly through a medium that lends itself to crude rather than sensitive handling."[45] The deadening effect of these stock responses is a threat to the moral life of the entire community: "the extent to which second-hand experience of a crass and inchoate type is replacing ordinary life offers a threat which has not yet been realized."[46] In *Practical Criticism* Richards again berates technology as the catalyst of cultural decline, warning that "mechanical inventions . . . and a too sudden diffusion of indigestible ideas, are disturbing throughout the world the whole order of human mentality."[47] Citing an erosion in "every department of literature, from the Epic to the ephemeral Magazine," he attributes the decay to the blinding pace of change in a technological society:

> The most probable reasons for this [decline] are the increased size of our 'communities' (if they can still be so called, when there remains so little in common), and the mixtures of culture that the printed word has caused. Our everyday reading and speech now handles scraps from a score of different cultures. I am not referring here to the derivation of our words—they have always been mixed—but to the fashion in which we are forced to pass from ideas and feelings that took their form in Shakespeare's time or Dr. Johnson's time to ideas and feelings of Edison's time or Freud's time and back again.

As world communication improves "through the wireless and otherwise," Richards predicts this heterogeneity will only increase.[48] The growing fragmentation of the culture, facilitated by the mass technologies of film, radio and the modern press, thus in Richards's view leads to a perilous standardization of response engendered, paradoxically, by the very complexity they help to create.

The means for countering these twin developments—in an argument that Richards forwards throughout his writings of the Twenties, from *The Meaning of Meaning* to *Practical Criticism*—is to educate people to a more sensitive use of language. Retraining our minds for the rich and complex operation that poetry requires to make meaning will reverse the trend toward standardization and the stock response. Richards's particular understanding of the Modern crisis helps to explain why he came to believe that *language* was the key to successful development in China. There, where the rapid transition to an industrial society promised to severely disrupt the fabric of traditional life, a mental preparation through literary training seemed even more urgent than in the West. Richards believed that a timely intervention of his linguistic methods could thus inoculate the Chinese against the demonstrable evils of mass culture, social fragmentation and total war that had followed technological advance in England and the West.

Given Richards's doubts about the benefits of technology, the embrace of science in his critical writings of the Twenties, and indeed in China, is surprising. As John Paul Russo points out, "Richards put a guarded faith in science and progress at a time when the sciences were in theoretical crisis and the idea of progress was all but dead."[49] His aggressively analytical approach to poetry, modeled on what he regarded as the latest methods of scientific inquiry, was a hallmark of his work in the Twenties; Isherwood was one of many contemporaries who saw Richards not as a cultural conservative, but one on the side of the "behaviorists, materialists [and] atheists."[50] That Richards consciously patterned his criticism on the sciences is clear. "It has long been recognized," he writes in *Science and Poetry*

> that if only something could be done in psychology remotely comparable to what has been achieved in physics, practical consequences might be expected even more remarkable than the engineer can contrive. The first positive steps in the science of the mind have been slow in coming, but already they are beginning to change man's whole outlook.[51]

This desire to annex literary criticism to an emergent "science of the mind," to elevate literary studies to the status of scientific inquiry, became the centerpiece of Richards's entire critical project in the Twenties, and it is for this program that he is best remembered today.

To appreciate the role that science played in his criticism and its consequences for the work in China, the particular meaning that Richards ascribed to the term must be clearly understood. In keeping with the rest of his cultural criticism, he sees science fundamentally as a question of language. Already in *The Meaning of Meaning*, he and Ogden define science in terms of their distinction between Emotive and Symbolic language. "The best test," they write, "of whether our use of words is essentially symbolic or emotive is the question—'Is it true or false in the ordinary, scientific sense?' If this question is relevant then the use is symbolic, if it is clearly irrelevant then we have an emotive utterance."[52] Science is, in its broadest sense, a special use of language, one that employs words for referential rather than emotive purposes. The scientific approach consists of a concern with the purely symbolic aspect of signs, independent of their evocative content. The first step of a scientific criticism is thus to distinguish these two registers of meaning in ordinary usage. "The recognition," they note, "that many of the most popular subjects of discussion are infested with symbolically blank but emotively active words of this kind is a necessary preliminary to the extension of scientific method to these questions."[53] It is in this special sense of the awareness of the separate functions emotive and symbolic language perform that Richards understood the application of science to literary criticism.

Along with his attacks on aestheticism and his borrowings from Sherringtonian psychology, Richards's (distinctly emotive) deployment of scientific metaphors buttresses the impression of scientific rigor in his criticism. In *The Meaning of Meaning*, the failure to distinguish between Symbolic and Emotive language is compared to an attempt "to sterilize our instruments without studying the habits of the bacteria."[54] In expanding upon modernity's "tempestuous turmoil of change," he characterizes poetry as "not a Rock to shelter under or cling to . . . [but] an efficient aeroplane in which to ride."[55] To illustrate the concept of mental equilibrium in *Science and Poetry*, he compares the mind to a series of magnetic needles, with the impulses described as perturbing magnets.[56] In addition to these rhetorical flourishes, Richards devotes great attention to defining poetry vis-à-vis science. In *Science and Poetry*, his most thorough discussion of the subject, Richards is careful not to promote the claims of poetry at the expense of science. The former, he argues, arose with what he calls the Magical View of the world—the ancient belief that nature is controlled through ritual and incantation. With the emergence of science, this conception of the world was decisively overthrown, and "in its place we [now] have the universe of the mathematician, . . . a field in which intellectual certainty is, almost for the first time, available on an unlimited scale."[57] Poetry still has a crucial role to play in this disenchanted age, but it no longer commands belief. Instead, Richards explains its value in a scientific age with reference to the notion of "Pseudo-statement." Science, as "our most elaborate way of pointing to things systematically . . . can tell us nothing about the nature of things in any ultimate sense. It can never answer any question of the form: What is so and so? It can only tell us how so and so behaves."[58] It thus falls to poetry to supply the attitudes or emotional states necessary for a fully human life. Its statements must be understood as pseudo-statements; "'true' if it suits and serves some attitude or links together attitudes which on other grounds are desirable."[59] With the concept of Pseudo-statement, perhaps the most hotly debated feature of his criticism in the Twenties, Richards unequivocally dismisses the idea that poetry reveals fundamental truths or adds to the stock of human knowledge: "it is not the poet's business to make true statements."[60] Rather, "poetry conclusively shows that even the most important attitudes can be aroused and maintained without any belief entering in at all."[61] Science and poetry, like emotive and symbolic uses of language, are consigned to two separate but equal spheres. Poetic truth and scientific truth are so different, in fact, "that it is a pity to use so similar a word" for each.[62] Properly understood, both work in tandem toward mutually reinforcing, but clearly distinguishable, ends.

But this apparent concordat between science and poetry obscures deeper reservations in Richards's criticism about the former's growing prestige. In a reversal of his original concessions to science, Richards concludes *Science and Poetry* on a distinctly apocalyptic note:

> The most dangerous of the sciences is only now beginning to come into action. I am thinking less of Psychoanalysis or of Behaviorism than of the whole subject which includes them. It is very probable that the Hindenburg Line to which the defence of our traditions retired as a result of the onslaughts of the last century will be blown up in the near future. If this should happen a mental chaos such as man has never experienced may be expected. We shall then be thrown back, as Matthew Arnold foresaw, upon poetry. It is capable of saving us; it is a perfectly possible means of overcoming chaos.[63]

As with his critique of the War and the cultural fragmentation that followed in its wake, Richards looked to language as an answer to the destabilizing truths of science. In his criticism over the course of the Twenties, he pioneered a unique linguistic solution to the problems of modernity centered on the key concepts of communication, mental equilibrium and complexity. In China Richards discovered what seemed to be an immense new field of application for these ideas. Reading the experience of a shell-shocked Britain into a modernizing China, he found a remarkable opportunity to put his theories to the test. The Basic English campaign in China would come to encapsulate some of Richards's most deeply held critical concerns of the Twenties, putting them into action in ways that he never could have realized in his own country.

IV

In China Richards found the problems of interwar Britain rewritten on a vastly greater scale. If the rate of social and technological transformation had been destabilizing in the West, the Chinese—struggling to adapt to centuries of Western development in a matter of decades—faced consequences even more destructive. However, because of the nascent state of modernization, Richards also saw a chance for the country to benefit from Western mistakes, appropriating its science and technology while avoiding their more ominous consequences. He was thus able to cherish great hopes for China's future while at the same time celebrating the virtues of a pre-industrial civilization. Paradoxically, while preaching the gospel of modernization he reveled in the architecture, philosophy and traditions of the very society he wished to see transformed. Through China, Richards found a way to express his profound doubts about developments in the West while still preserving a faith in progress. Part of the country's fascination for him was the chance it offered to look forward and backward at once. China came to represent for Richards a civilizing corrective to Western excesses while at the same time confirming his faith in the value of rationality and logical analysis he associated with Cambridge, and more broadly the Western tradition. In the attempt to integrate what he saw as the best of both civilizations, Richards developed a program that reconciled the more skeptical aspects of his cultural critique with the moral optimism of his literary criticism.

Insofar as Richards's perception of China depended upon prior values and assumptions, they were largely those of early twentieth-century Cambridge. To understand the effect this background had on Richards's interpretation of China, two Cambridge figures who shared his fascination with the Far East are particularly crucial. Goldsworthy Lowes Dickinson was in many ways the epitome of Cambridge humanism at the turn of the century. E. M. Forster, Lowes Dickinson's biographer, cites an acceptance of science, a reverence for art and a belief in human perfectibility as defining features of Dickinson's distinctly Cantabridgian cast of mind.[64] Richards absorbed many of these ideals during his time at Cambridge, later claiming to have committed Lowes Dickinson's *A Modern Symposium* to memory as an undergraduate.[65] His *Letters from John Chinaman*, first published in 1901, is a searing critique of Western culture and society cast in the voice of a Chinese official reporting on his observations of the United States. In using the character of John Chinaman to express his own discontents with the course of Western development, Lowes Dickinson indicates the ways in which Cambridge values could be mapped onto a specific construction of Chinese civilization. *Letters from John Chinaman* also anticipates many of Richards's own notions of China nearly thirty years later, indicating the degree to which the Cambridge context shaped Richards's understanding of his experience.

Bertrand Russell presents another dimension of the "Cambridge" China that Richards would carry with him to the East. In *The Problem of China*, Russell's account of his year-long tour of the country in 1920–21, he grapples with the complexities of modernization in China that would also absorb Richards. Disturbed by the anomalies in the Chinese rush to Westernize, Russell offers a cautionary vision for China's future in which the best of its ancient civilization may be preserved through a discriminating borrowing from the West. Russell's concern for China's transformation stems directly from his own sense of outrage over what he perceived to be the shortcomings and injustices of his own society. Like Lowes Dickinson, he presents a picture of China distinctly inflected by the values of modern Cambridge, owing as much to his sense of cultural crisis in the West as it does to his time in the East. In using China to articulate their own critical preoccupations and concerns, Lowes Dickinson and Russell suggest how Richards's Cambridge background provided a constellation of attitudes and assumptions about China that would pattern his own perception of the East. Their texts foreshadow Richards's ambitions in China and reveal the extent to which his hopes for Basic English were indebted to the humanistic ideals of the Cambridge milieu.

When Goldsworthy Lowes Dickinson first visited China in 1912, his admiration for the country and its people was total. "So gay," he wrote to E. M. Forster, ". . . beautiful, sane, hellenic, choice, human." He found the Chinese to be "a level, rational people—a kind of English with sensitiveness and imagination," governed by "no reaches into the infinite, but a clear, non-restricted perception of the beautiful and exquisite in the Real." Impressed by Chinese customs and institutions, he concluded: "If such a people could be lifted onto a higher economic level, without losing these qualities, we should have the best society this planet admits of."[66] Lowes Dickinson's enthusiasm is hardly surprising, given the nature of his preconceptions about what he would find. Twelve years earlier he had published *Letters from John Chinaman*, a critical comparison of Chinese and Western culture written without the benefit of having ever visited the East. The art critic Roger Fry had first suggested the idea of writing a critique of the West in the voice of a Chinese official on the eve of Lowes Dickenson's departure for the United States. The recent news of the Boxer

Rebellion there inspired him to adopt the fictional persona of a disenchanted Chinese official resident in the United States, addressing a series of open letters to a Western audience. The resulting account of the relative merits of Chinese and Western civilization establishes the pattern for a Cambridge discourse about China that would inflect Richards's later thoughts on the same subject.

Lowes Dickinson's commentator in *Letters from John Chinaman* is unequivocal in his judgment of Chinese superiority in nearly every aspect of its culture. His purpose, he tells us in the opening letter, is that of "explaining, as far as I am able, the ways in which we [Chinese] regard Western civilization, and the reasons we have for desiring to exclude its influences."[67] He adduces Western rapacity, religious hypocrisy, imperial aggression and social anomie as among the reasons for China's rejection of its ways. In a critique of Western economics more reminiscent of a John Ruskin than a John Chinaman, Lowes Dickinson claims:

> The salient characteristic of your civilization is its irresponsibility. You have liberated forces you cannot control; you are caught yourselves in your own levers and cogs. In every department of business you are substituting for the workman the tool, for the individual the company. The making of dividends is the universal preoccupation; the well-being of the laborer is no one's concern but the State's. . . . You produce, not because you will, but because you must; you consume, not what you choose, but what is forced upon you.[68]

As a result, the Western nations suffer from an "economic chaos" that stands in stark contrast to the centuries-old "moral order" of the East.[69]

China, by contrast, emerges as a culture of almost fantastical serenity and beauty, a society in which aesthetic cultivation is valued more highly than profit. In a famous passage from the *Letters*, Lowes Dickinson aestheticizes Chinese civilization in distinctly Paterian terms:

> A rose in the moonlit garden, the shadow of trees on the turf, almond bloom, scent of pine, the wine-cup and the guitar; these and the pathos of life and death, the long embrace, the hand stretched out in vain, the moment that glides for ever away, with its freight of music and light, into the shadow and hush of the haunted past, all that we have, all that eludes us, a bird on the wing, a perfume escaped on the gale—to all these things we are trained to respond, and the response is what we call literature.[70]

Paired with this heightened aesthetic awareness is an innate and age-old pacifism. Where the histories of the Western nations present "a long and lamentable tale of antagonism, tumult, carnage and confusion,"[71] the Chinese enjoy a benign Confucian ethic that has made them "the one nation in all the history of the world who genuinely abhor violence and reverence reason and right."[72] Consequently, Lowes Dickinson attributes the lamentable history of China's relations with the West to Western aggression and injustice. "You compelled us, against our will," his official points out

> to open our ports to your trade; you forced us to permit the introduction of a drug which we believe was ruinous to our people; you exempted your subjects residing among us from the operation of our laws; you appropriated our coasting traffic; you claim the traffic of our inland waters. Every attempt on our part to resist your demands was followed by new claims and new aggressions. And yet all this time you posed as civilized peoples dealing with barbarians.[73]

By the end of the *Letters*, John Chinaman has established China's superiority to the West by virtually every measure. Its social system, ethics and even aesthetic sensibilities set a standard that the Western nations cannot match. His assessment of the two cultures moves toward an assertion spelled out in the opening letters, that "left to ourselves, we should never have sought intercourse with the West."[74]

Significantly, the single point upon which John Chinaman concedes superiority to the West is its record of scientific achievement. "When I was first brought into contact with the West," he writes,

> what most immediately impressed me was the character and range of your intelligence. I found that you had brought your minds to bear, with singular success, upon problems which had not even occurred to us in the East; that by analysis and experiment you had found the clue to the operation of the forces of nature, and had turned them to account in ways which, to my untraveled imagination, appeared to be little short of miraculous. No familiarity diminished my admiration for your achievements in this field. I recognize in them your chief and most substantial claim to superiority, and I am not surprised that some of my countrymen should be advocating with ardor their immediate introduction into China.[75]

Lowes Dickinson's particular construction of China and the West hinges upon this point. The reason for Western scientific and technical superiority, in his view, has nothing to do with a more rapid pace of discovery, or greater access to natural resources, or a specific course of economic development. Rather, its successes in these areas are the product of a mode of rational, analytic thought that constitutes its sole claim to supremacy over the East. Even while conceding this point, John Chinaman expresses serious reservations about its advantages.[76] "Rationalization," he notes, "has taken the place of perception; and your whole life is an infinite syllogism from premises you have not examined to conclusions you have not anticipated or willed. Everywhere means, nowhere an end! Society a huge engine, and that engine itself out of gear! Such is the picture your civilization presents to my imagination."[77] Despite these criticisms, his observations underscore the point that rational, scientific thought is the exclusive preserve of the West. In defining the difference between East and West in such terms, Lowes Dickinson creates a dichotomy between Chinese and Western culture that reappears in Richards's later assessments of the East. On the one hand stands China: pacific, aesthetic, with stable traditions and a relatively benign history. On the other stands the West: aggressive, volatile, even barbaric, yet at the same time possessing powers of rational analysis virtually unknown to the Chinese. Science, and more significantly the tradition of rational thought that underpins it, becomes on Lowes Dickinson's account the single asset that the Western nations have which may be of some benefit to China.

Richards's aspirations for Basic more than thirty years later stemmed from nearly identical assumptions. His conviction that the Chinese required analytic training, a mental habit that Basic English was to provide, bears the mark of Lowes Dickinson's influence. Similarly, Richards's admiration for what he saw as a preference for cultural over military development in China also reflects a shared Cambridge background. Finally, in his insistence that China should serve as an example to the West, Richards paralleled Lowes Dickinson's own intentions in *Letters from John Chinaman*. The *Letters* conclude with a final plea from John Chinaman: "Learn to understand us, and in doing so learn better to understand yourselves."[78] The aim of Basic English was to provide a medium of communication that would make possible exactly such an understanding. Richards's hopes for a synthesis between Chinese and Western culture, in which the virtues of the one would check the excesses of the other, was indebted to the same body of ideas, values and assumptions that informs Lowes Dickinson's *Letters*.

Bertrand Russell also helps to illuminate Richards's interpretation of the East in several crucial respects. Russell first visited China in 1920 at the invitation of the Chinese Society for the Lectures on the New Learning. He thus arrived, as Richards would, in the capacity of self-conscious modernizer. Flouting convention by living openly with his lover, Dora Black, Russell lectured on topics ranging from Bolshevism to modern marriage for twelve months at universities across China, spending the bulk of his time in Peking. He was received with great enthusiasm, particularly among university students, in part because, according to Jonathan Spence, his "work in mathematical logic meshed with the effort made by many Chinese . . . to achieve a deeper understanding of Western scientific concepts."[79] Russell's tour coincided with the May Fourth Movement, a largely student-led protest calling for a sweeping program of modernization in education, politics and society. His popularity among Chinese reformists was such that during his stay cigarette advertisements in Peking began using his picture and a journal devoted to his thought, *Russell Monthly*, was launched.[80] Russell in turn admired the Chinese for their taste, manners and civility, which he understood in largely Western terms. "China makes the impression," he recalled in his autobiography, "of what Europe would have become if the eighteenth century had gone on till now without industrialism or the French Revolution. People seem to be rational hedonists, knowing well how to obtain happiness, exquisite through intense cultivation of their artistic sensibilities, differing from Europeans through the fact that [Europeans] prefer enjoyment of power."[81] While the novelist Lu Xun later accused Russell of "prais[ing] the Chinese when some sedan-chair bearers smiled at him at the West Lake," on the whole his reception gave him reason to think that he might speak with authority on the direction of China's future.[82]

In *The Problem of China*, written immediately after his return to Britain in 1921, Russell offered a prognosis of the country based on his observations over the previous year. In contrast to Lowes Dickinson's spirited defense of their traditional society, Russell encourages the Chinese to look forward. The real "problem" of modern China, in Russell's view, is how to adopt the necessary elements of modern Western science without losing the benefits that are uniquely Chinese. "Can Chinese virtues be preserved?" he asks in the opening chapter. "Or must China, in order to survive, acquire, instead, the vices which make for success and cause misery to others only? And if China does copy the model set by all foreign nations with which she has dealings, what will become of all of us?[83] In his conviction of the global significance of China's modernization, Russell anticipates Richards's own conclusions nearly a decade later. His particular view of the Chinese situation also has strong affinities to Lowes Dickinson's notion of the East in *Letters from John Chinaman*. Like Lowes Dickinson, Russell uses his description of China to criticize developments in the West. "The Great War," he writes, "showed that something is wrong with our civilization; experience of Russia and China has made me believe that those countries can help to show us what it is that is wrong."[84] What Russell finds "wrong" in the West is largely industrialization and its concomitant values. "Instinctive happiness, or joy of life," he maintains, "is one of the most important widespread popular goods that we have lost through industrialism and the high pressure at which most of us live; its commonness in China is a strong reason for thinking well of Chinese civilization."[85] He attacks contemporary Western civilization—in terms nearly identical to Lowes Dickinson's—for its "creed of efficiency for its own sake, without regard for the ends to which it is directed," attributing to "a superflux of the itch for activity" the cause of "our industrialism, our militarism, our love of progress, our missionary zeal, our imperialism [and] our passion for dominating and organizing."[86]

China, by contrast, Russell regards as "an artist nation, with the virtues and vices to be expected of an artist."[87] Its people retain "an almost unconscious effort after beauty"; an aesthetic impulse "that existed among ourselves before the time of the Puritans."[88] "The Chinese," he writes

> do not excel in the things we really value—military prowess and industrial enterprise. But those who value wisdom or beauty or even the simple enjoyment of life will find more of these things in China than in the distracted and turbulent West, and will be happy to live where such things are valued.[89]

As with Lowes Dickinson's *Letters from John Chinaman*, Russell's analysis of China depends upon a polarization of East and West in which the former is held up as a foil to the latter's excesses. China represents a corrective to Western civilization, but at the cost of depriving the Chinese of any claims to the characteristics that gave rise to "modernity" in the West. His idealized China exists essentially outside of time, innocent of history until its first contact with Europe. "Progress and efficiency," Russell claims, "make no appeal to the Chinese. . . . By valuing progress and efficiency, we have secured power and wealth; by ignoring them, the Chinese, until we brought disturbance, secured on the whole a peaceable existence and a life full of enjoyment."[90] Russell's China thus serves as an Other whose function is not to assert Western superiority, but to highlight its moral and intellectual failings. If his sense of the Chinese Other depends as much upon European values and assumptions as more explicitly imperial imaginings, its "otherness" is here deployed to critique the process of modernization that has led to its interference with non-Western civilizations.

Russell's China is as notable for its pacifism as it is for aesthetic refinement. Among the "ethical qualities in which China is supreme," he most prizes "the pacific temper, which seeks to settle disputes on grounds of justice rather than by force."[91] Confronted with the embarrassing fact of China's imperial history, Russell explains that "the persistence of the Chinese empire down to our own day is not to be attributed to any military skill; on the contrary, considering its extent and resources, it has at most times shown itself weak and incompetent in war."[92] Rather, China passively absorbed its "uncivilized" neighbors into its own rich culture. This presumed military incompetence on the part of the Chinese plays an important role in Russell's idealized picture of the East. While "our [Western] prosperity . . . can only be obtained by widespread oppression and exploitation of weaker nations," Russell claims that "the Chinese are not strong enough to injure other countries, and secure whatever they enjoy by means of their own merits and exertions alone."[93] Russell's sense of the Chinese incapacity for war resembles Richards's own appraisals of China's military inefficiency during the war with Japan nearly twenty years later. In characterizing the Chinese as artistic, pacific, pre-industrial and militarily incompetent, Russell availed himself of a Cambridge construction of the East that looked back to Lowes Dickinson and would influence Richard's later presuppositions about the Chinese.

Russell's characterization of Western strengths also follows a pattern familiar from *John Chinaman*. Despite China's moral superiority, Russell concedes that "its culture was deficient in one respect, namely science." Western predominance in technology, administrative efficiency and imperial conquest are all reducible to the capacity for scientific thought. "The fact," he writes, "that Britain has produced Shakespeare and Milton, Locke and Hume, and all the other men who have adorned literature and the arts, does not make us superior to the Chinese. What makes us superior is Newton and Robert Boyle and their scientific successors. They make us superior by giving us greater proficiency in the art of killing."[94] Like Lowes Dickinson, Russell considers the scientific world-view a profoundly dubious legacy and fears the consequences of its introduction into China. "The culture of China is changing rapidly," he warns, and Western ideas are destined to play a lasting role in its future. But he sees "two opposite dangers" threatening China in the process. The first

> is that they may become completely Westernized, retaining nothing of what has hitherto distinguished them, adding merely one more to the restless, intelligent, industrial and militaristic nations which now afflict this unfortunate planet. The second danger is that they may be driven, in the course of resistance to foreign aggression, into an intense anti-foreign conservatism as regards everything except armaments. This has happened in Japan, and it may easily happen in China.[95]

In either scenario, the Chinese risk losing the particular virtues that distinguish them from the West. Having identified the Western nations with science and the Chinese with art, ethics and a more satisfying appreciation of life, Russell now argues for a compromise between the two: "The distinctive merit of our civilization is the scientific method. The distinctive merit of the Chinese is a just conception of the ends of life. It is the two that one must hope to see gradually uniting."[96] Russell leaves the work of uniting the two, however, entirely to the Chinese. "I believe," he writes, "that if the Chinese are left free to assimilate what they want of our civilization, and to reject what strikes them as bad, they will be able to achieve an organic growth from their own tradition, and to produce a very splendid result, combining our merits with theirs."[97] While he hopes that "China, in return for our scientific knowledge, may give us something of her large tolerance and contemplative peace of mind," the "problem" of assimilation ultimately belongs to the Chinese to solve.[98] Its future, not that of the West, is the decisive one in creating a more stable global system. If China can effect a hybrid of Western science and Eastern contemplation, then it will have "played the part in the world for which she is fitted, and will have given to mankind as a whole new hope in the moment of greatest need."[99] It is in "the renaissance spirit now existing in China" that Russell places his hopes for "a new civilization better than any the world has yet known."[100] Though Richards would bring a different set of solutions to the "problem" of China, his sense of the dangers and possibilities of modernization echoes Russell's. For both, the question of China's future promised a marriage of scientific rationalism and those values of civility, artistic cultivation and pacifism that, to the Cambridge mind, offered the most attractive ideal for a new global consciousness. Ironically, the studied rationalism so dear to the Cambridge humanists gave way to a messianic optimism in their aspirations for an East-West cultural convergence.

Russell's and Lowes Dickinson's accounts of the East help to explain the unique place that China held in the Cambridge imagination. With its aesthetic cultivation, ethical superiority and capacity to enjoy life, China represented the last bastion of Cantabridgian sanity in a world threatened by a tradition of Western, rational thought developed at the expense of moral restraint or cultivation. To China fell the role of assimilating the best of Western science without acquiring the aggressive, materialist tendencies that had led to the tragedy of the First World War. Part of the appeal of this construction to Richards and his Cambridge predecessors is that it had the advantage of being at once conservative and progressive. In discussing China, they could criticize what they regarded as the gross excesses of Western development while simultaneously preserving their hopes for a better, more rational future. The legacy of this vision shaped Richards's Far Eastern project in several ways. First, the identification of Western rationality with scientific achievement responded to themes in Richards's literary criticism that posited rational modes of thought rather than particular social or economic reforms as the solution to China's future. Secondly, the notion of the East as more aesthetic and less militaristic than the West deeply informed Richards's sense of Chinese virtues and the necessity of preserving them at all costs, particularly through the course of the Japanese invasion in the 1930's. The hope that China could assimilate the best of both Western and Eastern civilizations in the process of modernizing shaped Richards's belief in the global significance of his linguistic program for China. Finally, Lowes Dickinson and Russell encouraged a pattern of thought that treated China as a mirror for the West; a way of articulating their cultural criticism through the idealization of an Other. While Richards found much to condemn in the East, he never lost his conviction that the Western nations had a great deal to learn about themselves through China. Basic English would provide the common language by which Chinese and Westerners could communicate and, in the process, create a synthesis of East and West that would be the basis for a truly global community. In this respect the Cambridge legacy significantly shaped Richard's own sense of the problems—and solutions—for China's future.

Along with his literary work, with its focus on themes of communication and its misgivings about the cultural impact of science and technology, the Cambridge background helps to explain how Richards—following his invitation to lecture in Peking in 1929—came to regard China as a testing-ground for realizing his most deeply held ideals.

3   ∽ A Moment in Paradise

The First Year in China, 1929-1930

I

> Tsing-Hua College, delightfully situated at the foot of the Western hills, with a number of fine solid buildings, in a good American style, owes its existence entirely to the Boxer indemnity money. It has an atmosphere exactly like that of a small American university, and a (Chinese) President who is an almost perfect reproduction of the American College President. The teachers are partly American, partly Chinese educated in America, and there tends to be more and more of the latter. As one enters the gates, one becomes aware of the presence of every virtue usually absent in China: cleanliness, punctuality, exactitude, efficiency. . . . One great merit, that belongs to American institutions generally, is that the students are made to learn English.[1]

Thus Bertrand Russell described Tsing Hua in 1920, during the course of his Chinese tour. Nine years later, Richards arrived at its gates to begin a year as visiting lecturer in English. Since Russell's visit the Kuomintang, under the leadership of Chiang Kai-shek, had won control of northern China and made Tsing Hua a national university. By 1929 the school was, according to one faculty member, "the apple of the Nanking Gov[ernment]'s eye, being considered the first university in the country and the only non-missionary one which pays salaries regularly."[2] Over the next sixteen months Tsing Hua would serve as Richards's introduction to the pleasures and obliquities of life in China. The experience of teaching brought him into contact with the rising generation of students, whose difficulties in understanding a foreign literature and mode of thought dwarfed anything he had encountered at home. Issues of communication that had exercised him at Cambridge existed here on an entirely new scale. By the same token, China seemed to offer a near limitless opportunity to put his criticism into action. The country was at a moment of profound transformation, struggling to adopt new forms of economy, science and government against a history of traditionalism and foreign interference. Richards found the possibilities for China's future exhilarating. "There is something which makes our old Renaissance seem a mere local agitation going on here," he wrote in his diary soon after arriving.[3] At Tsing Hua he also came to see the real obstacle to development in China as fundamentally linguistic. Absorbing the material technology of the West without its language—its technology of thought—seemed to him a serious bar to any lasting change. The year at Tsing Hua in 1929–30 strengthened Richards's belief in the power of language as an instrument of change, one that he felt was crucial to the Chinese experiment with Western models.

Before examining Richards's period at Tsing Hua, it is important to understand the cultural and political circumstances that framed his experience of the country. China at the time of his arrival was in the midst of a revolution. Within a generation the Chinese had reformed their centuries-old system of education, removed a dynasty in power since the 1640's, established a republic and opened the door to scientific and technological innovations from the West. Tsing Hua, as Russell's description indicates, was a direct outcome of these changes, and its history tells a great deal about the scale of change in China preceding Richards's arrival. What struck Russell most forcibly about Tsing Hua was its decidedly American flavor. From the style of its buildings to the character of its President, he found the school built firmly on Western lines. This "foreign" cast reflected a larger, and long-lasting, debate in Chinese society as to how the country might free itself from foreign influence. Although never officially a part of the empire, China historically had suffered greatly from Britain's imperial ambitions. First with the Opium Wars in the 1840's, which secured the British vast trading rights in China, and again in the 1860's, with the Emperor's call for European troops to quell the indigenous Taiping Rebellion, the history of China's contact with the West had been one of increasing dependence and concession. When Richards arrived in 1929 the major Chinese cities still had foreign quarters for Western traders and diplomats who were above the jurisdiction of Chinese law: a galling reminder of European ascendancy. As elsewhere in the empire, trade also brought missionaries. By the time of Richards's stay the missionary presence was a well-established feature of Chinese life, with mission-run schools, hospitals and bible colleges providing for many Chinese their first exposure to the West. Although many did undeniably good work in the country, their presence struck some as the imposition of a foreign creed.

At the same time, Chinese intellectuals had begun to look increasingly toward Western technology and science as the best hope for their country's future. The Japanese victory over Russia in 1895 starkly demonstrated to both Europe and the East what a non-Western nation, outfitted with modern weaponry and training, could do against a European army. The lesson was not lost on the Chinese. Beginning in the late-nineteenth century, a growing nationalist consciousness within the country sparked a widespread demand for modernization and reform. As never before, young Chinese began going abroad to study medicine, engineering, literature, languages and science in the hopes of absorbing the technical and medical knowledge to make China independent. The American-trained faculty that Russell noted at Tsing Hua was a product of this student diaspora, which extended to cities as various as Paris, New York, London, Moscow and Tokyo.[4] The reformist cause gained further impetus in 1919, when on May 4 groups throughout the country protested the signing of the Versailles Treaty for its concession to Japanese territorial claims in China. The resulting cultural upheaval, known as the May Fourth Movement, centered on the Peking universities and formed an important backdrop to Richards's time at Tsing Hua. In their "attempt to redefine China's culture as a valid part of the modern world," the May Fourth intellectuals looked primarily to Western arts and sciences as a means to national strength; a project that was given added urgency by Japan's growing imperial ambitions in the interwar years.[5] The spectrum of opinion over how China should pursue its modernization was wide, ranging from dynastic supporters to Moscow-trained Communists. But revolutionaries as disparate as Mao Tse-Tung and Chiang Kai-shek all came of age in a time of intense enthusiasm for Western models and a faith in their ability to secure an independent future for China.

Attitudes toward the West, then, were complex and conflicted at the time of Richards's arrival. Tsing Hua itself was a monument to this mixed legacy of foreign presence in China. The college was founded, as Russell points out, with indemnity funds from the Boxer Rebellion, one of the most violent anti-Western movements in recent Chinese history. Following the defeat of the Boxer uprising in Peking in 1900, the Western powers had demanded staggering reparations from the Chinese government: roughly $333 million to be paid over a period of forty years.[6] In 1908 the United States government chose to remit a large portion of its indemnity as part of its "open door" policy toward China. The money was to be used for sending Chinese students to American universities, and Tsing Hua was initially conceived as a preparatory school for this purpose. The American decision was a clear bid for influence in the country, and throughout the interwar years other nations followed suit. By the 1920's Soviet Russia was offering aid and military training to the Kuomintang as well as to the Chinese Communist Party. The missionary presence in China can be seen alongside these efforts as a further attempt to mold the country's future. Through schools, hospitals and charitable organizations they exercised a strong and lasting influence in the country. That Tsing Hua was "the only non-missionary [university] which pays salaries regularly" was a significant fact to Chinese nationalists, as it demonstrated China's ability to absorb Western forms of knowledge independently of missionary tutelage. The complex interplay of interests that formed Tsing Hua's history is emblematic of the struggle between the various Western powers to determine the future for China. It signaled the beginning of a new international situation, one far removed from the gunboat imperialism of the last century, in which the currency was no longer territory but cultural influence: an empire of the mind.

Within this context language played a key role. Russell had seen signs of this as early as 1920. His account of Tsing Hua makes an implicit connection between language and influence. The "cleanliness, punctuality, exactitude [and] efficiency" within the college gates—virtues "usually absent in China"—are in Russell's estimation clearly due to the American atmosphere of the college. He attributes this in turn to the fact that "the students are made to learn English"; language training is of a piece with Tsing Hua's other, distinctly American qualities. What Russell implies Richards would develop into explicit theory. The enthusiasm for Western ideas and models at Tsing Hua encouraged him to see China as an emergent modern nation burdened by the inertia of a centuries-old social structure and a legacy of imperial exploitation. By identifying language as the key to the transition, he found a field of application for his critical ideas that promised results of global consequence. If his experiment in "linguistic engineering" succeeded in China, it would endorse a vision of modernity in which nations could benefit peacefully and equally from technological advances. The spirit of cultural and political experimentation in China, the result of a tangle of nationalist and imperial pressures, made a propitious environment for Richards's literary and linguistic ideals. It was this climate of transition that nourished his scheme for a Chinese renaissance.

II

The entry in Richards's diary for December 9, 1928, reads as follows:

> Consequent headache all morning while Ivor sat in his dressing gown composing an intricate letter to China. Is it not a joke after all—this going to Peking? It seems wild—I wonder how Cambridge would take it?[7]

The passage is not in Richards's hand, but in that of his wife, Dorothea Eleanor Pilley. In Dorothea, Richards had found a match for his own formidable energies. A feminist, journalist, indefatigable traveler and renowned mountaineer, she shared with her husband a passion for climbing and a fiercely independent spirit. The two had been married the previous winter in the course of a world tour encompassing North America, Asia, India and the Alps. Dorothea kept a careful, if sometimes hasty, diary throughout the course of the marriage that contains a great deal of vital information about the couple's activities in China. Over the years she recorded impressions, plans and itineraries as well as transcriptions of important letters and scraps of conversation. Since many of the Richards's papers were destroyed in a basement flood in Cambridge, England, in the 1970's, Dorothea's diary, along with the surviving letters, is a prime source for tracing the Richards's thoughts and movements in the Far East.

The "intricate letter" to Peking was a response to the offer of a visiting professorship for the academic year of 1929–30. On the surface it seems an odd time for Richards to consider leaving Cambridge. By the late 1920's he was at the height of his fame. A constant stream of books and articles over the course of the decade had earned him a reputation as one of Britain's foremost authorities on literary modernism. To the generation coming of age in the Twenties, his influence was decisive and dramatic. Christopher Isherwood was only one of many students who felt that Richards "was infinitely more than a brilliant new literary critic: he was our guide, our evangelist, who revealed to us, in a succession of astounding lightning flashes, the entire expanse of the Modern World."[8] The critic William Empson, also a pupil of Richards's, could recall students spilling out of the lecture hall in the late 1920's, with Richards addressing the crowd from the street: a feat, it was said, "that had not happened since the Middle Ages."[9] Other successes might also have induced Richards to stay in Cambridge. The English School, which he had been instrumental in founding, was now firmly established, with F. R. Leavis among the first to receive a Ph.D. in the subject, in 1924. Richards's stock also promised to rise considerably with the imminent publication of *Practical Criticism*, the result of student protocols he had been collecting for nearly four years. Given these prospects, the consideration of a post in Peking at this time requires some explanation.

Certainly part of the reason for the decision lies with Dorothea, who found the transition from world traveler to academic spouse a difficult one. The tradition of the bachelor don was still strong at Cambridge in the Twenties, and a colleague's wife did not always fit easily into the round of teas, college dinners and late-night discussions at the heart of university life. Within a few weeks of returning from their honeymoon, Dorothea was already showing signs of dissatisfaction with Cambridge society. "I seem so dull," she wrote in the diary. "Notice my poor memory and powers of expression and don't really believe in others' interests except in their own immediate preoccupations."[10] It didn't take long for her to identify the company and not herself as the source of the trouble. Already by February she was writing: "In many ways I wish I could escape from this rarified atmosphere. I can never hope to be a scholar or really like people who allow themselves to be known so little, little in their factual or inner lives."[11] Dorothea never warmed to Cambridge—she once called it "a man-made world where women have privileges"—and later in Richards's career she would stay in London, joining him on weekends by train.[12] Her antipathy for college life must certainly have been a motivating factor in Richards's decision about Peking.

But Richards had reasons of his own for finding Cambridge confining at this juncture in his career. The world tour with Dorothea in 1926–27 was the symptom of a growing restlessness; he claimed to be "intellectually exhausted and badly [needing] a change of scene."[13] Their honeymoon, beginning in eastern Canada and proceeding through the Rockies to California, Honolulu (where the couple were married) and on to Tibet, India and the Alps, must have opened Richards's eyes to the insularity of Cambridge life. He also began to show signs of dissatisfaction with his teaching. After attending one of his classes at the end of 1927 Dorothea wrote:

> Somewhat struck by the uselessness to most of the audience of such lectures. What they want are tabloid rules for correct thinking—either practically as schoolteachers—or as complete aesthetes in the forefront of fashion—neither type can afford to be in the wrong. He needs snobbish certitude to achieve this mixed pride with pity—this exaltation. Ivor contends that he consoles himself with the thought that a few will be shown how to read and value poetry.[14]

The same sense of frustration pervades *Practical Criticism*, which was published in March 1929 just prior to the Richards's departure. The misunderstandings revealed in the students' responses to poems showed Richards how fundamental the problems of language and communication were even among Cambridge undergraduates, many of them reading for Honours. He found in the student protocols the same reliance on critical dogmas, the same tendency to fall back on pat formulas and dreaded "stock responses," that Dorothea observed in the lecture hall and that Richards had campaigned against so vigorously in his critical work. After dozens of examples of misreadings, slipshod analyses and dramatic failures in comprehension, he concludes *Practical Criticism* with the dismal observation that "the extraordinary variety of the views put forward, and the reckless, desperate character of so many of them indicate . . . how unprepared for such a testing encounter the majority of the readers were."[15]

Practical Criticism marks the beginning of Richards's shift in interest from literary criticism to problems of primary education. The change in no way diminished his fundamental sense of mission. "Ivor explains faith and the soul are bound to disappear for the next few generations," Dorothea recorded in a 1928 entry, just a month before the letter to China, "and his line is to give them standards of value without the old foundations."[16] By 1929, Cambridge no longer seemed to Richards the best place to accomplish this. As John Paul Russo says of this period: "The theoretical groundwork of his criticism had been laid down. He could even feel confident that the pioneering phase of the English School had ended and that consolidation, a phase that always interested him far less, had begun: the school reviewed its program and adopted new regulations just before he left."[17] Part of the attraction of the Far East for Richards was the chance to make a greater difference with his criticism. With *Practical Criticism* behind him, he was ready to take on a broader, more comprehensive challenge.

On January 16 an answer to Richards's Peking letter arrived. Arthur Pollard-Urquhart, a Briton teaching English literature at Tsing Hua University, wrote to explain the terms of the contract: twelve months' salary for the period of August 1, 1929, to July 31, 1930, with train fare for both Richards and Dorothea on the Trans-Siberian express. The arrangement called for two or three hours of lecturing a week at Peking University as well. Formal offers from the university President and the head of the Western Language and Literature Department would soon follow: "I have told them to lay it on thick about the honour we would have in obtaining such an illustrious light."[18] "Ivor wild with excitement," Dorothea recorded in the couple's diary. "I rather bubbling too at the thought of travel and adventure and escape from the Cambridge routine."[19] Magdalene College generously granted a leave of absence, and arrangements for travel were made. A scant five months after the publication of *Practical Criticism*, the Richardses were en route to China via Soviet Russia.

III

The couple did not leave for China entirely in the dark about the country's current situation. Aside from a steady diet of reading on the Far East, they had stopped briefly in Shanghai and Hong Kong on their way to the Himalayas in 1926–27. Their impressions then had not been entirely favorable. Although the stay was brief, it gave them a taste of the violence and political instability in the region. Richards also knew of Britain's checkered past with China and strongly opposed its imperial role. When a British gunboat opened fire on Shanghai, killing 2,000, the incident had left Richards "trembling with indignation at our [British] injustice."[20] A more direct experience of the political climate came on May 1, 1927. While leaving the harbor of Shanghai for Hong Kong, a short volley of bullets hit the ship, one shot actually grazing Richards's sleeve. The source of the gunfire could not be identified, but Richards was surprised to find the ship's officers nonplussed. The couple also found the cultural life disheartening. As Dorothea explained in a letter to her brother,

> China at the moment becomes more and more difficult to approach and
> less and less profitable to study as the war cloud gathers over it. There is
> no interesting battle of cultures (that is a European myth) because there is
> no contact. Everybody there is incredibly in the dark. All their looking
> into varied civilizations is v[ery] unsettling.[21]

The trip exposed the Richardses to many features of Chinese life that
they would encounter again in 1929–30: imperial bullying, the regular
threat of violence, the "looking into varied civilizations."

But the Richardses quickly revised their notions about the country
in their first year there. They developed a deep affection for the Chinese and their culture, with its strong respect for the past. Though
they saw much to criticize in Chinese life, the scale of change underway in the country astonished them. The situation impressed Richards as "all a mix of medievalism, the Renaissance and the Romantic
revival."[22] The time at Tsing Hua gave the couple a sense of the
enormous obstacles that the Chinese faced in their effort to shift from
an agrarian to an industrial society, but it also convinced them of the
country's immense potential.

Their excitement over the future possibilities for China began with
the train ride through the Soviet Union. In the twelve years since the
Bolshevik Revolution, Russia had committed itself to a rigorous program of economic modernization, and by 1929 signs of its progress
were everywhere. "Moscow was fascinating," Richards wrote to his
English friends. "There seems a chance of their pulling off their experiment and if so all the world will have to wake up. But one can't
on the spot admire too much the efforts they are making."[23] Though
not blind to "all the hateful aspects of despotism" under Communist
rule, he marveled at the sheer pace of change: "They had to crowd
1,000 years into 10 with a courage that makes one's heart grow
cold."[24] His impression of China would conform to a similar pattern.
The specific form of government was secondary in his mind to the
scope of work being done. In Russia, as later in China, this could lead
to false optimism or severe miscalculation. His astonishment at the
country's progress, for instance, led him to conclude that "a triumph
of prosperity on the A[merican] model is quite a possibility in the life
and time of our generation."[25] If the Soviet experiment succeeded, he
told a colleague, "we and the rest of the world will have to wake up
and change our mental habits."[26] As always for Richards, modernity

was more than simply technological change; it meant a new way of thinking, a reinvention of the world. The trip through Soviet Russia confirmed his view that lasting global transformations were underway, outstripping conventional responses and modes of thought. "I have the impression that the experimenting scope of Gov[ernment] there is something outside the scope of general principles and unpredictable," he wrote at the end of his Siberian journey. "Certainly the effort that is being made is titanic—and the material very intractable. But I don't feel sure that they won't succeed brilliantly."[27] Richards would face China's own efforts at modernization with the same conviction that he was witness to events of global consequence.

The Richardses arrived in Peking on September 14 ,1929. They were welcomed by Raymond Duloy Jameson, a faculty member at Tsing Hua, and Stanley Bennett, a climbing acquaintance of the Richardses' who held a post at the British Legation. Jameson was an American teaching English Literature in the Western Language department. A keen admirer of Richards's criticism, he was to become one of the couple's closest friends and an important collaborator in the Basic English project. At the station, Dorothea found herself "appalled again by the treaty port kind of foreigner—females over-dressed, males over drunk and both look[ing] self-indulgent and sulky to the last degree."[28] She was also struck by the clamor of the Peking streets, "what with rickshaws and bicycles and busses and trains and wheelbarrows and dogs and coolies with long poles balancing every kind of burden across their shoulders and funerals and weddings and none of them paying the least attention however much the horn is sounded."[29] Their temper quickly improved the next day with the trip to Tsing Hua, several miles from the outskirts of Peking. The contrast with the city was dramatic. The campus and its outlying buildings stood on a hundred-acre forested park at the foot of Peking's Western hills, with ancient Buddhist temples dotting the landscape. The Richardses would spend many weekends climbing the hills, visiting the temples and exploring the surrounding countryside where peasants worked the fields in a manner unchanged for centuries.

The couple were also delighted to find that they would be housed in an ancient Chinese temple, the Llama Miao, or "Temple of True Consciousness." The recently abandoned summer home of an important ex-minister, the Llama Miao had been subdivided and converted to faculty housing. The Richardses couldn't have asked for a more idyllic setting. The temple still bore signs of its monastic occupants; bronze incense burners, bells and a staggering variety of flowers filled the courtyard, which Dorothea pronounced "one of the loveliest gardens in the world."[30] "A perfect pleasure to live in," Richards wrote after two weeks there, "marble terraces leading between cassia groves to marble altars that are banks of flaming zenias now. Red lacquer pavilions whose fronts are all immense red pillars stand about the garden and we live in one of them."[31] At the Llama Miao the Richardses seemed to be living in an earlier China. As Dorothea described it to one friend: "The fairy tale feeling is so strong that one might at any moment wake up to find [oneself] in Cambridge."[32]

The "fairy-tale feeling" was a jarring contrast to the modern nation on the rise that Richards was there to advance. To understand his affection for the country, it is important to realize how much of his experience was filtered through the tranquility of Tsing Hua and the Llama Miao. Its bucolic charm tended to muffle some of the more troubling social and political changes taking place in the rest of China. Even the presence of a Nationalist army division within earshot of the Llamo Miao did little to dispel the fairy tale: "the 8,000 soldiers in the barracks a mile from here look about 15 years old dressed in grey cotton with cloth slippers on their feet so when they march past you only hear their heavy breathing along the dusty road."[33] The tranquility of life at the Llama Miao, abetted by the surrounding beauty of the Western Hills, would dominate the couple's impression of China for years to come. "Here," Dorothea assured a friend, "we are at the moment in Paradise."[34]

If the Llama Miao seemed a model of pastoral calm, Richards's first day of teaching introduced him to the turbulence of modern China. During the ceremonies that opened the Fall term, students and faculty gathered in a 2,000-seat auditorium festooned with political slogans and Nationalist flags. Before speeches began, the audience turned to an oversized picture of Sun Yat-sen, founder of the Chinese Republic, "while an officer shouted his will and gave the word of command at which we bowed solemnly three times."[35] The university President, Lo Mi Chin, then made what Dorothea described as "an emphatic and interminable speech" lasting three-quarters of an hour. Already the couple had heard rumors about Lo, a recent Kuomintang appointee who was said to be placing his own nominees on the faculty at the older teachers' expense. The politically charged atmosphere at Tsing Hua, as the Richardses soon discovered, was a typical feature of Chinese academic life, and it would contribute to their sense of the new values and principles the nation required. Afterwards they attended the President's feast, a grand affair ("6 round tables, hundreds of dishes succeeding one another [and] in the middle of each you help your neighbors with chopsticks while they help you") indicative of the scale of hospitality to which they would have to accustom themselves. By early October Dorothea complained:

> one becomes absolutely stunned in ½ hour by these feasts. Later in evening Ivor desperately depressed at the ease with which one becomes tired in this country. Probably the self-control required to tackle these foods robs one of all nervous energy.[36]

Aside from occasional homesickness—"we feel at present rather lost," Dorothea reported in November, "and Cambridge seems the home of tranquillity"—the Richardses found the social rhythms of Tsing Hua seductive.[37] They adapted quickly to the round of afternoon teas, dinners and weekend excursions to the Western Hills that filled academic community life. Their first acquaintances were their colleagues in the Department of Western Languages and Literature, who introduced the Richardses to some of the paradoxes of a modernizing China. The Department Head, for example, Wong Quincey ("very American, easy going") drove a new Ford and wrote English plays in the Shavian mode in his spare time.[38] Richards found him "very proud of his characterizations and utterly indifferent to any consequences of publication," though the seriousness with which he took his art was a running joke among the staff.[39] Another Chinese colleague, Wen Yuan Ming, had studied at King's College, Cambridge, and was a passionate admirer of H. G. Wells, Arnold Bennett and Katharine Mansfield, writers who were very much in vogue in China at the time.[40] Visiting Wen's home for tea, they discovered "a palatial place with Victorian foreign rooms, stiff leather armchairs and a small table giving an inferior hotel lounge effect."[41] Ming's Western tastes and education, however, did not preclude him from "presenting the case for ancestor worship, concubinage and Chinese scholarship," an incongruous blend of the traditional and modern that the Richardses found among many of their Chinese acquaintances.[42] One of these, a young faculty member named George Yeh (Keh

Kung-chao), struck up a close professional relationship with Richards that proved vital in the later Basic work of the Thirties.[43]

The foreign members of the faculty were also crucial social contacts and later formed an important source of recruits for the Basic English project. Arthur Pollard-Urquhart, a Scotsman, had come to China just after the First World War and was one of the senior Westerners on the Tsing Hua staff. Robert Winter, an expatriate Chicagoan who had known Ezra Pound at Wabash College in Indiana, was also a Tsing Hua veteran and the fiercely proud cultivator of a renowned Chinese garden. For the most part "old hands" in the country, they often assumed a breezy authority on Chinese matters that placed them in Dorothea's category of "denationalized Sentimentalists who love China."[44] Both were also homosexuals who found in China a more tolerant and congenial atmosphere than at home. Raymond Duloy ("Jim") Jameson was a more recent arrival from the United States who, with a wife and small child, was less eager to make China his adoptive home. On the train from Peking, Dorothea found Jameson "wildly keen on Basic English and Ivor and he got on at once very well and started making plans for teaching it."[45] All three became loyal friends of the Richardses and would be instrumental in future endeavors.

If the social milieu of Tsing Hua provided a sense of the familiar, Richards's contact with his students was a reminder of how foreign China could be. He began lecturing on September 19, 1929. Teaching mostly freshman English, Richards enjoyed great latitude in choosing his subject matter and took to the task with characteristic verve. The first weeks found him "haranguing his class on Aristotle, Longinus, Dante, Milton, Bordeau, Dryden, Coleridge [and] Arnold," explaining their relevance to the situation in contemporary China.[46] Other topics ranged from the influence of American advertising to problems of language and logic, pet subjects from his Cambridge years. In one lecture he explained how "the transplantation of peoples and the decay of the family puts a new burden on literature as the only vehicle of culture and superior mentality, just at the moment when the commercialization of printing and the diffusion of literacy have sunk its level lowest"; a crisp restatement of his cultural criticism in England.[47] How pertinent the analysis might have seemed to his Chinese audience is an open question. But in speaking about contemporary writers such as D. H. Lawrence, Walter de la Mare and George Moore, Richards discovered the same eagerness to learn about the current literary scene that he had met with among his students at Cambridge.

From the first, Richards viewed his Chinese students with a mixture of exasperation and awe. He found that "they have many times the European power of memory and a tireless application," and their deftness at retaining long passages of text, an ability highly prized in Confucian scholarship, was a continual wonder. In November he wrote to William Empson: "My pupils are incredibly nice. So attentive and good humoured—so anxious to learn and hard working. Very good minds many of them with a mental endurance and memorizing capacity that staggers belief."[48] Their manners and demeanor— "so respectful and patient"—reinforced his favorable impression. He found they responded sensitively to many kinds of poetry, growing "warm with pleasure over . . . descriptions of London evenings, lights, etc.," although "one never knows what they will find difficult or what say—in English poetry—they will take to or reject."[49] On the whole, however, Richards's relationship with his new students looked auspicious.

At the same time, a different set of cultural assumptions could lead to some jarring interpretations of Western texts. In teaching Thomas Hardy's *Tess of the d'Urbervilles*, for instance, Richards was mystified by student applause as he read out the final scene. He soon discovered that they had read the novel as a moral tale rather than a tragedy, interpreting Tess's death as just retribution for disobedience to her father at the beginning of the story.[50] Students were also apt to take writers at their word, investing literature with a kind of moral authority that hampered a more critical approach. In a letter to Empson, Richards lamented the fact that

> what we would say doubtingly and daringly after years of thought, they say 'of course' to even when it is quite, quite new to them as a thought. But equally some of our truisms they just don't believe—they think we are clumsy hypocrites about them. For example: nobody in their eyes does anything except for their own advantage and a man and a woman, if youthful, always misconduct themselves at once if alone together. When [George] Moore closes the Book K[erith] Chp. XXX with a remark about God as the last uncleanliness of the mind—they are apt to ask 'is that the right view, yes?'[51]

Such incidents led Richards to feel at times that his students were "incredibly charming but moving so much in another medium of thought than ours that they feel nearly as far off as fishes in a tank."[52]

What stands out about Richards's assessments of his Chinese students is that he attributed these differences not to intelligence or racial traits, but rather to language. "The great problem," he asserted

> is how they are taught to write and think in English. At present they learn an incredible pile of nonsense at school before they come to us. And their minds are half filled with useless lumber they can't handle. The familiar story in fact but on a new scale.[53]

Richards believed that his students' interpretive shortcomings were fundamentally no different from those of the Cambridge undergraduates whose misreadings he discussed in *Practical Criticism*. In both cases the causes of misunderstanding were the same: poor training in reading techniques and the mental operations that communication requires. In China, the problem was exacerbated by students' struggle to understand a foreign literature without being familiar with its attendant cultural assumptions. Richards blamed antiquated methods of language instruction for failing to take these difficulties into account:

> They have been taught the pluperfect subjunctive but can't work the present indicative. They say verdant abundance when they ought to say 'plenty of green'. Poor dears they have suffered from their teachers. . . . If I can knock on the head even three of the constructions they are taught and will never master, it will have been worthwhile coming.[54]

Many of the obstacles his students faced could, in his view, be easily avoided simply by improved teaching methods. An approach to language instruction more cognizant of their capacities and needs would be an enormous help in easing the process of cultural transmission. Greater access to language thus required a clearer grasp of its underlying concepts and assumptions.

While Richards faulted poor instruction for his students' difficulties with English, he also felt that the Chinese language itself was partly to blame. "Chinese leads them backwards up the stream of time, which is clearly too strong to be stemmed," he complained.[55] As he confided to William Empson, his pupils were certainly industrious and attentive "but with such obstacles linguistically and in their inverted oblique outlook to all our problems."[56] Although he knew almost nothing about Chinese, Richards quickly realized that the radically different syntax and structure of the language accounted for many of his students' more mystifying interpretive habits. Less than a month after arriving at Tsing Hua, he recorded that his "interest really lay in language ways and to get enough Chinese literature explained in detail to get the hang of the problems."[57] On November 30 he informed a friend:

> I'm trying to get up courage enough to tackle a little Chinese. Though some of them talk quite remarkably good [sic], their mental habit is not ours. They think in what look like traditional figures of speech, to which context alone gives specific meaning. Their logic seems more like our poetry (without the poetry) than logic. . . . I don't suppose I shall be able to find out anything about this in this short stay.[58]

For a critic as concerned as Richards with the nature of meaning, and in particular with the division between scientific and poetic modes of language, the differences between Chinese and English linguistic habits were fascinating. It was a subject that would occupy him more deeply in *Mencius on the Mind*, which he began work on toward the end of his stay. On the more practical classroom level, however, Richards saw that what his students most needed was a better system for learning how to put grammatical principles to use. It was his encounter with student difficulties at Tsing Hua that convinced him of the need for a type of instruction that would teach language not merely as a set of vocabulary and rules, but as an activity entailing specific processes of thought.

Richards began to think about new pedagogical techniques virtually from the moment he set foot in China. Less than a week after the couple's arrival, Dorothea wrote to a friend: "We had a Royal welcome and Ivor is much stimulated, enjoying teaching and starting a lot of wild experiments to teach the C[hinese] to talk."[59] Soon thereafter, Richards informed Frank Salter that "as to work it is mostly play but there is something interesting to be done with the teaching technique of English and composition. Also Ogden's Basic English is clearly going to alter the whole situation. It is exactly what the Chinese need and most of them know it in the universities."[60] Richards's actual use of Basic English during this first trip to China was minimal; its role in his later plans forms the subject of the next chapter. For the present, he concentrated on "find[ing] out what I can about teaching methods and possibilities, with a view to getting [the students] taught in the future something more useful than tenses which they don't ever think in or passive constructions they have to be told not to use."[61] The prospect of undertaking such pioneering linguistic work was exhilarating to Richards. "Teaching," as he described it to one colleague

> is like being an old Renaissance schoolmaster and indeed there is something which makes our old Renaissance seem a mere local agitation going on here. However it will be going on for a long time still and we needn't yet worry as to where it is going to; any movement in almost any direction seeming good for a people who have been, so palpably, stuck fast for so many centuries! It is a marvel that they haven't rotted away mentally but there is no doubt they haven't.[62]

Richards thus came to understand his own work in English instruction as part of China's larger advance toward modernity.

Apart from linguistic investigations and classroom experiments, the Richardses' schedule afforded plenty of time to enjoy the pleasures of the country. Foremost among these was the luxury of a servant staff at the Llama Miao. "One gets the attentions and services one has only dreamt of in dreams," Dorothea wrote home, facetiously complaining that the "difficulty is to create enough work for them to do. One tends to throw one's shoes about in odd corners and one's clothes on the floor so that they can collect, brush, press and put them away—it's unspeakably demoralising."[63] In their first week at the temple she also engaged a wizened Mandarin teacher ("Manchu, old, opium eater, very dignified, beautiful manner") and promptly began to keep the household accounts in Chinese.[64] "All rather like a fairy tale," she wrote, resorting to what was by now a favorite simile, "especially when at night the Boy pulls the great doors to . . . and he seems to vanish through the wall behind him. He goes off. We are not certain where, to some neighboring village to sleep."[65]

The round of life at the Llama Miao was punctuated by excursions to the Western Hills, visits to local temples, and long dinner parties with friends and colleagues from Tsing Hua. The territory around the university abounded in small villages and examples of ancient architecture which made China's history a living presence. "No foreigners about," Dorothea wrote after a typical excursion to the Tsing Hua walls for lunch,

> only peasants cutting grass and carrying it down in huge loads on a carrying pole. Had a lot of pleasant conversation in different languages with local people—a little begging went on. . . . Down to a temple near the

gate of the Pass. Broken golden tiles dusty. . . . Came round shoulder and found lots of blue people hoeing valiantly on terraces right high up.[66]

In addition to these idyllic scenes, frequent visits between members of the Western Languages faculty enlivened social life, with teas and cocktail parties often taking up the better part of the afternoon. Gossip was lively in such a tightly knit circle, particularly as social intimacy engendered a fair amount of sexual intrigue. In one very public incident, the wife of a Chinese lecturer discovered her husband's relationship with one of the servant boys. Their neighbors overheard the ensuing argument and word of the scandal soon spread to the rest of the faculty. Both Winter and Pollard-Urquhart, two of the Richardses' closest friends on the Tsing Hua staff, were frank about their homosexuality and the opportunities for practicing it in China. Their sexual orientation was more a matter of gossip than scandal; Wong Quincey's wife, for one, was full of information about Pollard-Uquhart's "private life in the village" and was happy to share.[67] Compared to the more formal, even formidable, social life at Cambridge, the relatively bohemian atmosphere of Tsing Hua seemed colorfully exotic.

Less pleasant were the endless series of factional struggles among the faculty. Chinese academia, as the Richardses quickly discovered, was far more explicitly political than anything they had known at Cambridge. President Lo was a direct appointee of the Kuomintang, and his cronyism was a source of bitter acrimony among the staff. Other disputes involved matters of patronage or simple envy. One Mrs. Chao, the wife of a lecturer in the Western Languages and Literature Department, told Dorothea that she and Mrs. Wong Quincey "had been very close friends for three years until a difference in a college appointment," after which she regarded Mrs. Chao as "a poisonous, coarse woman."[68] The Richardses managed to stay aloof from most of the strife, sexual and otherwise, and their circle of friends was wide. By the end of October, they were delighted enough with the country to consider staying for good.[69] Given the occasion for linguistic experiment and the pleasantries of social life at Tsing Hua, China's attractions seemed impossible to resist.

IV

Events in the following months forced the Richardses to revise some of their earlier views of the Chinese. Although still sanguine about the country's future, the realities of Chinese political and academic life began to blunt the edge of their optimism. One sign of the change was Richards's growing disillusionment with his students. Still impressed with their capacity and industry, he felt less certain that they were really benefiting from his teaching. In April 1930 he described his students to F. R. Leavis as having a

> good amount of memory but it is doubtful whether any but a few have any sense of what to do with what they learn or any power of learning a technique for handing their acquisitions. Their aim historically has never been to respond or think, but only to KNOW. It makes things seem absurdly simple but also simply absurd. I'm sure the best things we could give them would be techniques of various kinds but we haven't worked them out ourselves.[70]

Their linguistic habits proved more intractable than Richards had originally thought. "What is startling to find," he lamented to a colleague after seven months in China,

> is that they don't bother as we do about the sense. There is no impulse to ask 'Can it mean this'. They just say 'the meaning is . . .' and then the next minute they may say something quite different without the shock of the transition seeming to affect them. It's the generalized emotion (of a recognized traditional kind) and the neatness of a versification (triumph = a difficult game) and the high condensation of phrasing and the chant (which I fancy is very important—we should call it singing) its this whole thing which they enjoy and admire—NOT any fine nuances and subtleties. They are much more devoted to and concerned with mere technique than with meanings but AT THE SAME TIME they become flooded with rather vague and indiscriminate emotion.[71]

The new note of frustration reflects Richards's growing awareness of the depth of the gulf between Chinese and Western expectations from literature. A further disappointment was his continued failure to get behind his students' elaborate courtesies. Despite several months of poetry readings, classes, luncheons and more informal points of contact, the Chinese of his acquaintance seemed more impenetrable than ever. After one informal gathering to discuss *The Waste Land*, an exasperated Dorothea wrote: "They didn't contribute anything to the discussion and seemed like children. They did however suggest a little bowl of water under the lamp to reflect the light and catch the thousands of flies who fall in and are drowned."[72] In April she confided to a friend:

> We both enjoy our Chinese students still, but there comes a point when, after appearing to get very much in touch, one finds that one really doesn't know them at all. Years here seem to leave the same impression though—number of foreigners are very much in love with the Chinese. The country people have the winning ways of sweet animals—and their lives, too, poor things. But one doesn't manage to communicate much even with the most Western and modern of them.[73]

The Chinese approach to examinations was another source of distress. The Richardses found the open cheating, extortion and gross opportunism that surrounded end-of-term exams appalling. The whole process rendered the tests "an extraordinary farce as one isn't allowed to fail anyone, which would make the institution as well as the individual lose face. [The students] manufacture all kinds of excuses for not taking them so as to get a grade without any risks. Cheating is beyond anything we have dreamt of and its chief charm is its openness."[74] Student strikes were a traditional expedient for avoiding exams, as well as an accepted form of extortion: "Here they strike for books, for more heating in the classroom, against unpopular presidents and for political reasons we can't follow at all. . . . There is a very merciless and callow side to it all, intrigue behind intrigue, quite unscrupulous—rival factions in the staff using student agitations to further their own political ambitions and envies."[75] Part of the reason for the low level of academic integrity was that few students were at the university to become scholars. As Dorothea noted: "This place is rather like England as far as jobs for educated people are concerned, and all Chinese want to be officials with high salaries and nothing to do but be drained by the family, which is not a mere close relationship like ours but runs into fourth cousins and scores of people all of whom have a claim to their salaries."[76]

The students' attitude toward examinations confirmed the Richardses' more general sense of ethical irregularities in China. Their impression of university politics and administration continued to worsen. In February Richards bitterly remarked:

> China's idea of finance is a mixture of robbery and graft. From the lowest to the highest everybody 'squeezes' and if one gets one's salary it is only

because someone hopes to gain something from treating you in such an exceptional manner. The defrauded Chinese have to find someone to defraud in their turn. I've had 10% of my last month's salary and when I shall see the rest is in the lap of Buddha.[77]

Dorothea endorsed his view in a letter home in which she described the situation for a friend as follows:

If you imagine Chicago scale bribery with the comic opera eavesdroppers, hidden hand under the sofa kind of atmosphere you'll have fallen short of the actuality. Nobody can do anything on any line without making it worth somebody's while and demolishing, by slander or BLACKMAIL (the principal method of government here) half a dozen other persons who obstruct in the interests of their own hopeful little schemes. There is no idea of public service except in newspaper propaganda and blackmail is easy as there is unlimited occasion and when you haven't any facts, you invent them—the worse the better.[78]

The apparent lack of civic responsibility constituted one of the Richardses' main criticisms of the Chinese in their first year there. By April, Richards's view of Chinese ethics was so dire that he could write to T. S. Eliot: "I miss what we are accustomed to call morality—some influence of some principle of being, or aspiration, not merely of personal gain. It would be odd if I became a Christian out here."[79]

A coup d'etat near Peking in March 1930 confirmed many of the Richardses' worst impressions of Chinese political life. The Kuomintang had won control of northern China as recently as 1927, and their hold upon certain areas was still tenuous. In the spring of 1930 a cabal of warlords threatened to disrupt control of Peking. Tsing Hua, just outside the city, was well within the radius of hostilities. It was an important first-hand experience for the Richardses of the political instability endemic to China. On March 15, 1930, Richards sent word to friends and family back home of frequent changes in government following the vicissitudes of the military campaign. These shifts continued through most of the spring without much visible effect on Tsing Hua, aside from a group of students arrested for holding a Communist meeting in March.

The Richardses observed these political oscillations with a good degree of cynicism. Dorothea reported that "public interest is much absorbed in who will lose their jobs and who will lose their heads."[80] Matters became more serious in late May, when President Lo became "the only prominent supporter of the Nanking Government left in any office in or near Peking."[81] Soon thereafter, events descended into farce. A group of students, rumored to be employed by Tsing Hua's Dean, drafted a letter demanding Lo's resignation. Lo refused to accept the document, but immediately issued a response countering the charges and detailing his many services to the University. According to Richards, this reasoned rebuttal

> stirs violent resentment on two grounds: 1) That the style in which it is written does not flow very smoothly and is not very elevated (is not scholarly enough). 2) That it is stamped with a black oblong seal used for the most important official documents. The last point is considered to be a serious affront to the students! No criticism of the contents or of its being issued at all. Since the document, for these stylistic reasons has not commanded respect, the President is supposed to have lost much ground. This morning's rumour is that he has gone to Tientsin, to take shelter in the Foreign Concession there.[82]

The outcome of the student coup seemed emblematic of Richards's most serious criticisms of China. The preference for style over content, manner over meaning and selfish over civic interests paralleled many of his disappointments in the classroom. It also bred a certain cynicism about political developments in China which led him to emphasize language training over institutional change as a catalyst for future reform. In February 1930, Richards had written to friends in Cambridge that "amid much that is ridiculous and impossible there are some very hopeful things and it is quite certain that at present foreign nations can have a very good effect, if only as pieces on the board which won't follow the orthodox Chinese moves of the ancient game."[83] The events of the spring underscored the importance of this point for Richards, and in adapting Basic English for China he was determined to keep instruction as independent of political bureaucracies as possible.

In March 1929 Richards had accepted an offer of a semester's teaching at Harvard after his term at Tsing Hua. On January 5, 1931, he set sail for the United States to assume the new post. Dorothea remained in China for several months, splitting her time between Tsing Hua and Peking. The more negative aspects of the couple's experience in the country had in no way diminished their enthusiasm for its future. Facing the prospect of departing for Harvard, Richards wrote,

> There is an astonishing field of work waiting in China in every subject, for everyone with any wits. However the Chinese do very little—except

timorously follow some played-out Western line. They have abilities in some ways beyond ours (memory, industry, etc.) but very little intellectual courage. They are having to learn so much that they haven't energy to do anything with it. And they have hardly had any even 2nd rate people as yet to help them, in any of the social, psychological, anthropological lines.[84]

In the five years before his next trip to China, Richards took positive steps to provide the kind of help he believed the Chinese most needed. During that time he would refine his ideas on Basic English, work his observations into a more developed pedagogical theory and, crucially, enlist the support of the Rockefeller Foundation for enacting his plans. When Richards returned to Peking in 1936, he arrived well equipped to put his insights from the year at Tsing Hua to good use.

4   Both Sides of the Looking-Glass

Mencius, Basic English and the
Rockefeller Foundation, 1931-1935

I

In later years Richards remembered inviting T. S. Eliot to visit China in the hopes of exposing him to Confucian ideas. "I do not care," Eliot replied, "to visit any land which has no native cheese."[1] A letter from Eliot on August 9, 1930, sent to Richards during his first year in the Far East, suggests more serious grounds for his refusal. After expressing polite interest in Richards's investigations of the Chinese language, Eliot describes his own studies in Indian philosophy and Sanskrit some years earlier. "The conclusion that I came to then," he writes

> was that it seemed impossible to be on both sides of the looking-glass at once. That is, it made me think how much more dependent one was than one had suspected, upon a *particular* tradition of thought from Thales down, so that I came to wonder how much *understanding* anything (a term, a system etc.) meant merely *being used* to it. . . . And it seemed to me that all I was trying to do and that any of the pundits had succeeded in doing, was to attempt to translate one terminology with a long tradition into another; and that however cleverly one did it, one would never produce anything better than an ingenious deformation.

After citing the superficial "orientalism" of Shopenhauer as an example, Eliot goes on to conclude:

> In other words, I thought that the only way I could ever come to understand Indian thought would be to erase not only my own education in European philosophy, but the traditions and mental habits of Europe for two thousand years—and that if one did that, one would be no better off for 'translating', and even if such a feat could be accomplished, it didn't seem worth the trouble.[2]

Eliot's letter raises profound objections to Richards's pedagogical mission in China, and to his international vision generally. For what he attacks is not simply dilettantish scholarship—a kind of intellectual orientalism—but the very notion of translation itself. Eliot insists that intellection is primarily a matter of habituation, of "being used to" a set of values or ideas that receive their authority in part from a history of use. Communication, then, depends upon a shared sense of "mental habits" (a pet phrase of Richards's) formed by an education within a particular culture. To enter the mentality of one tradition after being raised with the language and assumptions of another is to be "on both sides of the looking-glass at once," a feat that Eliot finds "impossible."

Eliot expanded upon these themes in many of his other writings, and they form a crucial part of his poetics, which Richards deeply admired. His doubts about Richards's project in particular, however, center on the danger of treating translation as a matter of simply finding equivalent words between two languages. What concerned Eliot about this approach was its tendency to detach language from the particular, organic and ultimately irreducible cultural tradition that forms its meanings. Eliot's argument on this point bears a resemblance to those of contemporary critics who focus on the "silent" or untranslatable aspect of experience that language seeks to order and categorize. Seen in an imperial context, translation becomes a means of reducing one culture to the categories and terms of another in order to make it a subject of control. While Eliot's concern is with the futility of translation rather than its morality, his point is essentially the same: bridging the gulf between two cultures is an enterprise that can only take place in the language of one of the participants.

Richards, however, thought otherwise. In the years between his first and second trips to China, he articulated a case for the absolute necessity of a shared means of communication between cultures. His conviction was driven in part by his experience in China, where efforts to modernize introduced him to the growing international character of world events, and in part by the experience of the First World War, which left him with an abiding suspicion of barriers, both national and cultural, as arbitrary and artificial. In the years immediately following his return from China, Richards began to address these insights not only in his criticism but increasingly through his support for Basic English. He wrote over five books and articles on the subject in under six years in addition to his literary work and a teaching career that shuttled him between Harvard and Cambridge. It was also during this time that Richards enlisted the support of the Rockefeller Foundation, whose own efforts in China were in a process of redefinition. Through their funding Richards was eventually able to establish the Orthological Institute of China, with offices in Peking, which he joined to oversee personally in 1936.

This chapter concerns Richards's activities in the years before his second Far Eastern sojourn in 1936. It deals first with the immediate insights that he brought back from China in 1930 and with their influence on his ideas about the possibilities of language. In *Mencius on the Mind,* his first publication upon his return from China, Richards wrestled with many of the issues and concerns that arose from his experience in the country. *Mencius on the Mind* points the way to a more explicit interest in the philosophy of language, and the ideas that Richards worked out through his study of Mencius were to inform the rest of his work in China profoundly. The following section provides a brief history of Basic English and Richards's increasing involvement with it. The Basic English movement, founded by his close friend and colleague C. K. Ogden, gave Richards a vehicle for putting his ideas about China into practice. Finally, I will consider his relations with the Rockefeller Foundation, paying special attention to how its growing interests in the Far East intersected with Richards's own. Well into the 1950's, Richards's relationship with the Foundation was to have profound consequences for the Basic English movement. Under their auspices he was able to realize his plans for systematic English instruction in China.

II

Before leaving China in 1930, Richards had started work on a study that would summarize some of the linguistic and cultural questions raised by his time in the Far East. Throughout his stay he had shown a keen interest in learning about some of the traditional problems and approaches of Chinese philosophy. In the months before his departure he began working with a group of scholars at Yenching University on a translation of the Chinese philosopher Mencius, a figure who, in the Chinese tradition, occupies a place of importance nearly equal to that of Confucius. Richards's idea was to translate key passages from Mencius as literally as possible, including the variant meanings for troublesome words and taking into account the ambiguities and opacities that translators usually sacrifice to clear sense. With the help of Professor L. T. Hwang, Li An-che and Lucius Porter, all friends from Peking academic circles, Richards assembled a literal word-for-character text of several passages from Mencius amounting to some forty pages. It is this text, and the problems of translation it presented, that forms the basis of *Mencius on the Mind*.

In choosing a philosopher of Mencius's stature, Richards was attacking some of the thorniest problems of translation head-on. The first commentaries on Mencius were written in the second century B.C. and over the centuries the Chinese exegetical tradition had produced a baffling array of interpretations. Mencius's "terse utterances," as Richards points out, "remain, some of them, highly mysterious, even to the best equipped Chinese scholars."[3] He reminds his readers "that we are often not dealing with expressions whose meaning, to good Chinese scholars, can be said to be either settled or clear."[4] It is exactly this difficulty in affixing specific meanings to Mencius that makes him a perfect vehicle for Richards's own thoughts on language and translation. Richards understands as well as Eliot that in dealing with writings as complex as Mencius's, a simple translation of one set of terms to another is inadequate. In fact, the point of his study is not so much to provide a suitable translation as it is "to discuss, more explicitly than is usual, the difficulties that beset every translator and every student of any literature that is far removed in character from his own."[5] Through Mencius, Richards means to call attention to the futility of translating words or concepts before asking more fundamental, "Eliotic" questions about how a language, any language, operates to form its meanings. His purpose "is less to elucidate Mencius—which would be a task for another lifetime—than to bring into greater prominence an extremely puzzling set of linguistic situations."[6] In this respect *Mencius* is Richards's answer to the doubts that Eliot had raised about the possibility of translation between two different traditions of thought.

Ironically, the manuscript of *Mencius* was itself saved through a kind of miscommunication. Richards began work on the book shortly before his departure for Harvard, and completed a draft while still in

China. In Peking, however, the briefcase containing the manuscript was stolen by Chinese thieves. Richards then rewrote the text from memory in Cambridge, Massachusetts and submitted it for publication. While he was correcting the proofs a portion of the original manuscript arrived in the mail. It had been found on a rooftop in Peking as the pages blew down to the street, presumably abandoned by the thieves after discovering their loot to be sheets of foreign scrawl. Richards was able to check the proofs against his original manuscript, and the book was published in its final form in 1932.[7]

Richards's Foreword to *Mencius* defines translation as an issue with weighty consequences for both sides of the linguistic looking-glass. For the Chinese, he sees the study of ancient Chinese modes of meaning as a much-needed act of cultural preservation. Citing the opinion of the contemporary Chinese pragmatist Hu Shih that "Chinese Philosophy has nothing to contribute to modern thought," Richards writes:

> Chinese thought is now taking over and absorbing the whole developed Western logical technique; and it will do so more perfectly and in a more balanced way and make fewer avoidable mistakes, if it does not turn its back upon ancient Chinese thinking—relegating it to a position of historical interest. It will do better, I believe, to make as conscious and deliberate a comparison as possible between the purposes (and resultant limitations) of ancient thinking and the purposes (and resultant limitations) of Western logic.[8]

The sentiment reflects Richards's first-hand experience of the rapid and sometimes heedless pace of change he witnessed in China in 1929–30. His hope in *Mencius* is for a development that can negotiate past traditions with present technology in a way that improves upon both, a situation in which each element stands in critical balance with the other. Behind this sentiment one detects the concern that he felt for the temples and festivals and Mandarin courtesies that "modern" China seemed so intent upon destroying. But it also reveals Richards's skepticism toward Western technology and values, which he sees as a process that goes much deeper than economic or scientific change to effect a fundamental shift in mentality. Later in *Mencius* he writes:

> Before long there will be nobody studying Mencius into whose mind philosophical and other ideas and methods of Western origin have not made their way. Western notions are penetrating steadily into Chinese,

and the Chinese scholar of the near future will not be intellectually much nearer Mencius than any Western pupil of Aristotle and Kant. Unless the thinking which has been fundamental to historic China can somehow be explained in Western terms it seems inevitably doomed to oblivion.[9]

Richards's efforts on behalf of Mencius therefore begin with the assumption that Western ideas and ways of thinking are destined to become predominant in China. Modern China, he believes, will be essentially a Western China unless a conscious effort is made to preserve the voice of the past. Like Russell and Dickinson before him, he sees the problem of China as one of adopting Western scientific thought while still preserving indigenous customs and traditions. One aim of *Mencius* is to show that such a preservation is not a matter of libraries or museums, but of language. Without an understanding of the way that Mencius used language to communicate meaning, one quite different from Western logical techniques, the true content of his thought will be lost.

For the Westerner, Richards sees the value of his study as twofold. On the one hand, the difficulties encountered in translating Mencius force us to reconsider our own uses of language at a deeper level. "[T]hese linguistic situations," he says in the Foreword, "have an interest that spreads beyond the field of English-Chinese translations. A theory which could handle them would have direct bearing upon the whole range of our language purposes from the practice of the most elementary education up to the most abstruse enterprises of comparative criticism and philosophy."[10] The value in studying Mencius is to focus attention on the workings of language in general. In this respect, Mencius operates as a kind of mirror that lets us consider our own language from the outside. This use of a foreign culture to gain perspective on one's own is explicit in Richards, and an important part of his justification for the value of comparative studies. He illustrates the point by choosing a quotation from Shakespeare's "Troilus and Cressida" to open Chapter I:

> nor doth the eye itself—
> That most pure spirit of sense—behold itself,
> Not going from itself; but eye to eye oppos'd
> Salutes each other with each other's form;
> For speculation turns not to itself
> Till it hath travell'd and is mirror'd there
> Where it may see itself. This is not strange at all![11]

Secondly, by looking at our culture through the lens of a very different philosophic and linguistic tradition, Richards hopes to deliver a salutary check to the universal claims of Western thought and values. He expresses this view most explicitly in the book's Foreword:

> As to the increased knowledge of Chinese thought on the West, it is interesting to notice that a writer so unlikely to be thought either ignorant or careless as M. Etienne Gilson can yet, in the English Preface of his *The Philosophy of St. Thomas Aquinas*, speak of the Thomistic Philosophy as "accepting and gathering up the whole of human tradition". This is how we all think, to us the Western world is still the World; but an impartial observer would perhaps say that such provincialism is dangerous. And we are not yet so happy in the West that we can be sure that we are not suffering from its effects.[12]

Edward Said cites exactly this passage from *Mencius* as an instance of "a genuine type of pluralism" that is all too rare in Western encounters with foreign cultures.[13] It is also an example of the critical function that another tradition can sometimes serve for Western intellectuals approaching a culture regarded as "Other." As the passage suggests, Richards wants to use China as a critique of prevalent attitudes within his own culture. His East may be "invented" in the sense that what he finds important there is shaped by concerns originating with his own culture. But it is equally important to understand the purposes behind that depiction. For Richards, a key aspect of China's significance to the West is its ability to take us beyond the insularity of our particular history and habits of thought. As his study progresses, he uses Mencius to call into question some fundamental assumptions of European philosophy, and to expose them as linguistic conventions rather than "truth."

The critical direction of Richards's study becomes clear from his discussion of Mencius in the first chapter. Subtitled "Some Problems of Translation," it opens with the caveat "To a mind formed by modern Western training the interpretation of the Chinese Classics seems often an adventure among possibilities of thought and feeling rather than an encounter with facts."[14] The chapter then goes on to show how many of Mencius's most profound statements fail to meet the criteria of Western philosophical logic. In his first example, a brief and highly condensed passage from Mencius on causality, Richards stresses how many different interpretations the passage can bear when translated into English. The root of the problem for the translator is the Chinese word *Hsing*, which means something close to the word "Nature" in English. But, as Richards points out, because "*Hsing* stands both for Human Nature . . . and for Nature in general" in Chinese, it is extremely difficult to interpret Mencius's concept of "natural" causes in Western terms.[15] Does Mencius mean human or "external" Nature when talking about causality? Richards's point here is that due to its different linguistic resources, Chinese philosophy approaches the issue of causality with radically different questions. What appears to be an appalling lack of logical rigor to a Western philosopher is fundamentally a matter of language rather than "objective" knowledge. Following from this, Richards makes the central claim of his study:

> Chinese thinking often gives no attention to distinctions which for Western minds are so traditional and so firmly established in thought and language that we neither question them nor even become aware of them *as distinctions*. We receive and use them as though they belonged unconditionally to the constitution of things (or of thought). We forget that these distinctions have been made and maintained as part of one tradition of thinking; and that another tradition of thinking might neither find use for them nor (being committed to other courses) be able to admit them.[16]

This statement makes explicit the kind of critical self-examination of language that Richards wants to exploit through his use of Mencius. It also underscores an important aspect of his methodology throughout the book; by stressing the ambiguity of Mencius's philosophy to a Western-trained mind, Richards is able to point out an alternative register of meaning in which the passage makes sense. Reading Mencius independently of Western philosophic assumptions and with a sensitivity to the language he employs, other ways of seeing the passage emerge that make his purposes more clear.

Richards's explication of Mencius on this point bears a strong resemblance to his defense of poetry in the 1920's. The idea that a poem can say something "true" while not strictly adhering to purely logical or scientific standards of truth had been a cornerstone of his criticism since the *Meaning of Meaning*, and one that he pursued with exceptional rigor in *Science and Poetry*.[17] And, in fact, Richards goes on to equate Eastern philosophy explicitly with Western poetry. On the issue of *Hsing*, he writes:

> It is the extreme case which shows us—better than the average case—
> how interpretation of all language which is not strictly governed by an
> explicit logic proceeds. And more of our language than we suppose is of
> this kind. Perhaps apart from the language of mathematics we have none
> that is not. Certainly poetry uses this method—the indirectly controlled
> guess—for most of its purposes; and when poetry is highly condensed
> as, for example, it often is in Shakespeare and in much modern writing,
> the degree of implicitness may be as high as in any passage of Mencius.[18]

To drive the point home, Richards cites Shakespeare's lines from
Macbeth—"But here, upon this bank or shoal of time,/We'd jump the
life to come"—as an instance of an utterance from the Western tradition as logically tangled and evocative as any from Mencius. By putting Mencius's statements on a footing with Shakespeare's, Richards
wishes to shift attention from philosophical content to questions of
linguistic form, and to the very different approach that Mencius's
type of statements requires from readers. "[Mencius's] method," he
writes, "even when his aim is severely prosaic—is frequently the
method of condensed poetry. If we wished for a short description of
the difference between Confucian philosophic method and, shall we
say, Kantian, we could hardly do better than to say that the latter endeavors to use an explicit logic and the former an indicated guess."[19]

Simply by recognizing Mencius's special use of language, Richards believes that a Western reader has taken the most critical step in
appreciating his philosophy. He concedes that

> Those with a taste for clear, precise views (*itself a result of special training*)
> will accuse him of not knowing what he wants to say, or of having really
> no thought yet to utter. But there is another possibility—that a thought is
> present whose structure and content are not suited to available formula-
> tions, that these successive, perhaps incompatible, statements partly rep-
> resent, partly misrepresent, an idea independent of them which none the
> less has its own order and coherent reference.[20]

Again, this idea stems directly from Richards's notions of poetry,
which he treats in his criticism as a highly complex means of communication using resources of language other than the purely denotative. By showing *how* Mencius's statements communicate meaning
before going on to analyze *what* they say, Richards opens up possibilities of meaning that would be lost in a purely philosophical analysis. To expect, he suggests, that Mencius's writings meet the artificial
(and even arbitrary) standards of Western philosophy would be as
unjust as treating Shakespeare as a handbook in clinical psychology.

Further, the fact that Mencius's thought is taken seriously in the East *as philosophy* leads Richards to question those Western assumptions and categories that make it seem inadequate. In one of the boldest statements of the book he asserts:

> It is a possible suggestion that we perhaps Think and Feel and Will because we have for so long been talking as though we did and that if language and tradition professed a different set of psychic functions we might be conducting our minds otherwise.[21]

This passage points to a crucial motif in Richards's thought, and one that was central to his broad hopes for Basic English. In trying to work out an adequate theory of translation, Richards maintains that differences in Chinese thought stem directly from differences of language. What exists to Western minds as an intractable philosophic problem—such as the distinction between the human and the natural order—is not an issue for the Chinese because their language does not allow for it. Matters as fundamental to our identity as Thinking and Feeling and Willing, Richards suggests, are categories imposed upon the world through language. The "psychic functions" that we take for granted as an essential part of reality are in fact artificial boundaries created and enforced by our habitual use of language. These boundaries become so much a part of our ways of talking about the world that we cease to recognize them as boundaries and mistake them for natural limits.

This idea of course is not unique to Richards, nor is it entirely a product of his time in China. But what stands out are the uses that he feels it could be put to in developing nations such as China. Richards in no way accepts the pessimistic brand of cultural relativism that Eliot seems to argue for in his 1930 letter. Rather, he sees a vast, unrealized opportunity to re-engineer our understanding of the world through language. "To suppose," he writes, "that, because our conceptions and our purposes are of another fashioning from his [Mencius's], we must misunderstand him, would be to stop too short. What we need . . . if we are to go further, is a more conscious, and therefore more controllable, technique of interpretation for all cases where we may be comparing mental processes whose kinds as well as degrees of development may differ."[22] In the concluding chapter of *Mencius,* he sets out to provide exactly such a method.

The final section of Richards's study, "Towards a Technique for Comparative Studies," seems to have been written with Eliot clearly in mind. In places the language borrows directly from Eliot's letter of 1930. An opening passage reads:

> The problem, put briefly, is this. Can we in attempting to understand and translate a work which belongs to a very different tradition from our own do more than read our own conceptions into it? Can we make it more than a mirror of our own minds, or are we inevitably in this undertaking trying to be on both sides of the looking-glass at once? To understand Mencius, for example, must we efface our whole tradition of thinking and learn another; and when we have done this, if it be possible, will we be any nearer being able to translate the one set of mental operations into the other? Is such a translation, at best, only an ingenious deformation, in the style of the clever trick by which the children's entertainer makes with his fingers and thumbs a shadow really very like a rabbit?[23]

Richards, of course, goes on to answer these questions in the negative, and in this concluding chapter he offers an implicit refutation of Eliot's position. From what he had seen in the Far East, Richards could not believe that the efforts of his Chinese students to understand a foreign language and tradition were futile. Instead, he had found intelligent and eager minds undertaking a project that their language and training had not prepared them for. While drilled in vocabulary and the finer points of grammar, they were left unequipped to deal with the alien distinctions of thought that English, like any language, carries. In the earlier chapters of *Mencius*, Richards illustrates the importance of this wider conception of language by reversing the burden of understanding and asking Westerners to make sense of Mencius given only a literal translation of his words. Now, in the conclusion, he responds to Eliot's arguments by presenting a new theory of translation, one that will account for different intentions and purposes as well as words.

Richards's solution to the problems surrounding translation is a technique that he calls Multiple Definition. In the earlier parts of *Mencius*, Richards has shown that misunderstandings in translation stem from a failure to recognize how, not what, a given statement is trying to communicate. We read Mencius expecting Western philosophy, poetry expecting scientific certainty, and so on. "The danger to be guarded against," he asserts, "is our tendency to force a structure, which our special kind of Western training (idealist, realist, positivist, Marxist, etc.) makes easiest for us to work with, upon modes of thinking which may very well not have any such structure at all—

and which may not be capable of being analyzed by means of this kind of logical machinery."[24] Multiple Definition is "a plan for a technique" that would help to avoid these familiar circuits of interpretation. Richards defines Multiple Definition as:

> the habit . . . of accompanying any definition or distinction we make use of with a set of rival definitions in the background of the mind. Only so can we protect ourselves from the coercive suggestion of any one interpretation which seems for the moment to fit.[25]

Multiple Definition, then, is less a formal technique than a habit, a new way of understanding. The reader is asked to think in terms of "possible ranges of meanings"[26] rather than of a single, fixed meaning connecting the foreign word or phrase to familiar categories of thought. The idea owes something to Richards's cultural critique of the 1920's, when he defended the reading of poetry as a kind of mental exercise for processing the growing stimuli of modern life.[27] But the experience of teaching in the Far East, which forced him to confront problems of communication between two radically different cultures, gave a new context for these ideas and suggested a more ambitious scope for their application. By the end of *Mencius*, Richards has redefined translation as a habit of mind, a psychological training in cultural understanding. The consequences of such an approach, to Richards's mind, are far-reaching and potentially revolutionary.

One result of his theory is to counter Eliot's skepticism about the possibility of understanding ideas from another tradition. Behind Richards's notion of Multiple Definition is the assumption that all writing implies a desire to communicate. The aim of interpretation is to understand how a given utterance conveys its author's ideas. According to Richards, "The habit of mind required [for interpretation] is that of regarding all thinking—even the most seemingly autonomous—as purposive; and of expecting the form of the thinking to be not independent of the purpose." So a notion of purpose or intention is present in every statement. Following from this, Richards insists:

> With this habit [of Multiple Definition] we may be readier, when we analyse our thought, to treat any structure we find in it (or give to it in the course of analysis) as no more than an instrument convenient or not for the purpose in hand. The subject-predicate, universal-particular, relational, syncretic, discrete, or organic structures we use in the analysis, we shall regard as not necessarily structures that the thought intrinsically has (still less as necessarily the structure of the aspect of the world the

thought is 'of'), but merely as forms which it is useful, for certain purposes, to regard the thought as having.[28]

Here is the crux of Richards's objection to Eliot. In his 1930 letter, Eliot
sees the problem of translation as one of tradition; past usage gives
words their meanings and in turn shapes the ideas they can express.
In this passage, Richards maintains that language and the assumptions that it carries—the distinctions between subject and predicate,
universal and particular and so forth—are *incidental* to the ideas or
thoughts themselves. Mencius's statements may at first seem baffling,
but once we understand the purpose behind his distinctions—the
ideas that he is trying to get across with the linguistic tools at hand—
then we may be able to express the thought in different language
without misrepresenting his intentions. This view in no way contradicts Richards's earlier suggestion that "we perhaps Think and Feel
and Will because we have for so long been talking as though we did."
There Richards criticizes an unreflective use of language that mistakes
a habit of usage for a universal truth, one that blocks our ability to accept the possibility of other ways of seeing the world. Now, in his
conclusion, Richards advocates a kind of translation that communicates intentions rather than simply words, one that is supple enough
to distinguish a linguistic vehicle from its intellectual cargo.

The move is an important one, not only because it allows Richards
to circumvent Eliot's arguments about the weight of tradition, but
also because it forms the foundation of Richards's later case for Basic
English. If ideas can exist independently of the language used to express them, then that language can be simplified, stripped of its baggage of connotation and habitual associations, in order to present the
idea in a more naked form. Shakespeare's ideas about human existence can be abstracted from Hamlet's soliloquies and presented in
simpler language for an audience to whom the images and metaphors of Elizabethan verse are unfamiliar. The idea of Multiple Definition also indicates how Richards came to associate language with
world peace. In *Mencius*, he claims that Multiple Definition will put
an end to useless academic hair-splitting about words. "That our current procedure [of understanding] is inadequate," he writes, "is
shown by the ease with which any Cambridge-trained realist can
demonstrate the confusions in a product of Oxford idealism and vice
versa—a situation which would be comical if it were not so wasteful."[29] Richards's attitude toward philosophic controversy is similar

to his view of the First World War: both stem from the inability to realize that the other side is using the same words with different intentions. Richards's solution to the problem is much like his translation
of Mencius: a systematic listing of the possible meanings that key
words like Beauty or Good or *Hsing* might bear—"What is needed, in
brief, is greater imaginative resource in a double venture—in imagining other purposes than our own and other structures for the
thought that serves them."[30] Multiple Definition would provide "a
systematic survey of the language we are forced to use in translation,
of the ranges of possible meanings which may be carried by our chief
pivotal terms—such as Knowledge, Truth, Order, Nature, Principle,
Thought, Feeling, Mind, Datum, Law, Reason, Cause, Good, Beauty,
Love, Sincerity, . . .—and of our chief syntactic instruments, 'is,' 'has,'
'can,' 'of,' and the like."[31] Once the range of possible meanings is established, we can then sort out the speaker's intentions and examine
the way in which the particular word is being used. Multiple Definition becomes a habit of mind not limited to the field of translation but
applicable to any conflict where differing purposes are mistaken for
opposing ideas due to a limited view of language.

Richards's ultimate target in *Mencius* is the "combative habit of
mind," an evil with much broader consequences than Oxbridge controversies.[32] He reveals his own hopes for a wider approach to language in the following terms:

> The first effect of a general practice of multiple definition would be a
> strange peace in philosophy. A philosopher engaged in refuting an-
> other—not of his own party—would become a laughable spectacle. Ac-
> tually at the moment he is a more sinister figure. Nationalism in thought!
> The defence of the West! Of historic China! Poor little wretches that we
> are. For with the increasing pressure of world contacts we do pitiably
> need to understand on a scale we have never envisaged before. Warfare
> in the intellectual world as in the physical is a wasteful survival.[33]

By the end of *Mencius*, Richards has moved from questions of translation to problems of psychology and world conflict. His argument in
Mencius reveals how interrelated the issues were in his mind. Ultimately, what Richards advocates is a greater control over our uses of
language. A consciousness of how we use words to effect different
purposes is the first step in gaining control of those purposes. Concepts like "the West" or "historic China" could then be exposed to
critical examination, analyzed not for their truth or exact meaning but

for their purposes in a wider scheme of assumptions. And, having thus stripped them down, we would be free to change those purposes. Richards's approach to language thus allows for the possibility of questioning those traditional concepts, embedded in language, that present themselves as absolutes. It provides a critical stance on our set patterns of thought and perception. After China, Richards's ideas on this score took on an added urgency. The increasingly global context of development and trade necessitated new concepts that national boundaries no longer fit. With the theory of Multiple Definition, we refashion language to keep pace with our new concepts. By the end of *Mencius*, a theory of translation has become an instrument of world peace.

I have examined Richards's ideas in *Mencius on the Mind* in some detail because they are the essential ones underlying Basic English. An understanding of *Mencius* helps to make sense of the broad claims that Richards would make for Basic over the next decades. Basic was intended not only to make English more accessible but to change perceptions. It assumed that a more exact conception of language would eliminate the most intransigent barriers to communication. By focussing on purpose rather than tradition, it would close the gap between cultures and clear the way for truly global communication. Basic was also founded on the conviction, put forward in *Mencius*, that ideas are separable from their particular language and contexts. Ironically, Richards's enthusiasm for a limited, simplified language such as Basic was in part inspired by his recognition of the complexities involved in language and communication as discussed in *Mencius*. Basic would become a kind of shorthand for applying his ideas about Multiple Definition: a stripped-down language that would eliminate the need for long lists of possible meanings by reducing words to a more purely denotative function. China had first opened Richards's eyes to the practical possibilities of such an approach, and it was in China that Richards would make the most concentrated efforts to apply Basic in a systematic way. In the months after writing *Mencius*, he began finding the institutional support to realize his vision.

III

Between 1931 and his return to China in 1936, Richards spent much of his time putting the ideas behind *Mencius* into practice. The first

step in this direction was a growing involvement with the Basic English movement, then forming under the leadership of C. K. Ogden. In
1933 Richards attended the first Basic English conference in New
York and took a vigorous role in behalf of Basic at the Institute of Pacific Relations Conference in Banff, Alberta, that same year.[34] His
most significant achievement in these years, however, was to enlist
the support of the Rockefeller Foundation, which in 1934 agreed to
fund a program for Basic English in the Far East. The Foundation's
connection with Basic lasted until 1948, sustaining Richards's designs
in China through the Second World War and beyond.

Basic English was the invention of Richards's close friend and
collaborator, C. K. Ogden. The two had met as undergraduates at
Cambridge before the War, introduced by Richards's supervisor,
Frank Salter, after his pupil had informed him that he no longer
wanted to read for History because he "didn't think History ought to
have happened."[35] Ogden, a seasoned Classicist in his final year, was
called in to advise Richards on a new choice of subject. By the end of
their conversation Richards had decided on Moral Sciences, planning
to study with G. E. Moore. His next significant meeting with Ogden
occurred on November 11, 1918, the night of the Armistice. Ogden
now owned a picture gallery in Cambridge which was looted in the
general revelry because of his well-known opposition to the War.
Richards had witnessed the event, and Ogden called on him later that
night to see if he could identify any of the rioters. They soon discovered a shared interest in language, and talked on the stairwell "for
three hours, outlining the whole *Meaning of Meaning*."[36]

According to John Paul Russo, "the stairwell meeting [in 1918]
stood for commitment to a war-engendered antiwar consciousness
and the remolding of culture."[37] Basic English was to crystallize this
"antiwar consciousness" and become Ogden's and Richards's instrument of cultural change. The idea of a radically reduced version
of English first came to Ogden during the writing of *The Meaning of
Meaning*, the book that he and Richards began collaborating on soon
after their Armistice night meeting. In a 1973 interview Richards recalled:

> Ogden had been playing with artificial languages for perhaps ten years.
> . . . He'd read Wilkins and Leibnitz; he knew Newton's proposals back-
> wards. He was deep in it, and in all the artificial languages too. He had a
> gift for that kind of thing. And when he wrote a chapter in *The Meaning*

of Meaning, "On Definition," at the end of it we suddenly stared at one another and said, "Do you know this means that with under a thousand words you can say everything." If a word can be defined in a descriptive phrase of not more than ten words, you can substitute the descriptive ten words for the word and get rid of it. Over-simple, extremely—but, for most purposes, good enough. We found we'd worked out the principles for such rephrasings in writing that Chapter.[38]

Working out the details of such a language, however, took years. Between 1925 and 1929, in the midst of several other projects including the first English translation of Ludwig Wittgenstein's *Tractatus Logico-Philosophicus*, Ogden made progress on developing a vocabulary of essential words, one that would make it "possible to say all that we normally desire to say with no more words than can be made easily legible to the naked eye, in column form, on the back of a sheet of notepaper."[39] The project, as Ogden later explained, was "something more than a mere experiment in simplification." The condensed language he envisioned would serve as "an International Auxiliary Language, i.e., a second language (in science, commerce and travel) for all those who do not already speak English."[40]

Attempts to develop an international language had a long pedigree, one of the most notable recent instances being the campaign for Esperanto in the nineteenth century. But Ogden's approach differed from these by using for its foundation a living language that was already spoken by increasing numbers of people worldwide. By using English as its medium, Basic was obviously open to charges of "linguistic" imperialism. Although Ogden defended his choice of English as a purely pragmatic one, pointing out that "some form of English is already the national or administrative medium of over 500,000,000 people [and] English has long been the second language of the East,"[41] his general introduction to Basic, published in 1930, strikes in places a somewhat triumphalist note. "Standard English," he explained, "may be enriched and cosmopolitanized as the world contracts through the expansion of modern science; and Basic may meet the universal demand for a compact and efficient technological medium. If so, English will become not only the International Auxiliary language, but the Universal language of the world."[42] Such language roused the suspicion of many, and a distrust of the motives behind Basic would eventually plague the movement's efforts world-wide.

Fundamentally, however, Basic was rooted in Richards's and Ogden's shared vision of pacific, international scientific and technical progress. Ogden himself was a deep admirer of Jeremy Bentham, who had coined the word "international." Bentham's influence upon Ogden imparted a scientific and utilitarian bent to the entire Basic enterprise. Ogden insisted that the Basic vocabulary was "scientifically selected,"[43] and called his method of selection "Panoptic Conjugation" after Bentham's model prison, the Panopticon.[44] In 1929 Ogden published the first version of the Basic vocabulary. It contained an astonishingly compact vocabulary of 850 words. This brevity was both Basic's greatest attraction and the chief target of its critics. In *The ABC of Basic English*, published in 1929, Ogden asserted that "the complete word-list takes about a quarter of an hour on the records which makes it possible to get a rough idea of the sense of anything said or printed in Basic English after only one week's work."[45] The backbone of the Basic vocabulary was its six hundred nouns, ranging from general words like "substance" and "man" to "things which it is possible to get by pointing," such as "potato" and "table."[46] Ogden was able to abbreviate the vocabulary considerably by including several varieties of an object under a single, more general word: silk, cotton and twill, for example, become "cloth," marigolds, daisies and violets "small flowers."[47] The most remarkable feature of Ogden's system, and one that Richards cited as the "key to discovery of Basic," was its use of only eighteen verbs. By replacing the vast array of English verbs with simple "operators" and a directional preposition, Ogden reduced dramatically the number of words necessary to form workable English sentences. As John Paul Russo points out; "Ogden finally needed just sixteen verbs, such as *make, put, take, give, get, come* and *go*, plus twenty prepositions, to take over the work of innumerable verbs. *Abandon, abdicate, abjure, cede, desert, desist, forego, forsake . . . relinquish, renounce, resign, vacate, withdraw* and *yield* could be removed; *give up* could take their place." Richards described the simplicity gained by using this method in one of his later works: "If we jump, we go *up* and *down*, if we raise a building we put it *up*, and if we raze it we take it *down*. If we donate a thing we give it *to* someone or something."[48] A further advantage of conceiving of verbs as directional actions was that much of Basic could be taught through pictures, without the intermediary of a "home" language. Ideally, Richards and Ogden saw Basic as self-teaching, and much of Richards's later work on Basic aimed at developing pictorial techniques for linking concepts with words.[49]

The end result of Ogden's work was a simplified, readily useable language that read much like standard English (a favorite strategy of Richards and Ogden was to write their defenses of Basic in Basic). Beginning in the early 1930's, Ogden set out to publish a series of Basic books and primers that he hoped to distribute internationally. With this purpose in mind he established the Orthological Institute of London, which by 1939 had extended its operations to twenty-five countries, including the United States, Egypt, Burma and India.[50] Ogden also enlisted the initial support of the Rockefeller Foundation. In 1931 he approached the Foundation with a grant proposal for support in the publication of Basic literature, with a portion of the money earmarked for research in adapting Basic to Eastern languages.[51] It was Richards, however, who was responsible for extending the Rockefeller's commitment to Basic work in the Far East. In June 1932, Richards met personally with the Director of the Rockefeller's Humanities Program, David H. Stevens, in Cambridge and presented his case for the possibilities of Basic in China. Stevens was impressed and wrote to Richards warmly upon his return to the United States in September; "the various topics of our talk have been often in my mind since early June. In case I need your opinion on any of them during the autumn, I shall feel free to write. Also I guarantee prompt answers to any queries from you."[52] The relationship between Stevens and Richards developed rapidly, and Stevens's favorable impression of Richards motivated a good deal of the Foundation's support for Basic. Within seven months of their initial meeting, Stevens wrote to Richards: "Today the Rockefeller Foundation acted upon my recommendation for advancing cultural relations with the Orient through a grant for the basic English program for Japan and China as outlined by Ogden in a memorandum."[53] It was the first phase of a commitment to Richards's work in the Far East that would continue for more than fifteen years.

The initial Rockefeller Foundation grant-in-aid for Basic in China was to be administered through the Orthological Institute in London, and was treated officially as an addition to the Rockefeller's existing support for Ogden's proposals. But as Stevens's letter makes clear, the grant was awarded in the face of serious misgivings about Ogden and his more fantastical ambitions for Basic. "I count heavily upon you to see that the operating plans are basically sound from the outset," Stevens informed Richards, and that the research objectives [of the Far Eastern grant] don't get under others. I'm not impressed by Ogden's ideas on an American committee [for Basic]—for what ends I'm uncertain. . . . And as I told him, the program gains nothing by Bentham's blessing, even though the old gentleman's bones are still above ground. Those aspects of Ogden's method are not so good, in my judgement. But you know far more of the mixed possibilities than I and will conceivably be over to talk them out. At least you will be in on the organization of the work.[54]

Stevens's suspicion of Ogden's "methods" was echoed by many who worked with him over the years. That the Orthological Institute was a publishing venture as well as a philanthropic enterprise naturally called his motives into question. Ogden also tended to be possessive of what was, after all, his invention. As Stevens's comments about Bentham suggest, Ogden could be intransigent about his ideas for Basic. Later in the 1930's, his insistence on the final word in matters concerning Basic led to serious rifts with Richards, whom he accused of trying to take over the entire enterprise. Ultimately, however, Stevens's confidence in Richards managed to override any doubts he had about Ogden's opinions.

Aside from Stevens's support, Richards's success in enlisting funds for Basic depended upon recent changes in the Rockefeller Foundation's Far Eastern policy. The Foundation's involvement in China began in 1915 with the establishment of the Peking Union Medical College, a state-of-the-art facility for training Chinese doctors in Western medical techniques.[55] The PUMC reflected the Rockefeller's commitment to the spread of science and technology, particularly in areas of medicine and hygiene, an orientation that marked their philanthropic efforts worldwide. Beginning in the early 1930's, however, the Foundation began to reassess its Far Eastern mission. In 1931 Selskar M. Gunn, a Foundation official, traveled extensively in China to re-examine the Rockefeller's program there. Gunn's report to the Rockefeller Foundation offers an interesting contrast with Richards's own assessment of China in 1929–30, and helps to explain why the Foundation found Richards's proposals for a Far Eastern office of the Orthological Institute both feasible and attractive.

Like Richards, Gunn felt that the Chinese were entering a period of intensive change, not all of it for the good. "China," he reports, "is moving its ponderous mass. Experts agree that some of its oldest and most cherished traditions are beginning to give way. Ancestor worship, filial piety, family life, guild life, are all undergoing modification. The results will not always be happy."[56] Through interviews with high-ranking officials such as T. V. Soong, China's Minister of Finance, and C. T. Wang, Minister of Foreign Affairs, Gunn also received a dire impression of the political situation. According to his report,

> Instability of Gov[ernment], famine, civil war, banditry, communism, are all more or less constantly present. The Nanking Government really only has control over a small part of the country. An authority attached to the ministry of Finance stated that the Government actually received revenue from three of the twenty odd provinces. 90% of the revenue is used for military purposes according to a statement of T. V. Soong, the Minister of Finance. Illiteracy is the common thing, disease and premature death are met everywhere.[57]

"The government," he added, "is made up of a set of amateurs, far from being free from suspicion as to their honesty." Richards had also experienced what seemed to him the appalling duplicity of Chinese officialdom, though he tended to regard it as a troubling nuisance rather than a fundamental obstacle to change. Where Gunn's report differs most radically from Richards is in its assessment of Chinese attitudes toward the West. "Western civilization is under fire in China," he notes. "Many intellectuals, often trained in the U.S. or Europe, are among its sharpest critics." As a result,

> The demand is now to "Chinafy" Western knowledge. Every subject, except the exact sciences, is under fire. Nationalism is rampant and leads to exaggerations in act and thought. The Chinese have become touchy on the subject of inferiority. They have a heightened feeling of bitterness with regard to the rank injustices perpetrated on them by Western powers in the past years. They have exalted ideas of what they could do if given the opportunity.[58]

When Gunn tried to gauge Chinese feelings toward the Rockefeller Foundation itself, he found that "[t]he Foundation, along with all other foreign activities, has been accused of Imperialism and its motives undoubtedly have been, and still are, questioned."[59]

This ambivalence about Western knowledge and the suspicion of the imperialist motives behind it are almost wholly absent in Richards's accounts of his year at Tsing Hua. This in part may be due to his status as a visiting Western scholar in the somewhat rarefied world of Chinese academia; his Chinese colleagues might have been reluctant to express antipathy toward the West in the presence of a distinguished guest. Since it was a Nationalist-led institution, doubts about the political strings often attached to Western knowledge may also have been less acute. But Richards's failure to note anti-Western sentiments in China also illustrates his tendency to take Chinese courtesies at face value. As his later work with the Orthological Institute would prove, the attitude of some Chinese toward a project like Basic English was often more conflicted and less committed than appearances would suggest. Gunn's report is an important reminder of the latent Chinese hostility that a Westernizing project like Basic was likely to face.

In spite of Gunn's reservations about Chinese practices and attitudes, he ultimately agreed with Richards that the changes underway in China were of global consequence, and he encouraged the Foundation to aid the process of modernization. Regardless of their misgivings, he reports that contemporary China "has decided to use and adopt, with probable modifications, much of Western civilization."[60] Given this circumstance, a revamped Rockefeller program could be decisive. While acknowledging that "[w]ork in China under any circumstances means time and lots of it," he insists that "China cannot be neglected by the rest of the world. The Foundation would certainly not be living up to its ideals nor opportunities if it decided to withdraw from China. It can be useful in various fields." He then outlines a "total program of social reconstruction" that would greatly expand the Foundation's activities to embrace involvement in mass education, advanced scientific training, instruction in the social sciences, and a rural reform policy that would include "road-building, irrigation, possibly birth control" along with a thorough grounding in modern agricultural techniques.[61]

A salient feature of the proposal is Gunn's insistence that the Foundation work as far as possible along with the Chinese in instituting these reforms. He argues that Chinese-staffed programs, government agencies and institutions should be the prime media through which the Foundation distributes aid in order to stimulate local involvement. As a consequence, his program places a great deal of importance upon the emergent Chinese universities. Like Richards, Gunn saw these universities as an invaluable sign of China's modernization. "For many years," he reports,

> the colleges and universities maintained by the Missions have been without a doubt the leading educational institutions. Now, the Chinese them-

selves have launched an extensive program of National Universities. . . . I am of the opinion that these National Universities are the wave of the future.[62]

Gunn echoes many of Richards's frustrations with Chinese academia. He acknowledges that

> The difficulties in co-operation with National Universities are considerable. Political appointments have been very common on both the administrative and teaching staffs of the Universities. Thus, the universities have been subject to frequent and at times very extensive changes in personnel. Much trouble has arisen from the student body of the Government institutions. Frequently the students have often been ludicrous, and one must realize the exaggerated spirit of nationalism in order to understand the student movement.[63]

In spite of these caveats, however, Gunn believes that "in general the National Universities are becoming more stable," an impression that was confirmed upon a second tour of China in 1933. A further advantage of administering aid through the Chinese universities is that it would help to diffuse suspicions that the Foundation was acting in an imperial manner. Noting that "[o]ur [previous] contacts have primarily been with mission colleges and this fact has not strengthened our relations with the Government," Gunn declares himself "definitely of the opinion that the future emphasis of the Foundation in China in higher education should be in connection with the Chinese institutions. These are the institutions of the future."[64] In short, Gunn's tours of China in 1931 and 1933 convinced him of the decisive potential for Westernizing reforms. "Working in China," he concludes, "presents necessarily something of a gamble, but one which I believe we are justified in taking."[65]

The Rockefeller Foundation acted quickly on these proposals. Following his second report of 1934, the Foundation opened an office in Shanghai and prepared to institute Gunn's ambitious program of social reconstruction. Richards's concomitant proposals for Basic dovetailed perfectly with the new Foundation plans in the East. It involved education at both the primary and the secondary level, and depended upon close collaboration with the Chinese universities, where Richards already had many important contacts. To both Richards and the Rockefeller officials, it seemed the ideal chance to make a decisive change in China. This sense of optimism about the possibilities for Westernization was the product of a unique moment in

China's history, following the profound changes set in motion since the First World War and prior to the Japanese invasion in 1937, after which the Chinese approach to modernization took a radically different turn. When Richards departed for Peking in 1936, flush with a newly minted program for Basic English and backed with Rockefeller support, the prospects for change in China seemed bright. Indeed, they would never be brighter.

5 ☛ The Orthological Institute
of China, 1936

I

On May 7, 1936, the Richardses debarked for the third time in China.
Both were thrilled to be returning. Their readjustment to Cambridge
life had been difficult and incomplete. Less than a year after their return, Richards wrote to Pollard-Uquhart in Peking:

> We both feel that it would be fun to come back before long to your world
> that is not of this world as we undergo it here. Actually ours is acutely
> suspicious of some taint of China that seems to cling to us even after our
> brief immersion. Instead of being curious about the Far East, they show
> uneasiness, a faint apprehension. . . . It's the sickening, barely conceiv-
> able possibility of things not being all as they sure they are, which wor-
> ries them.[1]

A similar indifference greeted *Mencius on the Mind*, which Richards
complained had "slipped out with distinguished inconspicuous-
ness."[2] A review by Arthur Waley appearing in the *Times Literary
Supplement* confined itself to correcting Richards's translation of Mencius's text,[3] while a friendly but tepid review by Goldsworthy Lowes
Dickinson (one of the last he wrote before his death) was equally disappointing.[4] For Richards, the relative neglect of *Mencius*, which he
had hoped to be "revolutionary, epoch-making, fundamental etc."[5]
seemed to be indicative of a wider stagnation in British intellectual
life. He found himself out of sympathy with the contemporary literary scene, where "everybody [is] writing little books on Hopkins or
asking whether Eliot . . . is really sound as a critic. The youngest ones
re-worrying through all the old problems in new cruder than ever
terms of sur-realism [sic] which seems clearly to be about nothing at
all that hasn't already been better handled in other wrappings."[6] Nor
was he any better disposed toward the new generation of poets who

"seem definitely turning gentlemen communists, though some actually join the party and take their orders, which seem to involve a desperate amount of house to house propaganda and violent bouts of mutual criticism."[7]

In the midst of this dismal cultural climate, the Richardses kept abreast of political happenings in China, bemoaning the pro-Japanese slant of the British press in reporting the growing conflicts between the two nations. They also acquainted themselves with a growing number of Chinese students, whose views on the Far Eastern situation were often dismaying. "Cambridge is now happily full comparatively of Chinese," Richards wrote to a friend at the end of 1931. "That means there are 20, as opposed to when we left here in 1929. We are getting in touch with them gradually. And those we have met so far talk about Sandhurst and Woolwich and straight shooting as what China needs. It seems a pity if history is only to repeat itself."[8] Military developments in Asia were becoming more ominous. The long-standing Japanese presence in Manchuria culminated in the capture of Mukden in September 1931, giving Japan complete control of the territory. An attack on Shanghai the following January resulted in an armistice favorable to the Japanese. The situation grew dire enough to elicit a response from the Western powers. In 1931 the League of Nations dispatched a commission to China under the leadership of Britain's Lord Lytton following the incident at Mukden. Their report, which refused to recognize Japanese claims in Manchuria, resulted in Japan's withdrawal from the League and a renewal of its military efforts in Northern China.

Like many Westerners, Richards saw these developments as further evidence of China's need to enter the modern age. While deploring Japan's imperial aggressions, he also realized that the Chinese lacked the military and political means to resist them. Ironically, it was exactly this need for wholesale reform in China that gave Richards the greatest hope for its future. In November 1932, writing to a friend in China, he confided:

> I've been trying to suggest explanations lately as to why Japan found it so easy to remake herself as a 'Western' Power and China either finds it so hard or doesn't really attempt to. Do you think it can be that J[apan] made really only a very superficial change and that those in China who are making any change are making such a deep one that the temporary result is chaos? On this theory J[apan] was reformed like an army

(nothing irrevocably being altered) and China will reform, if at all, only like a family—nothing ever being the same again.[9]

Part of such a thorough-going reform, to Richards's mind, would be the adoption of Basic English. Toward this end he worked in tandem with Ogden's Basic campaign to secure funding for a separate Orthological Institute in China. From his return to Peking in May 1936 until his departure the following December Richards applied himself to assembling the necessary staff, research, contacts and teaching materials necessary to make Basic English workable in China. These eight months were incredibly productive, and under Richards's leadership the new Orthological Institute of China secured the reputation and expertise that guided their more sustained efforts of 1937–38.

Driving Richards's Basic work in the Far East was a consciousness of the darkening world situation. On October 20, 1935, he wrote to Dorothea: "I see tonight Italy has invaded Abyssinia and so . . . Great hours! And a chance, which it seems about as favourable as any could be, of showing that a reasonable policy can be stronger than any other."[10] For Richards, introducing Basic English to China was also a chance to affirm the power of clear, rational thinking in the face of mounting hostilities. If it could succeed there, it might serve as a model to the world.

II

In 1935, still in Cambridge, Richards published a short study outlining the benefits of Basic English for the Far East. In it he presents a case for the necessity of Basic in China and details some of its practical objectives. *Basic in Teaching: East and West* is thus a bridge between the theoretical insights presented in *Mencius on the Mind* and the kind of work he planned to undertake in 1936. Bringing together his personal experiences from 1929–30 and his more recent engagement with the Basic English movement, *Basic in Teaching* demonstrates how Richards had synthesized his reflections about language into a coherent program for change on the eve of his departure for China. Along with his correspondence to R. D. Jameson, an associate who came to figure largely in his Far Eastern plans, *Basic in Teaching* provides insight into Richards's goals on his arrival in China the following year.

His argument begins with a spirited defense of the utility of language theory. Richards points out that those disciplines most concerned with the study of language, namely Logic and Philology, treat words according to a fixed set of rules, logicians concerning themselves with permissible propositional forms and philologists with historically sanctioned definitions. What these disciplines overlook, he contends, is the active process by which words acquire meanings in everyday usage: the process of "how words mean, how they change their meanings, how they combine and separate them."[11] Following from his arguments in *Mencius on the Mind*, Richards insists that words are not discrete units of fixed meaning, but rather depend upon a complex tissue of assumptions and linguistic experience to make sense. "All our words and all our uses of language," he reiterates, "are knit together by countless filaments—some adamant, some cobwebby. From these connections, these partial, conditional equivalences, all discourse, all coherence, all order, all articulation in what we say comes."[12] By studying these connections and making them explicit, Richards maintains that we can elevate our language skill into a science.

This particular view of language greatly influenced Richards's approach to the teaching of English. For the native speakers of a language, he argues, the background of cultural information necessary for using a language comes naturally. We know how to use words "as we know how to do so many things—from whistling a tune to riding a bicycle—without any clear or precise ideas as to how we do them."[13] For a non-native speaker, however, this store of learning is not so obvious. The first step in teaching a new language is therefore to make explicit the "vast body of assumptions which [is shared] with all other users of the language they are working with."[14] The litmus test for gauging this kind of linguistic facility is not simply vocabulary size, but the ability to *substitute* one word for another. As it requires a more thorough comprehension of the work words do in a language, substitution measures to what extent a user of English perceives the "countless filaments" that give meaning to our vocabulary. "Substitution," Richards insists, "is the mode of action of all language, evidently. Utterances take the places of things and acts. In explanations one utterance (or sometimes an act, a demonstration) takes the place of another utterance."[15] Therefore to have Chinese students simply learn a list of words and their meanings is to neglect the very essence of how language operates. "If we admit," he writes, "that . . . every time we speak, or frame an articulate communicable thought, we are relying upon that host of assumptions which is reflected in the connections between words, we shall be in a better position."[16] In Richards's conception of language teaching, students would acquire a firm grasp of these assumptions before moving on to learn more complex grammatical constructions or vocabulary. Rather than memorizing terms like "democracy" or "justice," (examples that Richards uses elsewhere in the text[17]), they would first learn something about the concepts for which these words are a substitute.

Basic English, Richards argues, is a tool for exactly this kind of approach to language. Because of its limited vocabulary, Basic users can see the connections between words much more quickly than they could given the entire English lexicon. More importantly, the restricted vocabulary forces the substitution of simple words for more abstract concepts. Rather than relying upon the emotive force of a word like "justice" to convey meaning, Basic speakers must analyze the concept by parsing it into simpler constituent sentences. This habit of analysis is in fact the fundamental principle underlying Basic English. According to Richards,

> This analytic descriptive principle, on which the powers of Basic both as an auxiliary International Language and as an instrument in education depend, is a technical innovation in the deliberate control of language. What it makes possible could not be done without it—any more than an aeroplane could fly the Atlantic without the theoretical engineering behind its design. It is important, therefore, to keep the theoretical aspects in mind.[18]

Richards sees the analytic principle of Basic not just as an advantage for the Chinese, who have access to a workable vocabulary almost immediately, but also as a salutary check to native speakers inclined to use words out of habit rather than comprehension. English speakers who use Basic are forced to consider their meanings more carefully, as they do not have the usual array of synonyms to convey their ideas. Basic thus serves as a test of whether abstract words have any real meaning beyond their habitual associations. Non-native speakers learning Basic avoid the difficulty of "picking up words without learning quite what they mean, accepting them with indefinite and vague meanings that thereafter obscure their real uses."[19] The language in a sense stands naked; Basic is "designed to give *automatically* as much insight into the structure and articulations of our meanings as could be contrived."[20] Much more quickly than with Complete English, foreign speakers are able to *use* Basic to express ideas, instead of memorizing lists of synonyms without a feel for the contexts that give them their meaning.

In his second chapter, "The Cultural Crisis in China," Richards is more specific about the usefulness of this kind of linguistic training for the current Chinese situation. He begins by identifying some of the obstacles to modernization in China. One of the most significant to his mind is that the Chinese have turned to Western models out of necessity rather than choice. Their traditional culture and philosophy—a complex and coherent system of interpreting the world—are being abandoned on purely pragmatic grounds. Their interest is not in the truth of Western thought, but in its power. As he explains,

> The intellectual movement in Modern China is primarily a consequence of the political movement. The traditional Chinese outlook is being remade—not because it was felt to be unsatisfactory in itself, but because it plainly put China at a disadvantage in the world-struggle. In itself, it is probably—to those brought up in it—the most satisfying that has been developed in the world. Its historic stability is almost a proof of this, but to the new generation it has already ceased to be satisfying.[21]

To compare the changes taking place in China to a Renaissance would therefore be a misnomer, for "China is not to-day renewing contact with a past phase of her tradition, though a few scholars have set this as their program; she is being violently and reluctantly torn from it."[22] These sentiments highlight the unease that lies at the heart of Richards's work in the Far East. As in *Mencius on the Mind*, he acknowledges that by working to bring China into the modern world, he is at the same time undermining a tradition that offers a perfectly satisfying, and in some ways corrective, alternative to Western science and modes of thought. In this way *Basic in Teaching* repeats the tension apparent in Richards's feelings toward China in 1929–30: a deep admiration for its manners and culture accompanied by a perceived need for reform if the Chinese "are to take their proper part, undiminished, in the world's future."[23]

Despite his respect for the Chinese intellectual tradition, Richards feels that a purely instrumental approach to Western learning severely hampers China's ability to utilize Western systems of knowledge. The Chinese borrow the outward forms of Western learning without comprehending the assumptions upon which it is based. As in *Mencius*, Richards identifies the primary reason for this misunderstanding as a difference in traditions of interpretation. Richards writes:

> The purposes of Chinese philosophy have been different from ours, and therefore the problems and the forms of argument and the structures of ideas. The methods of comparing, analyzing, defining and uniting notions, which we know in the West as Logic (whose physical application is Science) never gained a permanent footing in the Chinese tradition. They developed instead another kind of subtlety.[24]

Here—like his Cambridge predecessors—Richards explicitly equates analysis and logic with the West, assuming these concepts to be foreign to the Chinese. In *Mencius on the Mind*, Richards had shown that different expectations of how a statement should be read are the prime source of Western misconceptions about Chinese philosophy. To expect that Mencius's philosophy should "make sense" according to Western standards of analytic logic is to grossly misunderstand the communicative purposes of the statement. Now Richards turns the tables and shows how Chinese expectations prevent them from perceiving the underlying assumptions and purposes required to truly understand Western statements. Not just language, but the assumptions about what language should do, hinder communication. "The root of the difficulty," Richards insists,

> is that the fundamental Chinese attitude to statements is unlike that attitude to statements which in the West led to the development of an explicit logic and that critical reflective examination of meaning which has produced modern scholarship and science. Quite briefly, the difference is this. The Western scholar, ideally, devotes himself, first, to determining, in the light of his relevant knowledge, and as neutrally, consciously, and explicitly as possible, what the meaning of a passage is, and secondly, to discussing by an open and verifiable technique whether it is true or false. But traditional Chinese scholarship has spent its great resources of memory and ingenuity upon fitting the passage into an already accepted framework of meanings. The framework need not be a traditional Chinese framework; it may be a revolutionary program, as we have seen, or a framework of Western ideas recently acquired by the scholar. But if so it will in almost all cases be used in the traditional Chinese fashion as something to which meanings . . . are to be *accommodated*.[25]

The crucial difference for Richards between China and the West lies not in racial or historical inequalities, but in opposing approaches to language. If the Chinese wish to benefit from Western science, they will first have to acquire an entirely new set of interpretive habits. Otherwise, Western subjects will fail to "give them, however perfect their command of English, that power of critical neutral examination and understanding which should be their prime purpose."[26]

Richards understands that "such a charge may well seem offensive," and his easy equation of Western thought with logical analysis and Chinese with a tradition of "accommodation" is indeed highly questionable. But it demonstrates Richards's tendency to attribute the disparity in power between China and the West to primarily linguistic causes. His belief in the power of language to shape thought, and in the ability of thought rather than technology or socio-political developments to effect change, informed his picture of China's—and the world's—future. More specifically, Richards defends his view of the Chinese interpretive tradition with the experience of scholars and teachers, both Chinese and Western, who have seen first-hand that "this tendency to accommodating interpretation is indeed a formidable obstacle to understanding [Western terms]."[27]

He devotes the rest of the chapter to enumerating the classroom problems faced by both himself and other expert teachers in the field. Many of the incidents are familiar from his letters and diary entries of 1929–30. He repeats the story of a Chinese Professor of English misreading Hardy's *Tess of the d'Urbervilles* as a moral tale about an unfilial daughter.[28] He criticizes the weighty university reading lists that expect Chinese students to comprehend Shakespeare and Katherine Mansfield "before they have acquired more than a very few glimmerings of insight into Western meanings."[29] "It is very clear," he writes, "that the mere process of deluging the student with more and more reading matter in English is no remedy unless this reading matter is going to be such as *to give him early some better power of making out our meanings*."[30] Richards's purpose in decrying "the peculiar fluidity, opportunism, and irresponsibility of the Chinese attitude to meanings"[31] is not to denigrate the Chinese or their cultural failings. His point is that the present method of teaching language in China works from a superficial notion of how language operates. By failing to acknowledge the different purposes to which English and Chinese have traditionally been put, educators are unable to teach students how to *use* English for understanding Western assumptions. In Richards's view,

> A better medium should, from the beginning, recognize that disparity (due to differences between Chinese and Western intellectual traditions) between Chinese and Western attitudes to language and its meaning. . . . It should aim at giving the Chinese learner of English what his own language does not (and perhaps never will) provide him with, an instrument of analytical discrimination between meanings. . . . The only way in which false and misleading approximations to Western units of meaning with Chinese 'equivalents' can be avoided is by giving these meanings through, and together with, an apparatus for comparing complex meanings—through an explicit analytic language.[32]

Basic is so crucial to China's future exactly because it will permit the Chinese to use for themselves the same medium of discourse in which Western logic, science and philosophy take place. Armed with these tools, and the ability to wield them for their own purposes, the Chinese will be able to "take their proper part, undiminished, in the world's future."[33]

By the end of *Basic in Teaching: East and West*, Richards has laid out the prime theoretical assumptions behind the Basic English program in China. His conception of language as an *activity* is a key tenet of Basic, and shifts the emphasis in teaching English from rule memorization or knowledge of a given syllabus to usage. The principle of substitution as a measure of facility requires that students understand more thoroughly the ideas and assumptions a word carries before it becomes a part of their working vocabulary. Finally, the abbreviated Basic word list forces English users of all levels to analyze abstract concepts, stripping them of their culturally specific emotive value in order to concentrate on the sense. These features of Basic, taken as a whole, provide the analytic training necessary for the Chinese to penetrate the constellation of Western presuppositions about logic, language and meaning without which its science and literature cannot make sense. Given this access to Western thought, the Chinese will be able to use it ultimately for their own ends. All of these assumptions had wide implications for the way he approached the teaching of Basic in China in the following years.

III

While Richards marshaled his arguments for *Basic in Teaching*, preparations for the Basic program in China were already underway. The catalyst for the operation was Raymond Duloy ("Jim") Jameson, Richards's American colleague at Tsing Hua University. Richards's ideas about language and literature had had a profound influence on Jameson since their first association in 1929–30 and over the next years he became one of the most devoted advocates of Richards's language teaching techniques. His direct involvement with Basic English began in 1933 when he undertook some preliminary research on teaching Basic in China for Ogden's Orthological Institute in London, which had just won funding from the Rockefeller Foundation to prepare a series of texts for the Far East. Between November 1933 and May 1936, when Richards arrived to oversee the operation personally, Jameson led the effort to inaugurate a program of Basic teaching in Chinese schools and universities. His letters to Richards and to the Foundation during this time give a keen sense of the difficulties that Basic faced "on the ground" in Peking. They also help to establish the ambition and scope of Richards's own goals in the following years.

Because of his position as an English instructor at Tsing Hua and other Peking-area universities, Jameson was able to begin experiments with Basic in the classroom almost immediately. By November 1933 he reported to Richards and Ogden that he was "making use of fairly fluent, though not particularly accurate, Basic in all of my lectures." He also began translating his first-year students' material into Basic, accompanied by examinations on reading comprehension. Their rapid improvement on the tests left him "more convinced than ever that Basic is not only workable but necessary in China."[34] At the same time Ogden's books on Basic, as well as some of his Basic editions of Western texts, began to circulate in Peking, where they stirred up a great deal of interest in academic circles. In November Tsiang Ting Fu, a professor at Tsing Hua with close ties to the Minister of Education, "announced that if he were the minister he would issue an edict requiring all graduates of the middle schools to have a demonstrable knowledge of the Basic words."[35] A group of Tsing Hua undergraduates also formed "on their own initiative" a Basic Association, asking Jameson to act as supervisor. At the end of 1933, the initial response to Basic in China seemed to be encouraging.

Not all reactions, however, were entirely favorable. Jameson cites Lin Yutang—"former Tsing Hua professor, doctorate in Germany and Harvard, Editor of the most widely circulated humorous reviews in China and member of several government boards"—as the "leader of the Anti-Basic movement" in the Chinese press.[36] Jameson declines to detail the particulars of Lin's objections on the grounds that "from his English articles it does not seem to me that his opposition is particularly serious." He is equally dismissive of other critics of Basic. On hearing that a Peking press is devoting a magazine issue to anti-Basic articles he writes:

> To what extent this opposition is due to the Esperantists and to what extent it is due to Chinese negativism is not clear. If there were more time to make investigations and carry the thing through in the only way in which work of this kind can be carried through in China, by lengthy conversations and a considerable number of dinner parties, the situation could be got in hand in a short time.[37]

Jameson's comment is revealing not only because it ignores the actual content of the case against Basic, but because it shows that Ogden and Richards were not alone in the international education market. "Esperantists" and proponents of other schemes for translating Western works kept up a steady barrage of criticism against Basic in order to promote their own products. Jameson mentions a large grant from the China Foundation made to Hu Shih, the prominent Chinese philosopher and translator, to publish foreign books in Chinese. Their plans included "a Chinese Shakespeare, a Chinese Synge, Berkeley, Kant and the like." "The project," he adds, "is a mess."[38] Although Chinese editions of Western texts might not be in direct competition with Basic, Jameson's mention of Hu Shih's venture is a reminder that Richards had no monopoly on schemes for making Western thought accessible to the East.

At the same time, Jameson's report of "Chinese negativism" suggests an opposition to Basic that he was readier to dismiss than to explain. Some hostility, he believes, is due to misunderstanding, some to self-interest—many Chinese academics being heavily invested in teaching English at the university—and some to a general distrust of change. In any case, Jameson did not feel that ferreting out the sources of opposition was particularly important. His clear distaste for the "lengthy conversations" and dinner parties necessary to "carry things through" in China indicates an unwillingness to meet his critics on what Jameson takes to be their own terms. This reluctance to promote Basic through accepted Chinese channels typifies an important aspect of Richards's Far Eastern project. Like Richards, Jameson believed that Basic would ultimately disarm its critics through its sheer reasonableness. Resistance was attributed more often to political motives or innate Chinese conservatism than to principled opposition. Jameson expresses a confidence characteristic of the Basic enterprise when he maintains that "the situation could be got in hand in a short time"; he cannot imagine rational critics holding out against such a sensible reform.

The following year, 1934, *Mencius on the Mind* appeared in China. Jameson wrote to Richards in December informing him of a less than enthusiastic Chinese response:

> Chin Yu Lin (philosopher!) is reported to have said that "Richards has succeeded in making Mencius ridiculous to foreigners." I had thought that this was due to the fact that Chin had not read the book through and that being what he is, he was not used to parallel interpretation. Certainly you make Western thought look as ridiculous as Mencius. . . . Mixed with this [reason] are many others which you understand such as, "No Westerner can ever understand China," and annoyance that anyone should have the temerity to attempt it and the like.[39]

More unsettling that Chin's comments were those of L. T. Hwang, a collaborator on Richards's translation of Mencius and one of the book's dedicatees. In a conversation with Hwang some weeks earlier, Jameson was distressed to find that he regarded *Mencius on the Mind* as a book that "grew out of a series of informal casual conversations and opinions offered by Chinese without recourse to the proper commentaries." Jameson felt that Hwang had missed the point of the whole book:

> With the tones of an excited lawyer who wishes to force a damaging confession from a recalcitrant witness [Hwang] demanded whether your method "was or was not to put all interpretation on the hinges of linguistic analysis." With equal enthusiasm I replied (remembering that an exposition of all your works was then out of place) that he should make his accusation even stronger, that your method was to show the difficulty of interpreting one set of words by another set, that his comments on Mencius showed clearly that you [Richards] had made this difficulty clear . . . and that if a foreigner of your competence had not succeeded in presenting the theoretical problem and illustrating it, it was equally clear that we could have little hope of finding Chinese who were competent in the interpretation of Western thought.[40]

Hwang parted from Jameson with the observation that "he had no fear that any Westerners would be much deceived about Mencius, even though Richards has written a beautiful book about him!" "So much," Jameson concluded, "for wasted effort."

Jameson's argument with Hwang is significant because it offers some insight into Chinese criticisms of Basic. Part of the grounds for Hwang's objection to *Mencius* is that it makes no reference to traditional Chinese commentaries; he sees Richards as ignoring the respected authorities and putting "interpretation on the hinges of linguistic analysis." Far from missing the point of *Mencius* as Jameson claims, Hwang here identifies one of the key concepts underpinning Basic. If English was to serve as an international language, Richards felt that it would have to be freed as far as possible from the nexus of cultural assumptions that supplies the vast majority of its meanings; a word like "freedom" cannot rely upon its customary historical and emotive associations to carry its meaning in a foreign culture. In the Basic vocabulary, which keeps such complex words to a minimum, the concept would have to be analyzed into a more fundamental set of statements. One result of this method, as Hwang points out, is that interpretation becomes a matter of "linguistic analysis," of abrading complex, emotive words down to their most primary denotative meanings. What his comments suggest, however, is that the Basic approach to interpretation fails to do justice to the rich history of accepted usages that help to shape the concept in the first place. An account of Mencius's philosophy extracted from its various traditions of interpretation is a misleading, even deceptive, exercise for Hwang. In discussing the limits of Basic in *Basic in Teaching*, Richards concedes:

> What are difficult to describe in Basic are not the ideas which may be divined and extracted from the original but the nuances of feeling which result from them and from such other factors as the rhythm. But in any exposition these are difficult to display; and there is, I believe, a very strong case to be made for saying that the exercise of attempting to describe them is not a valuable one. It too easily becomes a debauch, an expatiation of unregulatable sensibility. The valuable exercise is the analysis, the tracing out of sense items, the ideas and their articulations—for these are a main part of the springs of the effect. To study them is to penetrate to the body of poetry; to describe effects is to play with shadows.[41]

Although Basic is not Richards's explicit concern in *Mencius on the Mind*, his method there is the same; he wants to find a technique for comparing ideas independently of their cultural contexts. Hwang objects to this kind of appropriation of Mencius, which seems to remove his thought from the purview of Chinese interpretations. He complains of Richards's lack of "recourse to the proper commentaries" in discussing Mencius, an oversight that invalidates his interpretation. Or, as Chin puts it, Mencius's thought abstracted from its tradition looks "ridiculous."

Hwang's reaction to *Mencius on the Mind* illustrates the kind of misunderstandings that were apt to come between Richards's group and their Chinese colleagues, even the most sympathetic, and foreshadows some of the difficulties that Richards would have with his Chinese collaborators in the future. For the time being, the dispute with Hwang left Jameson more puzzled than angry:

> It is damnably hard even out here to keep in mind the differences of approach. So often we have the feeling that we are standing on the same ground with these people, working out common difficulties, when the chasm between us opens and we find ourselves so far apart that any progress towards common understanding seems impossible.[42]

The progress toward understanding at all levels was an arduous one, and obstacles could often appear in unexpected places. In trying to make sense of these "misunderstandings," Jameson cites objections to Basic less scholarly than Hwang's. "I fear," he writes, "that not enough room is left here for the literary snobbery of China. The first thing a $20 a month clerk wants to read is 'literature.' One of the objections to Basic is that having learned the 850 [words], students can't understand Shakespeare." Elsewhere in the same letter, he advises Richards against changing his theories to accommodate Chinese criticisms:

> To me the paper has been tremendously stimulating. If the imperialistic considerations were omitted, the good it does would no doubt correct the offense it gives. Neither Hu nor the interpreters of Chu Hsi would be happy. But they aren't happy about your views anyway. . . . Inasmuch as any contribution a foreigner makes to anything is treated with envious scorn, I see no particular advantage to be gained by adopting the methods of courtship in a matter of this kind.[43]

Echoing Richards's position in *Basic in Teaching*, he laments: "Perhaps we're too optimistic to expect anyone in China—in view of the traditional lack of analytic tendencies—to get matters which so few Westerners, despite our analyses, are capable of understanding."[44] Richards himself was more adroit in dealing with Chinese resistance to Basic, but he shared Jameson's tendency to equate criticism with error, and disagreement with a failure to understand.

Yet despite these theoretical objections, the prospects for Basic seemed to continually improve. A more immediate threat than its critics was the proliferation of pirate texts. By November 1933, Jameson was writing to warn Ogden and Richards that "every Chinese publisher I have ever heard of has been pirating us and it will be extremely difficult to get protection, except for material prepared specifically from China."[45] The difficulty of enforcing copyrights was to plague the Basic movement worldwide; in China, where both "copyright protection and centralized pedagogical institutions through which we can work" were lacking, the problem was particularly acute. In response, Jameson suggested two courses of action. One was to authorize a single Chinese publisher to distribute Basic texts. In return, the publisher would have to submit to the approval of a "feed association of Chinese and foreign teachers and students, chosen both because of their competence and their *authority* in China," to assure that "the material is being presented adequately from the point of view of theory." While this wouldn't eliminate the problem of pirate editions, it would assure "that at least one presentation is adequate and, on the somewhat doubtful hypothesis that the best man always wins, should be of considerable advantage." The other response was to step up the pace of legitimate Basic publications within China. Although desperately pressed for time by a heavy teaching load, Jameson outlined plans for a Basic Reader consisting of "narrative reprints from [Ogden's] English publications [and] general scientific articles written in Basic" as well as a selection of readings "written by natural scientists in China on the nature and purpose of their subjects." He also discussed the need for a Chinese edition of *Basic Words*, a new *ABC of Basic* "pointed at middle school teachers rather than students," and several translations of Chinese works into Basic English. "As we are in the center of a whirlpool," he warned, "we must, if we intend to keep Basic from becoming an utter mess, work with extraordinary speed and vigor."[46]

The problems of piracy lent an added urgency to the pace of the Basic enterprise in China. But the very demand for texts inspired optimism about its chances of success. With "general supervision and planning," Jameson was confident that "Basic could be put into the middle schools here within a couple of years, but the preliminary work necessary to get it there is, of course, entirely apart from the linguistic research that is necessary to make it effective." Unfortunately, as promising as the situation seemed, Jameson simply could not undertake the work alone. Aside from sixteen hours of teaching at Tsing Hua per week, along with supplementary classes at two other Peking-area schools, the customs of Chinese academia required his participation in the same round of dinners, cocktail parties and extracurricular socializing that the Richardses had found so trying during their own stay. Any work that Jameson undertook for Basic from 1933 until 1936—classroom research, reviews of Basic materials, letters to the press—was strictly on his own free time. In addition to these other pressures, throughout 1933 and most of 1934 he was at work on a book that, as he explained to Ogden, "is of enormous professional importance to me if I am ever to do the work in the West that I want to do."[47] What made the situation more frustrating was that Basic seemed to be booming. Critics aside, by August 1934 Jameson was able to report that "China is more completely Richardsised than any other country," with Tsing Hua taking the lead in advocating the work of the Cambridge semasiologists. "*Practical Criticism* is in all the Peking and several of the other government universities," he wrote.[48] It was clear that in order to capitalize on the moment, Basic would need more attention and resources. But by the end of 1934 much of the agenda for instituting Basic was set: classroom research to test Basic's effectiveness in the Chinese setting, publication and propaganda to counter criticism and, above all, Basic materials for middle school teachers and students to put Richards's ideas into operation in the classroom.

Early in 1935, Jameson contacted Selksar Gunn of the Rockefeller Foundation, then in the midst of his third tour of China. Although the Foundation had been funding the Orthological Institute in London since 1933, with a portion of the grant earmarked for developing Basic in China, plans for a separate branch of the Institute were not within the scope of its support. Jameson discussed the position of Basic in China with Gunn, presenting him with a detailed report of its progress over the last year and a half. Gunn was deeply impressed. He wrote to David H. Stevens, director of the Rockefeller Foundation's humanities program, in New York in March:

> It would appear that real progress has been made in the last year in China. In fact Professor Jameson is a little afraid of the speed with which interest in Basic is proceeding here. There is some danger that it might get out of hand. It certainly started off in China on the wrong foot, with

pirating of Ogden's books and their apparently abominable translations by the Chung Hwa Book Company, the Commercial Press and others. However, this difficulty seems to have been overcome. . . . Professor Jameson strongly urges you to come out here.[49]

Stevens, already favorably disposed to Richards's Far Eastern plans, received confirmation from Gunn of how much could be accomplished in China given timely support. Jameson's attached report, which detailed the scale of Basic activity in China already underway without the benefit of direct Foundation funding, helped to convince Stevens and other Foundation officials that Basic in China was a safe bet.

Jameson's report begins with a restatement of Basic's key purposes in China:

> First, we are trying to devise ways of teaching to students in Middle Schools and Colleges an English which will be of use to them and at the same time save them two years of word learning with the thought that these years can be put on more profitable work.
>
> Second, at the same time we are trying to present the material in such a way that an analytical—as opposed to the temperamental Chinese synthetic—habit of thought will be acquired.[50]

In support of these objectives, he identifies the problems with English teaching as it currently stands in China. "At present," he complains, "the teaching of English is in the hands of men with literary ambitions. Youngsters aspire toward an elegant obscure style before they have the root senses of the words they use." More profoundly, Jameson reiterates Richards's sense of the cultural gap between Western and Chinese thought:

> One of the reasons why Chinese and Westerners generally fail to understand each other is this: though they may use the same verbal symbols in speaking each other's language, these symbols refer to entirely different fields of discourse. The problem is less abstract than it appears in this discussion. It is part of Chinese mentality and permeates all activities. It explains why Chinese are said to be good technicians but bad originators. Without an understanding and correction of this, attempts have met with only slight success when they were directed towards rebuilding China's rural and social structure along Western lines. A knowledge of the mechanics of the Western scientific procedure and an ability to parrot Western terms can be of no value unless this ability is implemented by our habit of analysing complexes into their elements and reconstructing the elements into general principles.

The mention of "rebuilding China's rural and social structure" alludes to the Rockefeller Foundation's own newly instituted program of rural reconstruction in China, which sought to improve the condition of the Chinese peasantry by introducing modern agricultural methods and other technical reforms. Since the Foundation's first involvement in China in 1915, its aim had been to foster medical and scientific development. The Foundation's recent commitment to a broader program of reform still centered on imparting technical knowledge in areas like engineering, agriculture and sociology. Basic's success in garnering the Foundation's interest depended upon the argument that such development could not proceed without prior training in the habit of "Western" analytic thought. Jameson continues:

> Language is the tool of thought. The Basic vocabulary and the linguistic theory upon which it is built make the fullest possible use of our Western analytic tendency. One of the most important ways of giving Chinese learners ability in analysis is to make use of the Orthological technique. When Chinese read, whether philosophy, poetry or science, their purpose is not to get the author's thought in detail, but to let the sacred characters pass through their consciousness in order to get a totality of effect. That some attempt is being made to face this question will be seen below.[51]

In trying to win the Foundation's support, Jameson adhered to the familiar Richardsian line that language comes prior to technology, and that Chinese attempts to make use of Western advances will be futile without training in analytic thought. Basic seemed the necessary step prior to clearing the ground for any more thorough-going reforms.

At the time of his report in March 1935, Jameson was already able to point to a solid record of Basic achievements. At the end of 1934 a Far Eastern office of the Orthological Institute had opened with funding from London, consisting of Jameson, a "worker on fellowship named Liu Pao Tung, and a Chinese typist." In February 1935, one month before the meeting with Gunn, the new Orthological Institute of China founded the Western Languages Association of China, an organization "sponsored by some sixty college and middle school teachers from cities in Eastern China." The purpose of the WLAC was to discuss innovations in language teaching techniques through regular meetings and a newsletter. Although technically independent of the Basic enterprise, it operated under the auspices of the Orthological Institute as a way of forming a network of Chinese teachers and administrators interested in educational reform. The Institute also continued to carry out research on adapting Basic English for Chinese classrooms. Through the help of friendly academic contacts, Jameson was able to report that "some five hundred students in universities and middle schools in Peiping, Tsingtao and Changsha have been and are being given a 'Basic Vocabulary Test,'" consisting of a list of Basic words for which the students are asked to write equivalent Chinese characters: "The kinds of error made are investigated and the results will be used in the preparation of texts. Thus far some 250,000 of 425,000 responses are ready for examination."[52]

For many of these operations, Jameson could boast a considerable amount of help from important Chinese academics. Hung Shen, Dean of the English Department at the National Shantung University in Tsingtao and former director of an important Shantung film company, was writing and translating plays into Basic. Chao Yuan Jen, head of the Department of Linguistics at the Academia Sinica, had recently produced a set of twelve Basic phonograph records currently "being made use of in several schools." A professor of philosophy at Tsing Hua, Shen Yu Ting, was at work on a translation of Mencius that employed "the Basic method of tracing ambiguities and outlining the configurations of Mencius's thought." Finally, Professor Shui Tien Tung, "one of our field representatives," was completing a book of "Good Stories from Greece and Rome." Shui played a crucial role in later Basic endeavors; in 1935, Jameson notes that "it is largely due to Shui's initiative that we hold so favorable position in the National Shantung University. He is also annotating our other publications and is formally responsible for the negotiations with publishers. He has offered to put Basic [in the province of] Kansu, where his father is Minister of Education, if the project is worthwhile." In addition to academic support, plans to include Basic in the freshman English course at Tsing Hua were also underway, as well as in the Mass Education night school and nurses school at Changsha. In fact, the growing enthusiasm for Basic exceeded the powers of the small Institute staff to monitor:

> Information as to how widely Basic is being made use of experimentally in schools is incomplete. . . . I am giving sixty fourth year students, prospective teachers, in the National Normal University Peiping, training in Basic and experiments are being made in other schools, in Peiping, Tientsin, Shanghai, Soochow and Hong Kong, to my certain knowledge. Al-

though many inquiries have come in from other centers, I have no knowledge as to what is being done, nor does it seem profitable at present to do more than express an appreciation or interest.

With this impressive roster of associates, Jameson was able to paint a picture for the Rockefeller Foundation of a vibrant, mushrooming program with an impressive amount of local support.

In short, by 1935 Jameson could assure Gunn that "the enthusiasm and controversies of 1933 have given way before a realization that we are neither an emotion nor a fad but that we are offering a reasoned approach to an important question."[53] His detailed presentation of the array of Basic activities underway in China gave empirical confirmation of the program Richards had outlined for Stevens in 1933. Moreover, as Gunn pointed out in his letter to Stevens, the Institute's projected budget "is a modest one": $40,000 over a three-year period, exclusive of funds required to send Richards to China, which both Gunn and Jameson were anxious to do. The Foundation had already made a commitment to Ogden's Basic program and shown themselves receptive to Richards's ideas. With their own plans for reform in China stepping up, Foundation officials ultimately agreed to support the Institute's work. In January 1936, a grant-in-aid of $2,000 was awarded to Jameson "for cooperative work with Chinese scholars on the teaching of English, during the twelve months beginning February 1, 1936."[54] By February, a separate grant of $15,000 was assigned to the Orthological Institute of China for the period ending June 30, 1937. In its official resolution the Foundation stipulated:

> One purpose of this proposal for aid to the Orthological Institute of China is to give application to the work of the group in London under Mr. C. K. Ogden, whereby within the same period materials will be prepared for a series of Basic English books for Chinese readers. As these are completed, they will be taken over by the group in China to assist in the reorganization of the teaching of English now going forward in schools, colleges and universities.[55]

Three months later, Richards arrived in Peking to oversee personally the Basic program that Jameson had set in motion.

IV

On February 23, 1936, Richards informed the Master of Magdalene College that the Rockefeller have decided to help Basic on a considerable scale in China.

They have asked me to go out for them to see what should be done. They are making a useful one year grant at once and if I can report that the right body exists out here they will be prepared to subsidize it through some years quite heavily. They are treating me rather magnificently over the visit and there seems a good chance of doing something with their aid.[56]

Less than two weeks later the Richardses were en route to China, arriving after a brief stopover in Japan in early May. They found their Peking circle much as they had left it. Winter and Jameson were eager to greet them, delighted by their return and showing a promising enthusiasm for Basic.[57] Wong Quincey and Y. C. Mei, President of Tsing Hua, also gave the Richardses a warm welcome.[58] On May 16 they celebrated Pollard-Urquhart's fortieth birthday at the Llama Miao, their previous temple residence near Tsing Hua.[59] In a short time the Richardses had settled back into a familiar Peking social routine, entertaining friends and colleagues, both Western and Chinese, at cocktails, dinners and teas. They were pumped for information on developments at home, "all wanting the tip on literary winners," as Dorothea recorded in their diary.[60] In mid-June Richards received word that Cambridge had granted him a leave of absence for the fall. Certain that they would be staying until Christmas, the Richardses took a house in the East City section of Peking. "Picture me," Dorothea wrote to her father, "at the Chinese Auction, not a bit the kind of thing you get at the Army and Navy stores or at Christmas but a house just vacated by the owner and packed full of warm, half-naked coolies, fat, perspiring Chinese clerks, ladies in hundred pounds worth of jade hesitating if she bid 50 cents!"[61] But a few weeks of this local color, living "among street cries which must be like the middle ages," as Dorothea put it, proved too much of a strain.[62] At the end of July they moved to quieter quarters in a house formerly occupied by Osbert Sitwell.[63]

Despite the pleasures of returning to Peking, Richards wasted no time in getting down to the business of Basic. On May 12, less than a week after his arrival, he wrote to Stevens at the Rockefeller Foundation's New York office to present his "first impressions of the Basic situation here." On the whole, he found much to be pleased with. The Orthological Institute was comfortably housed at 7 Hsien Hsiao P'ai Hutung in Peking under the leadership of Jameson with four Chinese associates, including Shui Tien Tun.[64] Due to an arrangement with the Chung Hwa Book Company, in which the Institute agreed to give their imprimatur to the publisher's editions in return for the right to approve the contents, the damaging effects of piracy were largely curbed.[65] The prospect of institutional support was also encouraging. Tsing Hua along with several other Chinese universities expressed a strong interest in adopting Basic for their Freshman Composition classes in the autumn, while in a recent interview with the Minister of Education in the capital at Nanking, Jameson had been given "a very encouraging reception and an indication that when the Institute is ready, anything it can do will be welcomed."[66]

Given this level of demand, Richards was confident that "the promotion side of the work required up to this stage can be considered covered." What they needed was supply. Because of Jameson's other teaching demands as well as the limited resources available from Ogden's grant, the Institute was woefully behind in developing Basic texts for the classroom. Now, with separate Foundation funding, the top priority was to develop the "Chinese primers, and readers and classroom materials" necessary to put Basic to work in schools. Richards immediately mapped out two main objectives for the next eight months. The first was to concentrate on teacher training. Richards felt very strongly that Basic required *"above all*, good teachers who know their stuff and can use and develop and criticize the material and aids the Institute is now working out for them." He was eager to ensure that teachers of Basic were proponents as well, and understood the theories behind the word-list. The second objective was to direct the Institute's efforts toward Chinese middle schools rather than the universities. Despite Tsing Hua's interest in using some form of Basic for their freshman program, Richards anticipated that "the students there are very likely to resent, or profess to resent, being treated in a special way. Someone may call Basic a 'baby' or 'pidgin' language, or some university colleague, who is not feeling friendly at the moment, may upset them with a word and then the work—except as experience to the teacher—is wasted. My experience makes me confident that the Middle Schools are much solider ground to build from."[67]

The decision to focus on the middle school rather than the university level reflected in part Richards's experience of the volatile academic atmosphere in 1929–30. Then he had complained of the factions, jobbery and political unrest rampant at Tsing Hua. Five years had done nothing to revise his opinion. "I wish I could sketch for you," he wrote to Stevens on July 24,

> something of the extravagant complexity of the internal politics of a Chinese University. Jealousies, ancient feuds, pressures from influential persons with a friend who would like a professorship and a long bad history of sinecurism, absentee tenure, plural livings and many less easily imagined factors come in. All complicated by *opera bouffe* interventions from students who make patriotism an excuse for refusing to sit for examinations, while demanding their degrees and who manhandle timorous professors. Therefore one can never know with certainty what is behind anything.[68]

The announcement of a student protest in Peking in June, which prompted the Minister of Education to recommend an early close to the term, did nothing to bolster Richards's confidence in the university environment.[69] This distrust of Chinese academia shaped a good deal of the Institute's long-term strategies in China. Richards and his colleagues were convinced that Basic could not rely entirely upon the support of existing Chinese schools for its success. Rather than integrating Basic wholesale into university or middle school curricula, Richards felt that the Institute would have to train its own teachers and to make Basic independent of any particular institution. The program was to be, as far as possible, self-teaching: texts to train teachers, teachers to train students, and minimal dependence upon the surrounding educational environment. Later, as war with Japan interrupted the school system, Richards was still able to hope that Basic might have a chance since efforts had been made from the beginning to make it self-sustaining.

One difficulty the Institute faced, however, was finding Chinese colleagues who shared their commitment to the Basic enterprise. Richards felt strongly that Basic should eventually be independent of the Institute, and attracting Chinese support was a large part of its purpose. Jameson had formed the Western Languages Association of China in order to foster local interest, while Richards took pains to ensure that "young teachers really see the *why* of what they're doing with Basic, as well as the how, and its difficulties, before they start their classes."[70] But in July Richards admitted to Stevens that "keeping C[hinese] assistants on the boil is no light business. Less than a certain constant supply from the West—and nothing happens. . . .

[Jameson] will have to be full out all the time or they will just patter and plan, no more." He found that the Chinese staff "require an immense amount of sustained diplomatic handling or they end in talk. But the drive has to be given in C[hinese] modes, which usually means that the arrangements have to be remade 6 times and then changed completely at the last moment. I go on feeling it a miracle when anything happens."[71] The problem of working in "Chinese modes" was a persistent one, and Richards's vexation echoed that of Jameson during 1933–34. In June he lamented the diplomatic "absurdities" he confronted in promoting what seemed to him a simple curricular reform. As he confided to Stevens,

> One can't say what one thinks, as one can elsewhere, without raising personal antagonisms which may very easily become very formidable local obstacles to all future efforts. The people most responsible usually occupy commanding key positions in Schools and Departments, and are ruined if they *lose face*. The few foreign teachers, and the even fewer Chinese, who know enough to expose such nonsense, dare not say anything; they would lose all their influence if they did by going against the current code of 'face saving.'[72]

The Institute did what it could to apply indirect pressure through channels such as the Bulletin of the Western Language Teacher's Association. But the problem of operating within accepted Chinese codes of behavior remained a continual source of frustration. "It's all very amusing," Richards wrote, "but the tact required at times is prodigious."

Nevertheless, over the following eight months the Institute managed to achieve a great deal. Richards quickly recruited Bob Winter and E. K. Smith, a professor of English at Yenching University and according to Jameson "one of the most experienced and best elementary English teachers in China," to help with the work load.[73] Both set to work on developing a Chinese-Basic primer as well as a Basic wall chart that would include the entire vocabulary and rules of grammar on a single banner. Richards did not expect to accomplish much else during the murderous Chinese summer, when the heat drove most of the Peking intelligentsia to the hills. But on July 2 he was able to report to Stevens that Shih Ta, "The chief [teachers'] Training College of North China has just offered us its Summer Session of a fortnight to run—about 100 teachers."[74] The Shih Ta summer program, a two-week intensive training session aimed at the improvement of provincial middle school English teachers, had been mandated by the Ministry of Education the previous year; Shih Ta's invitation to run the 1936 session was an excellent chance for the Institute to make a favorable impression in government circles. With only two weeks to prepare, Richards and the entire Institute staff assumed leadership of the session on July 19, lecturing from 7 A.M. until the early afternoon. Although Richards saw it primarily as "a good chance of judging what our assistants can do," the Institute's successful management of the session augured well for Basic's future. It also gave Richards a chance to gauge the teachers' reaction to Basic, where he believed Chinese support most counted. The response was optimistic, with the "livelier" of the teachers almost "pathetically ready to be helped."[75] At the end of the two-week session Shih Ta asked the Institute to plan a new curriculum for them, an offer which Richards's staff was in no position to accept. In addition, demonstration classes for Basic were underway at two Chinese Middle Schools by the end of May, accompanied by bi-weekly meetings with the teachers.[76] By the end of the summer, Richards was declining offers to teach classes at other schools for the purpose of "concentrating upon producing teachers and primers and other materials to supply them with." Capping the summer's progress was a warm letter from the Ministry of Education at Nanking. On August 21 T. C. Woo wrote

> to assure you that the Ministry is following with great interest the work O.I.C. [Orthological Institute of China] is carrying on. You will undoubtedly receive support from the Minister and those like myself, who would like to see that this very serious business of English teaching in the Chinese secondary schools is put on a sound and scientific basis, thereby obviating much waste and (I'm sure) suffering among young people.[77]

Coming just three months after Richards's arrival, Woo's endorsement confirmed that Basic was proceeding with remarkable smoothness.

As research and work on the primers progressed throughout the summer and fall, Richards grew more optimistic about the Institute's opportunities. In a jubilant letter to Stevens on August 17 he confided:

> At times I divert myself with the idea that there is a world-wide field for constructive remedial work in the conduct of English teaching (with all it implies.) If Public Health is an international affair, Orthology, the conduct of interpretation, elementary thinking, General Education—what-

> ever it is called—seems to have equal scope. Why not an international
> service of sane curricula and examination models to study the haphazard
> improvisations of term-worn teachers? That is a dream: but here in China
> we do seem to have our opening.[78]

For all the Institute's success thus far, the scope of Richards's ambitions caused Foundation officials some concern. In October Stevens reminded Jameson that the Institute's work was to be a joint collaboration between Chinese and Western scholars, preferably being turned over to a Chinese institution at the end of the grant period.[79] At the time of his letter the Institute seemed nowhere close to this goal. Adding E. K. Smith and Bob Winter to the staff, along with a new Chinese Fellow, Lu Pao Tung, cost more than the Institute budget had anticipated. In November Richards and Jameson requested a budget increase for "Simple Science in Basic for China," a series of four texts for ages 14 to 17, undertaken "with the aid of Chinese collaborators trained for the purpose," that would "present scientific developments not as something peculiar to Western thought, and to be painfully mastered as an alien mystery, but as the outcome of historical influences such as those which the present generation in China is now experiencing."[80] Aside from the growing expense, the leadership of the Institute was also uncertain. Richards had to return to Cambridge in December, and it was doubtful that he could interrupt his academic career to take charge of the Institute if the Foundation grant were extended. Jameson, the nominal Director, was also committed to Tsing Hua, which began to resent his and Winter's absorption in the Basic movement.[81] If Jameson were to leave Tsing Hua, the Foundation would be committed to his support indefinitely. Moreover Jameson, who was going through a bitter and rather public divorce in Peking, was known to be "temperamental" and did not inspire the Foundation's confidence. In short, Basic in China threatened to require more support than the Foundation had initially planned. Addressing these concerns in a letter of November 18, Richards assured Stevens: "I note and recognise the weight of your remark about there being a term to the Foundation's interest in the Institute. There should be no risk of any misunderstanding. But may I plead that diminuendo is not necessarily part of a finale?"[82] Ironically, by the end of 1936 the most pressing obstacles to Richards's Chinese plans were coming from the Western side of the collaboration.

With the end of the year approaching, the Institute continued to extend its activities. Richards spoke to the Rotary Club and the University Women's Association in October to make sure that "the foreigners in Peking are at last becoming aware of Basic."[83] By November the Institute staff was developing a radio program for middle schools. An important new middle school just opening in Chungking asked Richards for a group of Basic-trained instructors to teach in the Spring; an opportunity, he felt, for "trying our stuff out on a fresh and uncontaminated field."[84] By December he was confident enough of Basic's chances in China to consider leaving Cambridge in order to stay in Peking. "Basic," he confided to a friend in England,

> has been doing well. Now there is a solid organization here to look after its spread, and a reasonable chance that the whole educational programme of China will be doubled in efficiency (and time) as a result— which seems more than can easily be believed. The temptation to hang on to watch the next few further steps is pretty hard to resist.[85]

Certainly the cultural atmosphere of Peking heightened the temptation. Richards and Dorothea spent their free time visiting Buddhist monasteries and temples just as they had in 1929–30, and vacationed at the peak of the Peking summer in an idyllic resort near the Gulf of Pei Chi Li.[86] Visits from Jameson, Winter and Pollard-Urquhart, as well as a diverse array of friends and acquaintances, were a regular feature of their social life. In the summer they received a visit from Virginia Woolf's nephew, Julian Bell, whom Richards found had "got over his romanticism about China which means going through phase two and being rather skeptical,"[87] while Dorothea renewed her friendship with Ida Pruitt, a journalist and author of several popular books about China. These attractions made it more difficult for the Richardses to resign themselves to leaving. "We are in a restless mood," Richards wrote in early December,

> being torn by a desire to stay on here almost to the point of saying goodbye forever to Cambridge. Seduced by the lovely house D[orothea] has created here. It's hard to break up after only a few months in it. Spoilt by good fortune I suppose we are.[88]

That Richards was willing to entertain the notion of leaving Cambridge reflects the extravagant promise of Basic by the end of 1936. After eight months of research and development, he was understandably reluctant to abandon the projects set in motion. "The grim foot of time," he complained, "is getting ready to boot us out of

P[eking] (via the Trans-Siberia) in to Cambridge once more. It is a sickening sensation waiting for the kick."[89]

In the midst of these reflections, Selksar Gunn visited Peking from the Rockefeller Foundation's new Shanghai office. The Institute's grant was due to expire at the end of June 1937; one reason for Gunn's trip was to assess its progress and advise the Foundation on the possibility of a three-year extension. In a letter to Stevens on December 10, Gunn struck a note of cautious support. He found that the Institute had made "considerable progress" in following Stevens's exhortation to attach more Chinese scholars to the enterprise. Through a recently established Committee on Control, Richards began to integrate leading Chinese educationalists such as Chancellor Yuh of Yenching University and Dr. P. C. Chang of the university at Nankai into the Basic movement. While the Committee members were not to be involved in the day-to-day workings of the Institute, they would be asked to "sit at the meetings when policy, budget and matters of this kind were up for discussion and consideration."[90] These contacts were essential to the Institute's prestige and also forwarded its plans to make Basic an independent Chinese enterprise. Aside from important data collected on the effectiveness of Basic in the classroom, the Institute staff had finished the Basic Wall Chart for use in middle schools, and a considerable portion of the Chinese-Basic primer commissioned from E. K. Smith was now completed. These achievements, along with the interest shown by the Ministry of Education in Nanking, inspired Gunn's confidence in the future success of Basic.

But Gunn expressed significant reservations as well, anticipating some of the difficulties that would plague the Institute in the future. First among these was the question of funding. For all of its advances, support for the Basic project still fell squarely on the Foundation's shoulders. "I do not see at the moment any likelihood of material appropriations from Chinese sources," Gunn told Stevens, though he added that "I doubt it is fair to expect them so soon."[91] Yet he realized that without some kind of commitment from the Chinese themselves, the Institute would depend upon Foundation resources indefinitely. Though interest in the capital was important, Gunn found it necessary to remind Richards and Jameson that "while it was highly desirable to have the confidence and backing of the Ministry of Education, . . . they must be careful in this matter as the Minister, knowing that the Rockefeller is financing the Orthological Institute, might anticipate further grants from the Foundation which might not be possible to realize." Gunn was understandably concerned that the government's interest in Basic might have as much to do with Foundation backing as with Richards's theories. The issue of leadership was also still pressing. When Richards mentioned the idea of remaining in Peking, Gunn grew suspicious. As he told Stevens:

> Richards stated that he is becoming so interested in the work in China that he is ready to consider staying out here for a period of several years, and he may be writing you on that subject. I have no doubt that this would be a desirable thing for China if it can be arranged, but it would mean, of course, that the Foundation would have to finance him. Without encouraging him at all to believe that you might be interested in a scheme of this kind, I quizzed him about his relationships with Cambridge and pointed out that in no event would there be a possibility of the Foundation's undertaking the responsibility to take care of him indefinitely.

In fact, Gunn felt some misgivings about both Richards and Jameson, the two personalities at the center of the project:

> I had a private conversation with Richards concerning Jameson. . . . His general statement was to the effect that while Jameson had "jittery" periods of a day or two occasionally, he felt he was doing a good piece of work and was safe. I might add that Richards himself is something of an "odd duck." You know him better than I do. I am not sure just how far to value his judgement. With his desire to remain in China he becomes more than ever an "interested" party in the whole business.

Richards's later efforts on behalf of Basic showed Gunn's suspicion to be misplaced. But his observations serve as a reminder that most reports of Basic's success came from members of the Institute itself. His comments also highlight the extent to which the organization depended upon the personalities who ran it. Certainly at the end of 1936, the Orthological Institute of China seemed less an institution than an organization dependent on Richards and his predominantly Western colleagues. As long as the Institute's initiative came from the Westerners who headed it, the future of Basic English in China would be fragile at best.

On the same day that Gunn posted his letter to New York, Jameson wrote to him from Nanking with news that seemed to put many of his immediate doubts to rest. On December 3 he had received a message from Wang Shih-chieh, the Chinese Minster of Education, expressing the Ministry's willingness "to receive from the Institute, at any time when it is ready to do so, a comprehensive report of its own findings on the present status, and proposals for the improvement of English teaching in Chinese middle schools."[92] Hinting at an impending "systematic modification" of the middle school curriculum, Wang ended his letter on an exceptionally accommodating note. "I must thank you," he wrote,

> for offering the resources of the Institute, and wish to assure you that the Ministry will always be glad to render it such support and facilities as it requires. Please send along your translation of the revised curriculum for English, and I shall be glad to have it looked into, to have the questions cleared up, if any.[93]

Within a few days, Richards and Jameson were in the capital at Nanking meeting with the Divisional Heads of the Ministry of Education. Jameson assured Gunn that official interest in Basic was even greater than Wang's letter had suggested. In a series of meetings with key Ministry officials, they found that in addition to Wang both Tai Yin Kwang, Chief of the Section on Secondary Education, and Ku Shu-sen, head of the Division of Elementary Education, shared Richards's sense of the problems facing English teaching in China, and were anxious to benefit from the Institute's advice. According to Jameson, "[t]he Divisional chiefs, on whom Minister Wang naturally leans heavily, were almost embarrassing in their eagerness to be of assistance."[94] Most significantly, the meeting culminated in an offer to help shape government policy. The Ministry revealed that plans for a sweeping reform of the national curriculum were getting underway, and while the details were still unclear, they would involve a major overhaul of the current Chinese system. Jameson noted that Minister Wang

> looks toward a revolution, or at least a reform, of the methods of teaching English and feels that the Ministry is now sufficiently in control of the situation to implement the lines it decides upon. "When a curriculum is chosen finally, there will be no wavering." He urged Richards to return and formulate his suggestions. He intends to set up early in the year a Committee for the Improvement of English Teaching in China and expressed the hope that Richards and the Institute will be of assistance. ("The Institute will, of course, carry on its own work, but there will then be a formal connection.")[95]

This kind of government interest in Basic was a crucial step toward the tangible support that the Rockefeller Foundation hoped for from the Chinese. The Ministry solicited Richards's and Jameson's advice on "the selection of vocabulary, teaching material and teaching method" for English, and arranged for a Ministry official to attend the Institute's meetings so as "to formalize on our [Wang's] side the relations between the two bodies." More immediately, Wang consulted Richards on the organization of a government-sponsored summer school scheduled to begin the following year "which will embrace a third of the English teachers in China." In the meantime it was agreed that Institute members would join a Committee for the Improvement of English Teaching in China scheduled to meet early in 1937. Whether Richards would be in China at this time or not was still uncertain.

By the end of 1936, Richards had reason to regard the Orthological Institute of China as an unmitigated success. Eight months of classroom research, teacher training and demonstration classes had culminated in the opportunity to shape a national English curriculum for China. In the midst of all this promise, the Lent Term at Cambridge began. As late as December 28, just two weeks before the start of classes, the Richardses were still torn over whether or not to stay in Peking. "Heartache whichever foot we end on," Dorothea wrote in the diary.[96] Ultimately they decided that it was "wiser . . . not [to] lose the Cam[bridge] pulpit and sounding board,"[97] and in January they boarded the Trans-Siberian railway once again en route to Cambridge. By the 19th Richards was giving his first lecture of the term. He had left just as the Basic situation in China seemed to be reaching its peak, and his original vision looked well on its way to becoming a reality. If Basic could work in China, Dorothea pointed out, "there seems a good chance of it making an enormous difference to education everywhere."[98] As Richards told Stevens in June, "It's grand to be able to do something definite instead of feeling just a man with some crotchets."[99] By year's end the sentiment seemed amply justified.

6 ⌒ War and the Flight
to Kunming, 1937-1945

I

Richards spent the first months of 1936 back at Cambridge lecturing on English literature. His thoughts, however, were still very much with China. Soon after the beginning of the Lent Term he petitioned for a one-year leave of absence to continue his work in the Far East. On February 3, 1937, the General Board of the University honored his request with an unpaid sabbatical for the period lasting from April 1937 to the end of September 1938.[1] Their decision guaranteed him eighteen months to devote to Basic in China, the longest continuous amount of time he had yet had. In the meantime Richards set to work drafting a report on English for the Chinese Ministry of Education, keeping in close touch with the Institute's affairs through cables with Jameson. He also let Stevens at the Rockefeller Foundation know that he was eager to return to China, where the Institute's work seemed likely to result in a revised national curriculum for English. "I often wonder," he wrote to Stevens in February, "what itch makes me want to joggle about the world interfering with other people."[2] With Basic's recent advances in China, the feeling was never more insistent.

On February 23, Richards's concerns about the year's funding were put to rest when the Rockefeller Foundation elected to extend its support of the Orthological Institute of China through June 1938. The grant included a separate allotment for Richards's salary and travel expenses over the next sixteen months.[3] A solid year of Basic work, from April to September, was finally possible. "This is a short and harassing time," he assured Dorothea as the term wore on, "but it will be repaid with a grand long spell in China. Two Yunnan summers [of mountain climbing] and a whole autumn winter spring in

Peking. . . . And after all it's exciting, being the spear point at the moment, of the contact between the West and China, isn't it?"[4] At the Foundation's request Richards agreed to attend a conference on Basic English in New York that April, proceeding from there directly to Peking. Dorothea left Cambridge in advance of Richards at the beginning of April 1937 via the Trans-Siberian express. In eastern Russia and again in Manchukuo, then under Japanese control, her luggage was searched with unusual rigor and incivility; a portent of mounting diplomatic tensions in the region.[5] Richards joined her in Peking in late May, just missing the lavish celebrations for Coronation Day at the British Embassy, complete with an Anglican service, polo announcements and fireworks.[6] Feeling "as if I hadn't been away for more than a week," he settled down to what he fully expected to be Basic's most rewarding year.[7]

Less than six weeks later Japanese troops were on the outskirts of Peking fighting for control of the city. The attack took foreigners and Chinese alike by surprise. Japan's long-standing military ambitions in Northern China were well known, but actual war had seemed a distant prospect to most. Stopping in Japan (where a translation of *The Meaning of Meaning* had just won a prize) on his way to Peking in May, Richards had heard "that there is a great change in [Japanese] policies, Liberal opinion becoming much bolder, and the army has its back to the wall at home."[8] When hostilities broke out at the Marco Polo Bridge on July 7, 1937 (Lugouquiao), such hopes for peace evaporated. The Chinese army was woefully unprepared; at the end of the month they abandoned Peking and retreated to defend Shanghai. The fall of Peking began a war that was to last in China for the next eight years, driving the government and the Northern universities into a retreat of more than 3,000 miles across the provinces of the central and southwest interior. Remarkably, Richards and his colleagues managed to continue their work in China throughout most of the war. In September 1937 Richards left Peking to join up with Nationalist officials in Changsha, where he hoped to continue meetings with the government's recently appointed Committee on the Teaching of English. By 1938 he had relocated the Institute's main office to Kunming, capital of the rural, semi-independent province of Yunnan, where the Peking-area universities were gathering for the duration of the war. The survival of the Orthological Institute in China during this period, and the reasons for the Rockefeller Foundation's continued support of its work during the war, are the central concerns of this chapter.

The war years brought some of the strengths and weaknesses of Richards's ambitions in China into high relief. That he hoped to continue with Basic through the war attests not to a naïve optimism, as some of his more spirited plans during the worsening conflict might suggest, but rather to an ongoing belief in the key assumptions underpinning the Basic enterprise. Richards saw Basic as a way of cultivating rational individuals, and his idea of communication took the individual as its primary unit. His conception of language, in both poetry and pedagogy, emphasizes not the communal or social aspects of linguistic formation but the process by which individuals manipulate language to communicate their thoughts. In China, this translated into a focus on texts rather than institutions or model schools. Insisting upon Basic's essential clarity and accessibility, Richards labored to develop a series of primers that would make Basic nearly self-teaching. He wanted to ensure that Basic would not simply supplant one pedagogical system with another, or impose a new set of equally arbitrary rules for the teaching of English, but give students the tools to use and learn language on their own. With an adequate classroom text for students and teachers, he was convinced that Basic could take hold in China even without effective academic or governmental support.

Even after the Nationalist's pre-war commitment to a revised, Basic-oriented curriculum, Richards continued to perfect the Basic instructional texts by testing them among Chinese students and teachers in the classroom. He saw to it that this research survived throughout the war with Japan, tailoring materials to meet classroom needs. Because of this empirical bias, and the reliance on texts and teachers over sweeping institutional reforms, Basic was less threatened than it might have been by the severe disruption of the war. Although Richards quickly saw that no real advances could be made until peacetime, he believed that diligently tested primers and teachers' handbooks would ensure Basic's spread after the war regardless of the political situation. The textual and empirical emphasis of his work meant that Richards could continue to make a good case for the value of Basic in China even when its political future seemed uncertain. Finally, the tenacity of Richards and his staff through the war stemmed in part from his equation of communication and world peace. Born out of the disaffection following the First World War, it seemed fitting that Basic should remain in China to mitigate the effects of the Second. Because Basic was intended not just as an educational reform but as a means of international harmony, the Institute was able to maintain its sense of purpose during the rigors of an escalating global conflict.

But if the war demonstrated Basic's strengths, it also exposed some damaging flaws. First among these was the shortage of staff, particularly Chinese. The failure to cultivate an effective Chinese leadership left the Institute in constant danger of evaporating when its Western support ended. Ironically, this was due in part to both Richards's and the Rockefeller Foundation's desire to ensure that Basic did not become another Western missionary venture. Their continued insistence that the Institute's work be taken over by the Chinese government as soon as possible meant that it never became very deeply rooted in the country. Working with a limited budget, the Institute had to perpetually justify its existence to the Foundation and could spare little time or resources for developing an effective Chinese staff. As a consequence, Basic came to rely on a narrower band of Chinese support, depending upon the personal agendas of reformers within the provincial or central governments. Along with this development came a growing alienation from the Chinese universities. Particularly after the retreat to Yunnan, when the Peking-area universities consolidated into a single body, the Institute failed to win over those critics who felt that Basic was a patronizing "dumbing down" of English or an offensive cultural imposition. Instead, the Institute responded by looking increasingly to the provincial Commissioner of Education for support, hoping to make Yunnan a model of Basic education for all of China after the war. As a result, the Basic project during the war was a somewhat quixotic combination of the short- and long-term, its designs at once minutely local and vastly national, even global, in scope. On the one hand Richards and his colleagues were tantalized by large-scale, immediate gains like those promised by the Ministry of Education before the war, and continued to court key officials in hopes of more far-reaching change. On the other hand they worked to institute Basic in a handful of obscure rural middle schools with a skeleton staff and budget, trying to make Yunnan a seedbed of future reform. Both aspects of the enterprise represented an effort to keep Basic active in China under highly unfavorable circumstances.

Ultimately the war transformed the Basic enterprise in China in ways that neither Richards nor the officials at the Rockefeller Foundation could foresee. As the political situation fluctuated in these years, the place of English teaching generally in China's future became uncertain. The competing pressures of Soviet Russia, the Chinese Communist Party and the Japanese presence all pointed to a very different constellation of influences for postwar China. The Nationalist government had little time for English-teaching reforms while fighting a losing war, and it was uncertain that they would return to such plans even in the case of a victory. In the occupied areas English was ousted from the middle school curricula in favor of Japanese, while in many of the Communist-held territories Russian seemed a more logical second language. These developments made it increasingly clear that whatever the outcome of the war, the English-speaking nations would wield less influence in China than they had previously. If Basic could succeed in Yunnan it was likely to assume explicit political value as a conduit of Western influence in the postwar reconstruction.

Anticipating a diminished role for English after the war, Richards became more aware of Basic's usefulness as a token link with the Anglo-American world at a time when the Chinese were turning to other solutions in their drive to modernize. This growing politicization of English in China left less scope for the progressive ideals that had originally fueled the Basic project, and it presaged the new challenges that Basic would face as World War II shaded into the Cold War.

II

Richards's mood upon returning to Peking in May 1937 was one of unmitigated optimism. His month in the United States in April had resulted in promises from Groton and Andover to try Basic in their classes for the following year, a prestigious advance.[9] In China he found "prospects too rosy to be entirely reassuring."[10] The Ministry of Education proved receptive to all of the Institute's proposals for educational reform, with a marked absence of the obstructionism and internal politicking that Richards had come to expect from Chinese officialdom. Describing his meetings with Ministry officials in late May, Richards told Stevens:

> I was afraid there might be a political side—that the Ministry might be wanting to say, "Look how open-minded, modern and progressive we are!", or might just want a potent bit of paper from us, or be hoping to use us as a shield against something. But I'm satisfied—as one rarely is satisfied in China—that all it wants is that the Committee not only recommend but "do" what it thinks will be helpful with a free hand and, if possible, a really drastic program.[11]

On June 8, T. C. Woo of the Ministry of Education formally invited Richards and Jameson to join a Committee on Middle School English Teaching scheduled to meet in the capital on June 26. Other members included George Yeh and Y. R. Chao, long-standing friends of Richards's from Tsing Hua, as well as P. C. Chang and President Luh of Yenching, both of whom sat on the Orthological Institute's Committee of Control. Woo himself, another Basic sympathizer, was also an appointee. The Ministry's Charter invested the thirteen-member Committee with an impressive amount of authority. They were expected to decide upon a comprehensive English vocabulary suitable for Chinese middle school students, and to edit all dictionaries and textbooks used at each level. In addition, the Committee was empowered to revise current standards in English for students as well as teachers through a new series of exams. Finally, they were asked to investigate how the middle school curriculum might be better integrated with the University system, a commission that suggested some jurisdiction over university affairs.[12] Although the Ministry charter made no reference to Basic English, its intentions were clearly pro-Basic, as ten of the thirteen Committee seats belonged to known adherents of Richards's ideas.[13] The government Committee was, in Dorothea's words, "to recast the whole system."[14] Ivor was equally enthusiastic: "It really looks as if the Chinese G[overnment] were going to make Basic E[nglish] official in the schools and set to work on a whole new English teaching program. A tremendous thing, if they do, so soon!"[15]

By June 30, which marked the eighteenth-month anniversary of the Orthological Institute in China, Richards and Jameson were in Nanking for the first meetings of the Ministry's Committee on Middle School English Teaching. Despite the overwhelming majority of

Basic supporters, Richards encountered unexpected opposition from some of the other members. Of the four middle school teachers appointed, two, W. Luh and Chang Shih Yi, opposed the Basic tenor of the proceedings. Since technically the Committee was not affiliated with Basic, Richards had to proceed diplomatically. "We've not yet come to openly discussing Basic," he wrote to Dorothea from Nanking, "but one after another of the Principles we are arguing about points to Basic."[16] Confident that he could "win over the two doubtful folk . . . in a few days," Richards expressed great satisfaction with the Committee meetings.[17] He was also gratified to hear that the Ministry planned to allocate somewhere between $20,000 and $50,000 for the Committee budget, a sign of their commitment to reform. On June 28 a Subcommittee on Vocabulary Selection for Middle Schools was appointed, with Richards elected as its head. Consisting of George Yeh, Y. R. Chao, Beauson Tsing and Chang Shih Yi, the Subcommittee was to draft a list of English words for use in middle schools and present them before the full Committee in January 1938.

Vocabulary selection was a crucial initiative for Basic, which depended upon the 850-word list for its effectiveness. With Richards, George Yeh and Y. R. Chao sympathetic to the Institute, a decision in favor of the Basic vocabulary seemed likely. Beauson Tsing, "a brilliant and admirable young Changsha Presbyterian Middle School teacher," soon showed a vigorous interest in Basic as well and promised to be a great support. Chang Shih Yi, however, remained obstinate. A veteran middle school teacher and former Ministry advisor, he opposed Basic schemes in favor of the "old regulations and textbooks," many of which he had helped to design.[18] Characteristically, Richards refused to see Chang's opposition as insurmountable, but it did mean that Committee work "will have to go slow and educate the members as it goes."[19] As the next meeting was scheduled for January, there seemed plenty of time to win over Basic's opponents.

Richards and Jameson had no illusions about the Ministry's ability to institute a uniform school system for all of China. Aside from the administrative problems involved in a country so large, Jameson realized that "gov[ernment] edicts in China are not always well received" and saw government support as only a first step in Basic's advance. Accordingly, they returned to Peking in early July planning to concentrate on developing textbooks and teacher's handbooks so good "that the teachers will be unable to resist them."[20] Although they both hoped that the Ministry would eventually take over the Institute's work, the immediate advantage of government interest to Richards's mind was the chance it offered of introducing more Chinese teachers to Basic. To this end Richards and the Institute staff assumed instruction of the Summer School Session for Junior Middle School Teachers at Yenching University, some three miles outside of Peking, as agreed upon the previous December. Shui, Jameson and Richards left the city daily at 7 A.M. to lecture an assembly of middle school teachers from across China. After the month-long session, to be followed by another at the Shih Ta Teacher's Training College later in the summer, the Richardses planned to holiday in the mountains of Yunnan, returning to Peking in the autumn. Altogether, Richards's first six weeks in China in 1937 had presented the greatest opportunity yet to effect his language reforms. The Nationalist government seemed intent upon making Basic a part of its official curriculum, and Richards was now in a position to expose a number of English teachers across China to Basic through the government-mandated summer schools as well as his work on the Committee. "A very exciting chance," Dorothea enthused at the end of June. "There must be a catch somewhere."[21]

On July 7, two days after the first teachers' training session at Yenching, Japanese troops opened fire on the Chinese Army at the Marco Polo Bridge, 10 miles west of Peking. The incident, which culminated in the occupation of the city three weeks later, is considered to be the first battle of World War II. For several days the outcome of the skirmish at the bridge remained unclear. A confused Chinese policy of negotiation and counterattack left the inhabitants of Peking in the dark about the situation for several days. Richards continued to lead classes at Yenching, leaving the city gates each morning uncertain if they would be open when he returned.[22] On July 11 he and Dorothea walked through the streets after admiring the sunset outside the city gates to find soldiers "sandbagging the crossroads and an air of expecting battle."[23] That night the sounds of machine gun and artillery fire were audible from their Peking home. Describing the martial atmosphere to her brother-in-law in England, she wrote

> We have no idea what is really happening and can hear fighting just outside the city all round. The trains have been stopped. There are any number of Chinese troops without any equipment or organization and it

is likely to become another Abyssinia if it comes to fighting more than these minor skirmishes.[24]

The state of the Chinese army was a constant concern for the Richardses and their friends over the next several days, as they believed that a protracted battle with the Japanese would be a slaughter. Nor was it clear how the encounter would affect their year in China. "Naturally," Dorothea conceded, "it puts all our Basic English and most plans into uncertainty."

Richards returned to Yenching the next day to find his entire summer school class assembled as usual. Conditions were remarkably calm within the city as well; Richards spent the evening of the 12th on the roof of the Hotel du Nord with Dorothea, drinking lager and admiring the view. Rumors of an impending Japanese defeat were even beginning to circulate.[25] On the 16th Richards assured a friend:

> The local situation is so far harmless to such activities as there are of the Institute. Its possibilities are impossible to forecast here on the spot as they are everywhere else. There seems good reason to suppose that Chinese equipment is totally insufficient to make equal combat possible. The spirit seems fairly high. Peking remains remarkably tranquil. Gunfire audible from various sides of the city most nights. Minor skirmishing only. It is very likely that the Chinese forces will retreat to Shanghai without attempting to hold Peking.[26]

Aside from a cancellation of the summer's mountaineering, it was still hard for the Richardses to tell how the war was likely to change their plans in China. For the moment at least they felt safe in Peking. "There seems no likelihood of a siege or of popular rampaging," Richards reported to his brother, "and we could, in need, quickly get into the Legation Quarter," which offered diplomatic immunity in the event of occupation.[27] By mid-July, the Richardses were even persuaded that the skirmishing around the city might not lead to war given the disarray of the Chinese Army. "It seems to be almost even betting whether this will become a general Sino-Japanese war or not," Dorothea wrote. "By all accounts the Chinese should make, at least for the present, almost any terms. It is very humiliating but better than a massacre."[28]

Remarkably, the training classes at Yenching continued throughout late July. When some suggested that the students adjourn to Peking, a patriotic teacher "harangued them and told them it was their duty to go on at Yenching."[29] Because of train stoppages, news from the front was scarce. On July 26 Richards returned from Yenching as usual and accompanied Dorothea to Bob Winter's house near the West gate for a quiet evening in his famed Chinese garden. At 7:45 P.M. loud volleys of gunfire sounded just over the city wall. A phone call confirmed that fighting was taking place all around Peking. The Richardses opted to stay with Winter for the night, listening to news on the wireless until two in the morning.[30] At 5:20 A.M. they woke to cannon fire as Japanese troops assaulted the Chinese barracks near the city. That morning the West gate was shut for the first time since the outbreak of hostilities. Later that day the French and German embassies summoned their citizens into the Legation Quarter in anticipation of Japanese bombing. "It's an odd life," Richards reflected, "but represents our age well."[31]

The following day, July 28, the *Peking Chronicle* reported that the Japanese ultimatum had been rejected, and the Chinese government demanded an enemy withdrawal. More intense fighting now seemed certain. The British Embassy ordered all of their subjects in Peking to be in the Legation Quarter by noon. After "a miserable two hours having breakfast under the big tree listening to bombing and cannon fire,"[32] Richards and Dorothea packed and left for the Embassy by rickshaw at 10:30 A.M., where a film crew recorded the crowds entering the Legation barricades.[33] One of the more colorful refugees was Sir Edmund Backhouse, the famed hermit of Peking and former advisor to the Empress Dowager during the Qing dynasty, who made a dramatic entry through the barricades with a Tolstoyian beard, shaved head and dark sunglasses.[34] By evening the Chinese military leaders opted to withdraw to the south, thus averting the danger of heavy fighting in Peking. The Richardses were able to return home two days later, finding it "strange to see so little change in the streets after such cataclysmic happenings."[35] The most pressing difficulty in the aftermath of withdrawal was provisioning the large number of wounded soldiers that flooded Peking from the surrounding countryside.

Deeply frustrated by recent events, Richards resumed his work at the Institute with remarkable intensity, which he acknowledged "as the most immediate task to fill and steady our minds."[36] On August 1, just two days out of the Embassy, he completed four stages of the Basic Primer.[37] He spent the following morning at the Institute office with Chao and Shui, finding the former deeply upset but the latter "just as usual."[38] Richards was despondent about the invasion, to the point of questioning the value of his own work. As he admitted to Stevens,

> It is a sadly inert world that permits greed so outrageous without check. There are moments when I feel ridiculous to be scribbling here at a school book while such things go on around me. Just as I wrote "go on" I heard a dull distant thud that might mean anything one's imagination could picture. I suppose that is all an argument for pressing forward with remedies for stupidity and ignorance—but it is not always clear to an outsider like myself.[39]

With the cancellation of the sessions at Yenching and Shih Ta, the situation for Basic began to look even bleaker. Life in Peking was becoming intolerable. Japanese troops now patrolled most areas of the city; on their way to the Summer Palace on August 4 the Richardses were stopped and questioned, eventually turning back "after twenty minutes jibbering" with the Japanese soldiers.[40] The weeks following the Chinese retreat also revealed the scale of July's slaughter. A trip to Yenching on the 4th gave Richards some sense of the devastation in the countryside surrounding Peking. His friend Lucius Porter was in charge of caring for the refugees, where houses were being robbed and recalcitrant shopkeepers bayoneted.[41] Within Peking, Dorothea heard "stories of journalists and educationalists being carried off and houses being searched."[42] Bob Winter occupied the time by collecting wounded soldiers from outside the city gates, while Dorothea made bandages with mounting anger at the Chinese military for fighting at all. "Fists against machine guns," she wrote to her father, "aren't much good."[43] The death of so many poorly equipped Chinese soldiers must surely have bolstered Richards's sense of the need for modernization in China, linguistic and otherwise.

On August 8, 3,000 Japanese troops officially entered Peking, "parading the streets in thousands, with cavalry, machine guns, bicycle corps, generals in motor cars, [and] large flags."[44] For several days the Richardses were divided about whether to remain in the city or leave for the south. Although the sight of occupation left them both "very upset," the relative stability in Peking following the Chinese withdrawal persuaded Richards that much could still be done. As he noted to Stevens,

> The political tension and military anxiety disturb the work in the Institute surprisingly little. The Chinese have an amazing capacity to forget

their personal and national problems. . . . So I see no reason why a very fruitful period of text-production should not follow. (All this assuming that fighting in or very near Peking does not break out again. We still hear gunfire at night from Nankow.) Our job will be to prepare, on a really adequate scale for the educational reconstruction which will begin when peace comes. Our guess is that this may be in two years' time.[45]

Counting against this relative peace was the state of the Peking-area universities, which, as Dorothea recorded, looked "like becoming shadows of their former selves. The new rulers will certainly frown on any traditional studies and regard the students as the source of all anti-Japanism."[46] In addition, Japanese censorship had made Peking an "isolated news-less pocket," so that contact with the world outside the city was difficult. A diary entry of Dorothea's on August 12 describes their mood during the occupation:

Hate Peking, spiritually dominated, everywhere closed—Suspicion—hills a thousand miles away. Makes one feel starved. . . . We are virtually prisoners—news in and out censored, no cables—and one over-crowded train a day.[47]

Despite the city's stability, the notion of remaining in Peking eventually came to seem as unrealistic as it was abhorrent.

On August 15 the Japanese launched an attack against Shanghai. It was now clear that the military situation would escalate into a full-scale war. Richards, who still hoped to continue meetings with the Government Committee on English Teaching, realized that he would have to make contact with officials outside of Peking. He had no illusions about government interest in Basic lasting through a protracted war. But he felt the important groundwork for future reforms could still be laid. "Even if another government were in power in Nanking or elsewhere," he assured Stevens, "the general trend towards this type of reform which has been created is so strong now that there is no risk of our work being wasted." In fact, in some respects the disruption created a more favorable opportunity for the Committee's work. Shui, for one, felt "that the people in the Ministry [of Education] may find this a heaven-sent chance to do fundamental work—since the squabbles between University dignitaries, and such-like things, which usually distract them, are suspended."[48] Ultimately Richards resolved to leave Jameson, Chao and Shui in Peking to continue with the Institute's work while he and Dorothea proceeded south to find the other members of the Ministry Committee. His sense of Basic's usefulness was still undaunted. John Paul Russo cites Richards's suggestion that the Institute might continue its work in occupied Peking and "thus find a new channel into Japan" as "surely the wildest example of his optimism."[49] But it also reflects Richards's long-standing assumption that with a completed course of textbooks and teacher's manuals, Basic could be effective under any political circumstances. This belief played a key role in his ambitions for Basic during the war years.

On August 31 the Richardses left for the port city of Tientsin, intending to find passage to Hong Kong. Joining them was William Empson, who had arrived in Peking at the end of August to assume a teaching post at the Peking National University, or Pei Ta. Over the past several years Empson had played an oblique but significant role in the Basic enterprise. As one of Richards's most outstanding students at Cambridge, he had adopted many of his teacher's ideas about language and literature; his first book of literary criticism, *Seven Types of Ambiguity*, was the result of a paper undertaken for Richards's tutorial. In 1929, while Richards was at Tsing Hua, Empson lost a bye-fellowship at Magdalene College after a maid discovered condoms among his articles as he changed rooms. With Richards's help he managed to secure a job lecturing in Japan, where he taught English literature from 1930 to 1934. During this time he exchanged several letters with Richards on the subject of Basic, often exercising his former teacher on the more philosophical aspects of language theory. When Richards considered designing a dictionary based on a more complex model of how words operate, he gave to Empson the job of defining the word "honest," a project which closely resembles Empson's later analysis of socially nuanced words and their various connotations in *The Structure of Complex Words*. At the outbreak of hostilities with Japan Empson cabled Richards from England to see if he should still come. After receiving no answer (Richards was unable to get a cable out of the city) he left for Peking on the Trans-Siberia express at the end of July. Finding the city under Japanese occupation upon his arrival, he decided to join Richards on his journey south in hopes of finding the Pei Ta faculty, which was then in retreat in Changsha.

Tientsin was crowded with refugees. After a four-day wait the party finally found a berth to Hong Kong. There they planned to meet Victor Purcell, a British civil servant who headed the Protectorate of Chinese at Penang in Malaya. Purcell, who later wrote several books about China and Malaya and was appointed U.N. Consultant on Asia after the war, had intended to visit the Orthological Institute in Peking under a Commonwealth Service Research Fellowship before the Japanese invasion.[50] With his plans interrupted by the war, he was currently collecting intelligence on the Japanese position from Hong Kong.[51] On September 10 he met Richards's party arriving from Tientsin. The war in China continued to escalate; heavy fighting around Shanghai nearly prevented them from making the necessary transfer to Hong Kong, especially as British women were now barred from entering the region.[52] As Chinese resistance to the Japanese strengthened, the violence of the conflict began to increase. In Hong Kong Richards soon learned more about the horrors of the military situation:

> The Japanese have been striking at communications everywhere regardless of the non-combatants and helpless refugees they blow to bits. They seem quite mad and I do hope feeling in America and England will be with the Chinese, who, in spite of their many failings, are doing incomparably better than they would have done even five years ago.[53]

After a few days in the city, Richards received word from Hu Shih that all but one of the Middle School Committee members were now in Changsha, the capital of Hunan province and well behind the combat zone. The Northern universities were also gathering there in search of a refuge from the Japanese persecutions in Peking. Richards decided to join the government and university officials in Changsha. On September 21 he and Dorothea, accompanied by Empson and Purcell, flew the five hundred miles to Changsha in three hours. Just after their arrival they heard news of the bombing of Canton, less than eighty miles from Hong Kong, which they had missed "by five minutes."[54]

The stay in Changsha gave Richards a chance to take stock of his situation. Students and faculty from Tsing Hua, Yenching and Pei Ta Universities were collecting in the provincial capital. Their immediate plans were as uncertain as Richards's own. The atmosphere in Changsha, "a sprawling and rather ugly town with a damp climate" in Richards's estimation, was chaotic. As he reported to Stevens,

> Just now all the intellect of the North is gathering here. I don't see how the faculties of three very jealous universities are going to combine (with perhaps no more than some 200 students) very harmoniously! In many

ways the inappropriateness of intellectuality in a war-time world is being evidenced here again. (Yet they are the makers of the future in China.)[55]

Finding George Yeh, Beauson Tsing and Y. R. Chao in Changsha, Richards began meetings of the Subcommittee on Vocabulary Selection almost immediately. Over the next days they conducted "nearly continuous" debates on questions of vocabulary and grammar, arguing over matters such as "whether a mastery of 'shall' and 'will' is a prime requisite of English teaching in China."[56] Russo cites Richards's "seeming aloofness in the midst of political turmoil" as he continued Basic work during wartime, and his drive under such dire circumstances does seem incredible. Russo explains Richards's actions by pointing to the long focus of his vision for Basic: "He was thinking not in terms of years or even decades, but of half-centuries; not in terms of cities or countries, but of continents and world politics."[57] But Richards's comments to Stevens about the situation in Changsha suggest more immediate reasons for carrying on with the enterprise, ones that show his growing awareness of politics as well as linguistics:

> All of [the committee members] and others of the extraordinary concourse of the dislodged University big-shots which is assembling here, insist that 'after the war' China will need English speaking friends more than ever, and that therefore there will be more demand for good English teaching. There is a fear of Russian influence in this. If Russia helps China more than the other powers she will expect a reward, that is their feeling. And they look to an increased knowledge of English to be one counterpoise.[58]

On August 21 Richards's concern about a postwar Russian influence was confirmed with the signing of the Chinese-Soviet non-aggression pact, which made the Soviet Union China's most important wartime ally. The Russians certainly provided the Chinese with more concrete military aid than any other Western power, a fact the Richardses were well aware of. "We gather that a good number of aeroplanes are coming in from Russia," Dorothea wrote to her brother on September 27, "and that 100 Russians are being naturalized in Nanking while a lot of the young Chinese are being trained in Russia."[59] Such reports suggested that a strong Soviet influence, both cultural and political, could well be a part of China's future. The need to promote Basic English became even more imperative as the axis of China's attention promised to shift away from the West.

Richards may have had other political concerns in mind at this time as well. The struggle between the Nationalists and the Chinese Communist Party had been largely confined to South and Central China during the Thirties; Richards seems to have received little news of it in Peking. In Changsha, however, signs of the conflict were more readily apparent. "Much destruction in '27 and '33 by Communists and anti-Communist," Richards tersely noted in his description of the town on September 23.[60] Moreover Beauson Tsing, who was proving to be an extraordinarily helpful and intelligent member of the Subcommittee with important family connections in Hunan, was discovered to be a "modified Christian Communist,"[61] exposing Richards more directly to the impact of the Left in China. Richards himself was not necessarily anti-Communist; as Russo points out, in some respects "part of him longed for a strong central government that would enable him to spread Basic throughout China."[62] His later enthusiasm for the Communist regime in 1950 showed that he was not ideologically opposed to its political ideals as such. But the possibility of a Communist China after the war clearly meant that the cultural and linguistic balance would swing away from the English-speaking countries in favor of Soviet Russia; a concern that would increasingly trouble Richards as the conflict developed.

Richards was also almost certainly aware of the political reasons behind Purcell's interest in Basic. As the former Assistant Director of Britain's Education Department for the Straits Settlements (which included the cities of Singapore, Malacca and Penang), Purcell had a first-hand knowledge of the political importance of English teaching for Britain's colonial interests. As he explained later in his *Memoirs of a Malayan Official*, the large Chinese population of Malaya was using their schools as organs of propaganda for Chinese political causes. Staring in 1925, classroom texts in Chinese schools began to express strong anti-British sentiments, representing scenes of the Opium War of the 1830's and British troops burning the Summer Palace in 1860. To stem the tide of anti-British propaganda, the Department of Education began requiring registration and control of Chinese schools in Malaya and the Straits Settlements, adopting a policy of training teachers who would instruct students to regard Malaya rather than China as their homeland.[63] Purcell's grant to study Basic in 1937 was therefore part of the broader British effort to regain control of propaganda in the classroom.[64] While Richards may not have been aware of the details of the Malayan situation, the colonial government's interest in Basic must have given him added cause to consider the political dimensions of English teaching. This is not to say that Richards endorsed an explicit political agenda for Basic, but neither was he simply the "curious mixture of the adventurous, the committed, the naïve and the ingenious" that Russo presents.[65] His work on Basic in these years was a conscious attempt to preserve a cultural presence in China that seemed threatened by the politics of war.

During their stay in Changsha, the Richardses lodged at the Yale in China mission, whose American character reminded Richards curiously of Ann Arbor, while Purcell and Empson retired to a "low German dive with lots of drinks."[66] Daily Committee meetings were held at the local Bible Institute, a missionary school that would soon house the newly consolidated Peking area universities. Richards found the Committee members to be less tractable than he had hoped. He complained to Stevens of the "gentle pressure and persistent coaxing and convincing [that] will be needed if the Committee is to produce anything like as good a piece of work as it might."[67] At times he found them "ready for what I want to give them,"[68] at others he encountered "lots of queer resistances and fears that Basic was pushing everything else out."[69] Dorothea also complained to her brother of Richards's difficulties in "smoothing the vain Chinese over. They correct your English and tell you how to pronounce your own words."[70] Aside from Committee meetings, Richards observed classes at a local girls school[71] and lectured to sixty middle school teachers on English teaching with the permission of Dr. King Shu, the Commissioner of Education for Hunan.[72] Richards realized that the opportunities for Basic in a province like Hunan were limited; the Nanking government didn't wield enough centralized authority in the semi-independent southern provinces. Here again, his hopes were for the possibilities in China after the war.[73]

Meanwhile the Richardses kept abreast of the darkening military situation. On September 25 an air raid at Hankow, less than 200 miles north of Changsha, killed 606 civilians.[74] Soon after, word came that the Japanese had bombed the Public Hospital Building at Nanking, crippling the manufacture of vaccines and other necessary medical supplies. This sparked a debate in Changsha over whether the local hospital should display a Red Cross flag in case of bombing; in the end, the decision was not to, "in case it proved a magnet to the Japanese."[75] Changsha was no longer a safe retreat. As the Universities sought a new place to relocate, the Richardses determined to wait for further developments, resolving to spend the rest of the year in the mountains of Yunnan. With most transport commandeered for military purposes, they were fortunate to meet one of their Chinese student acquaintances from Cambridge in Changsha, who introduced them to the Chinese Vice Minister of Communication, Hsu En-tseng. They managed to secure a ride with the Minister's motorcade as far as Yunnan-fu, the provincial capital of Yunnan.[76] Despite the intensification of the war, Richards was optimistic about the chances for improvement upon his return. In relaying to Stevens news of the situation, he wrote:

> The conscience (and the self-regarding sentiment) of the world does seem at last to be seeing the significance of what is being done here by the Japanese, and perhaps some effective aid to China will come in time. Our feeling is that it is something of a miracle that she has been able to resist so effectively. The general spirit surprises those who knew the old China. In a society that has been corrupt so long there are bound to be some rats and traitors but on the whole a new spirit is emerging.[77]

On September 30 the Richardses left Changsha with the Vice-Minister, accompanied by Empson and Purcell. As they headed for the mountains, occupied Peking seemed a distant world.

III

Within two weeks of leaving Changsha, the Richardses were in the mountainous region of Yunnan preparing for a month of climbing. Their travels with the Vice-Minister and his motorcade are amusingly related in Victor Purcell's memoir *Chinese Evergreen*, where Richards appears as "Edwards" and Empson as "Dudley." Purcell provided a telling character sketch of the couple in the period following their flight from Peking. After traveling with them over a four-week period from Hong Kong to Hanoi, Purcell recalled:

> I can make no approach to a character study of Edwards [Richards] because he is as elusive as a will-o'-the-wisp. It is only when he waxes warm in one of his enthusiasms that I have felt that I was nearing contact with him, but in a trice he had regained his old distance. Mrs. Edwards [Dorothea], a lady with both feet firmly planted in the present and impervious to any suggestion which might deflect her from her few well-defined objectives, made an admirable shield for her husband and de-

fended him from those who would diminish the established distance between them and his personality. She was a lady of great cheerfulness, energy, determination and powers of endurance.[78]

Richards's aloofness no doubt stemmed in part from his tightening time schedule. With the Rockefeller grant expected to end in June 1938, his work in the coming months looked like the last chance to put Basic on a strong footing in China until after the war, however long that might last. During the Minister's week-long stopover in the town of Kweilin en route to Yunnan, Richards used the time to interview the provincial Commissioner of Education and considered the possibility of relocating the Institute there. "Kweilin is the new model Province of China and General Pei, its genius and concealed dictator, is now No. 2 in China," Dorothea informed her brother. "After the war Kweilin ideas in education are certain to be very important."[79] In the event, the city was bombed three days after the Richardses' departure. But the incident shows that Richards's central goal was now to find a place that would shelter Basic from the present situation and encourage its spread after the war.

On October 11 the Minister's party crossed the Chinese border into Hanoi, which offered the most direct route to Yunnan. Dorothea found the city a welcome respite from the rigors of traveling in provincial China: a "well-planned, spacious capital with broad avenues with trees and shops around a lake," offering the unaccustomed luxuries of "clean beds, baths and food."[80] In Hanoi Purcell took leave of the Richardses to resume his post at Penang. They proceeded with Empson by rail to Yunnan-fu, the provincial capital, arriving on the 15th. After a frustrating series of delays, Empson decided to abandon the expedition and left for Changsha on the 19th. Three days later the Richardses set off from Yunnan-fu for Tali, high in the mountains of western Yunnan. For the next eight weeks they traveled by foot and horseback through the snowy ranges between China and Tibet. "We get no war news," Dorothea wrote from camp; "it's like being off the map and most of the country round on the borders of Tibet has never been surveyed."[81] Among the tribesmen of Tibet Richards had a unique opportunity to test his theories of communication by using the local picture language: "The trick is, when they've got an idea that hasn't a picture—'Think' for example, to hit on something that sounds like it has a picture. 'Sink' say."[82] China and its war seemed centuries away.

Meanwhile the Orthological Institute faced a different set of challenges in the occupied North. Its staff now consisted of Jameson, Shui Tien Tun, Chao-chao Hsin and Wu Fu-heng, with additional help from Winter. Because of their status as members of a private body with foreign funding, their work on the Basic primer and teachers' handbook was able to continue undisturbed. But the Japanese presence in Peking made the city an increasingly hostile place to work. With the bulk of its students and faculty in flight, the Japanese began looting at Tsing Hua, where Winter stubbornly kept a list of items taken.[83] Jameson grew so frustrated with the situation that he resolved to leave the country. In November he informed Stevens:

> My only reason for staying in China is the work of the Institute. When the work is finished, I am planning to return to America, as I no longer feel that the sorts of lectures I am asked to offer in Tsing Hua or would be asked to offer in any other university here, have anything to do with anything that is important.[84]

On the same day that Jameson wrote this, Shanghai fell to the Japanese. By now it was becoming clear that the Institute would have to relocate in order to accomplish anything substantial; it needed to be closer to the central government and "more progressive workers," as Jameson told Stevens in December.[85] Soon thereafter he left for Changsha to consider the possibility of moving the Institute there. The visit convinced him to keep the Basic operation going in Peking; aside from the increased fighting around Changsha, he discovered that the Universities were planning a move further south, to Yunnan. Remarkably, Shui, Wu and Chao continued to work for the Institute despite the personal losses brought to their country by the war. But Winter's concern with the Japanese looting and Jameson's darkening mood through the occupation suggests that the Basic presence in Peking by the end of 1937 had become a holding operation only.

When Richards returned to Yunnan-fu in late December he immediately set about making plans for the coming year. On the 23rd Dorothea recorded that he had resumed work on the Primer; the next day he gave a speech on Basic to a gathering of provincial government officials, followed by a larger lecture (with a translator's aid) to an assembly of 2,000 middle school teachers on the 27th.[86] The Commissioner of Education for Yunnan, Kung Tze-chih, showed an encouraging interest in Basic, and his later support would prove vital in keeping the Institute operating throughout the war years. For the moment, Kung's openness convinced Richards that Yunnan was the ideal location for the refugee Institute. Safely behind the line of fire and increasingly populated by students and faculty from the war zone, Yunnan seemed the perfect place to prepare for Basic's spread after the war.

Officials at the Rockefeller Foundation, however, proved less willing to accommodate this idea than Richards hoped. While planning to spend the winter in Yunnan-fu exploring the possibilities for Basic, he and Dorothea were summoned by Gunn to Hong Kong to discuss the Institute's future. They departed reluctantly on December 29, spending the first weeks of 1938 in conference with Gunn and other Rockefeller officials in Hong Kong. Their chances of staying in Yunnan did not seem good. After a lunch with the Gunns on January 4, which left Dorothea with "the ghastly feeling of talking to dummies,"[87] she wrote to her brother John:

> We are again in a state of not knowing what the next months will bring forth. I had been hoping that we should return to Yunnan-fu, away from the war zone, where China is still something of what she was, . . . where all the intellectual life of China is likely to retire to voluntary exile, where the Universities and Committee for Education for Middle Schools are anxious to give Basic English a trial, where there is still something which can be done for China—But it seems the Rockefeller suggest it is not the moment for launching out on fresh schemes.[88]

The Foundation's reluctance was all the more frustrating given the chances for Basic not only in Yunnan but also in Hong Kong, where the Vice Chancellor of Hong Kong University was willing to train middle school teachers in Basic for the first two years of English instruction.[89] In addition, Richards received word from the North that the Hautes Etudes College in Tientsin, a Jesuit-run middle school at the major port serving Peking, had agreed to test the Basic primers and handbooks in their English classes over the coming term. Before the outbreak of hostilities, the Nationalist government's acceptance of Basic had outstripped even Richards's expectations. Now, important officials ranging from the Vice-Chancellor of Hong Kong University to provisional Commissioners of Education in Yunnan-fu and Kweilin expressed an interest in using Basic in their schools. Despite the war, Richards had grounds for believing that a great deal could still be done "to help in building up a seed bed" for China's future. With the northern Universities in exile and the Nationalist government engaged in a large-scale war, Basic's success depended upon a few well-placed advocates, "like germs to wait their time," that could nurture Basic and be ready to institute it at the end of the war.[90]

Nevertheless, the Rockefeller Foundation remained wary of Richards's optimism. "I am pleased with the spirit Richards shows in his letter of the 19th," Stevens wrote Gunn from New York. "He goes very far, however, in implying that he himself might be willing to stay in Hong Kong for five years."[91] Given the course of the war, Steven's reservations about a long-term commitment to Basic seemed well founded. On November 20 the Chinese government retreated from Nanking to Chungking, a distance of nearly 800 miles. After the fall of the capital on December 13, there followed a seven-week period of Japanese atrocities that rank among the worst of the war. With the Institute's grant due to expire on June 30, the Foundation officials decided that Richards's remaining time in China would be best spent in supervising work on the Basic primer at the Hautes Etudes College in Tientsin. On January 29, 1938, Richards left Hong Kong to return to the North. Dorothea, feeling that "Peking under the Japanese is just ashes in the mouth," opted to return to Yunnan, proceeding from there to Burma for the spring.[92]

Richards arrived in Tientsin on February 6, following a brief stay in Shanghai. While in Shanghai he met with Jameson, who was traveling to Yunnan to see if the Institute might relocate there. Richards found him in an agitated mood, unnerved by the weeks spent in occupied Peking.[93] Since he had accepted an offer to lecture at the University of Wisconsin in the fall, his tour of Kunming would be his last undertaken for the Institute in China. Jameson's manner indicated some of the difficulties Richards would find in Peking. From Shanghai he wrote to Dorothea that the "general view here is that the war is going on indefinitely—and that all the North is being organized (and armed) by the Communists so that there will be a vast explosion in due course. All this points to finishing off quickly by April."[94] His visit to Peking twelve days later confirmed this view. Although the city was still "quite calm," the outlook for Basic was decidedly grim:

> All the schools in Peking are having to provide teaching in Japanese. I've little doubt that time given to English will eventually be cut down a lot.

> Its official importance in the schools seems likely to diminish. All the
> more need therefore to improve the technique of teaching it.[95]

Since the outbreak of the war Richards had oriented his plans to the
future peace; now, with China facing either a long period of Japanese
control or a Communist insurgency, the scope for English promised
to be considerably narrowed. The pressure to complete the Basic
texts was greater than ever.

But the situation in Peking presented Richards with unexpected
obstacles. Foremost among these was the Japanese occupation. "I
can't help being glad for your sake that you didn't come here," he
wrote to Dorothea upon his first visit to the city since August. "It is
horribly depressing. . . . There is not much prospect of any sort of
free life for any one—except for folk who stay indoors and just go on
with some job."[96] Shui, Wu and Chao all continued to report at the Institute office, now located in the Foreign Concession; Chao in spite of
having received no word from his parents since their flight from Peking. Despite their persistence, however, work on Basic had not progressed as Richards had hoped. "I don't feel there is any doubt," he
confided to Dorothea, "that RDJ [Jameson] has completely gone to
pieces since the War began. None of his people up here has done
more than a week or two's work since August I suspect. And if we
get our texts through as I hope I'll have to do 9/10ths of it, I fear."[97]
Winter also promised to be of slight help. He fell sick just before
Richards's arrival with what looked like scarlet fever but proved to
be an abscess. His somewhat histrionic recovery in the weeks that
followed left the burden of completing the primer largely on Richards's shoulders.

Adding to this workload was the pressure of time, as the Rockefeller Foundation expressed no intentions of funding the Orthological
Institute past June 30. On March 8 Richards received a letter from
Stevens requesting that he close the Institute's books by the end of
June, which "meant the unpleasant job of telling Winter, Shui, Chao
and Wu that they are out of a job from June 30 on."[98] Although this
did not necessarily signal the end of Foundation support (Stevens explained that he simply wanted no outstanding commitments before
discussion of a "renewed program"), it did mean that Richards
needed to have the Basic texts as close to completion as possible before the end of the grant, particularly if he hoped to make a case for

its extension. In addition, although Richards was on leave from Cambridge until October, Stevens was eager to bring him to the United States for a series of conferences on teaching English as a second language. Given the uncertain future of Foundation support in China, Richards felt it impolitic to refuse. But accepting these engagements in the States meant that he would have to leave China in May. On March 8 he booked a ticket on a steamer leaving Tientsin on May 16, due to arrive in San Francisco on June 1. This left a total of three and a half months to complete the primer and accompanying teacher's handbook at the Hautes Etudes.

Fortunately, the work in Tientsin progressed exceptionally well. Richards moved into a campus dormitory with Chao and two other Chinese, writing and lecturing for up to sixteen hours a day.[99] Scarcely two weeks after his arrival he assured Dorothea:

> All goes well and very industriously and steady progress in overhauling the Primer is being made. I'm clear, now that I'm actually watching classes that would have been impossible, without that, to make the theory nearly as practicable as I can now make it. Also Father Petit's criticisms and suggestions are extraordinarily useful. Most useful of all is seeing how the boys respond to the various ways teachers behave. I can now see to it that the Primer supplements the teacher's deficiencies at the most glaring points and in the Handbook for Teachers I can do a lot, I hope, to make them see why certain habits they all seem to have are bad or wasteful.[100]

The students' response to the texts ("many encouraging things said about the ways certain passages have worked like magic on the boys," he recorded in February) further convinced Richards that an adequate English textbook and handbook could help to make up for "teacher's deficiencies" in the classroom.[101] The textual issue was an important one, especially as the Institute's future in China looked doubtful. Aside from the war and the uncertainty about funding, Richards was wary of his Chinese colleagues' ability to lead the operation in his absence. "With someone on hand," he told Dorothea, "a lot can be got out of Chao and Shui—but on their own they do pretty characteristic Chinese *nothing* most of the time, I fear."[102] While impressed with Chao's industry on the Hautes Etudes project, he complained that "he hasn't the drive to run everything and the next day is as good as today if I don't keep track of every bit of paper that has to move on a stage." His solution was to produce an adequate text covering the first year of Chinese instruction so that Shui, Chao and

Winter "could very usefully go on with a largely mechanical job on second year stuff right through six months with great profit."[103]

Richards's failure to train adequate Chinese leadership for the Institute must be seen in light of his emphasis on texts over institutions. Ideally Richards felt that Basic would not need a university or Foundation to ensure its spread: rather, it would demonstrate its own value by its efficiency. In a letter to Dorothea during his period in Tientsin, he compared Basic to other socio-scientific "breakthroughs" like sanitation:

> Really one often asks oneself why past generations never (or hardly ever) tackled sanitation (or Swiss villages, the problem of mud in the village streets; or Cambridge the problem of a reasonable insurance scheme for everyone; or Europe in 1920 the real problem of disarmament) and then looking in at any class one sees that teaching is utterly primitive and chaotic and 80% wasted time and effort—for lack of some continuous thinking about how it might be done better. I expect to be on that job of showing how to make things easier to learn the rest of my life.[104]

The statement gives a sense of how Richards conceived of his project in China, and reflects his equation of rationality with peace in his writings of the Twenties.[105] Hence the time invested in practical tests of Basic through programs like the one at the Hautes Etudes; Richards wanted to ensure that its authority rested on firm empirical, nearly scientific certainty. Given this assumption, the particular leadership or political environment of the Institute were not of primary importance. With an adequate series of "scientifically" tested texts, the benefits of Basic would be as unequivocal as the advantages of antiseptic or village drainage.

By late March Richards was still pleased with the rate of progress at the Hautes Etudes. "All goes nicely with the work," he wrote Dorothea near the month's end; "I'm well ahead of schedule so far." Anticipating a hernia operation in April, he made plans to place Wu in charge of the work at Tientsin while Shui and Chao helped him in the hospital "on the translator aspects of [the] Reader which now is beginning to look all and more than I hoped for. Astonishing how much it improves every time it's redone, and most of it has been entirely reconstructed at least five times now!" In an expansive mood, he recalled Auden's recent lines in *Letters from Iceland*:

> To I. A. Richards who like a mouse
> Nibbles linguistics with the cerebral tooth

> We leave a quiet evening in the boarding-house
> Where he may study the facts of birth and death
> In their inexplicable oddity . . . [106]

"Auden's legacy to me, 'a quiet evening in a boarding house,' I've happily had many times over," he told Dorothea.[107] With the Primer and Teacher's Handbook "now about half done or more," he looked forward to Dorothea's return to Peking in April, after which they would leave together for the United States.

What the Richardses would do after China, however, was still an open question. The Rockefeller Foundation now showed a strong interest in promoting Basic in the United States, particularly among foreign-born Americans, where Richards felt there was "quite a chance—with the new text and Handbook—of nailing something big with the Washington officials."[108] He was also considering Basic plans for Latin America, which he intended to discuss along with other matters in person with Stevens in June. But any Basic work undertaken in the United States would have to come to an end in October, when he was due to resume his position at Cambridge. After the exhilaration of the last year in China, the return to academic life was a prospect that Richards was reluctant to consider. In an extraordinary letter to Dorothea written soon after his arrival at Tientsin, he expressed his reservations about leaving China for Cambridge in no uncertain terms:

> That whole world of Post War Lit Crit. has quite vanished from my interests now. On the other hand I do believe in the Primer—which is getting enormously improved in every day's work upon it—and, in a less degree, in my American tinkerings with school antics. Why shouldn't I be a Rimbaud of criticism (who fled as you recall from being the leading new French poet to being a trader in the Sahara)! Why shouldn't I resign from Cambridge and Magdalene—giving the needs of the China of the future as my main reason, as it would be—and, after this spell of Primer work here and a Summer in California, New York, come back to Yunnan-fu, live in a boat or a temple with you—bring my trained young teachers from here and make Yunnan—in 8 years—the leading intellectual center in (shall I say) the world. If the Primer is any good it'll do that—or I'm wasting my time, sadly! Soberly there is much to be said for NOT squandering more of one's remaining last years on heavily immunised public school boys in a swamp. . . . I do think we'd be fools to tie ourselves down to Cambridge with what we saw in Yunnan available to us through our active years.[109]

In light of the war, there is something fantastical about Richards's vision of living "in a boat or a temple," transforming rural Yunnan into a global intellectual nerve-center. But behind the extravagant tone lies a real dissatisfaction with the prospect of abandoning Basic in China to return to literary criticism. His letter also underscores the hopes that Richards still invested, even at this late date, in Yunnan. "I've begun a campaign with Stevens," he confided to Dorothea, "in favour of moving all my workers [in the North] down to Kunming to start in with the Primer in the autumn."[110] Whatever the rate of progress in Tientsin, Richards continued to feel that Basic's future in China was tied to that of Yunnan.

Jameson's report of the situation in Yunnan confirmed Richards's hopes in this regard. After six weeks in the provincial capital prior to his departure from China, Jameson gave Stevens a favorable report of Basic's chances there. Conditions in the province were decidedly rugged:

> In Yunnanfu fourteen professors are sleeping in one vermin filled room. The Universities would be willing to call a halt for a year but they have to take care of some 800 students who can't be sent home because their parents are either killed or in refugee camps. They can't fight because the Kuomintang will have only party members and the government hasn't yet had time to take in untrained individuals.[111]

Nevertheless, he felt that in many ways the region was ideal for continuing Basic work through the war. In a later letter Jameson summed up Basic's position in China as follows:

> The war in China has not greatly reduced our opportunities for experimentation. Not only do the Middle Schools even in conquered territory show a remarkable persistence, but both in conquered and in unconquered territory there are a great number of private schools, Chinese and Mission, which are happy to cooperate with the Institute. Mr. Chen Li Fu, the new Minister of Education [for China], has informed Mr. George Yeh of the Central Government's Committee of Thirteen on the Reform of Elementary English Teaching, that the Ministry wishes the Committee to continue its work and will give financial assistance in calling a meeting of the Committee whenever the Chairman thinks a meeting is advisable.[112]

With revived government interest, the chances of the Foundation extending its support of Basic improved considerably. Most significantly, Jameson reported that Richards's trust in Yunnan's Commissioner of Education had not been misplaced. On March 20 Kung extended a request to the Institute to "undertake formal cooperation with the educational authorities in the province for the teaching of

Middle School English," with the understanding that the provincial government would eventually assume management of the Institute.[113] The following day Richards received a letter from Commissioner Kung warmly commending the Basic work in China thus far, and expressing hopes for its further success in his province:

> Since the opening of the Institute there has been great progress in many ways. The principals of the schools where the Institute has been conducting experimental classes have all sent in reports of the success of the work and their hope is that it may be continued. The winter school for teachers held here last month was of great help to those teachers who attended it as they were able to receive scientific methods of teaching and were also introduced to better textbooks. I have also learned with pleasure that the middle schools of Tai Li, Shing-Ping, I Liang, and Chu Ching [all in Yunnan] have adopted your text. I hope that in a few years time your work will be extended all over the province.[114]

On April 9 Richards received a cable from Stevens in New York "saying he'll support four workers for another year if I ask it. So I've asked it." Due to the interruption of the war, a surplus of $11,000 remained from the Institute budget for 1937–38. On April 12 the Rockefeller officials in New York resolved to apply the balance to a further year of Institute funding, an extension of their existing appropriation rather than a new investment on the Foundation's part. Assured of support through June 1939, Richards could now move the Institute south. "With Kunming developments I'm hoping that will be our centre," he wrote to Dorothea upon news of the extension. "When you come we'll consider whether I can—by now—drop Cambridge and see the job out in Yunnan or not."[115]

When his ship departed for San Francisco on May 18, however, Dorothea was still in Hong Kong trying to find a berth to Tientsin. Held up in Burma with a case of ptomaine poisoning and plagued by a series of frustrating administrative delays, she missed her rendezvous with Richards, who had to sail without her. As late as May 13, less than a week before his departure, he still felt the need to justify his reasons for leaving. Noting that the "whole China program is to be decided in that week while Jameson is there" and citing a Basic conference in New York, Richards felt he had no choice but to go.[116] When Dorothea finally reached Peking, she found herself bewitched once again by its beauty: "In spite of the neon lighted brothels and the endless military parades, I find this the most bewitching city in the world. There are moments when you quite forget the Asahification of the town and when you know clearly that it is impossible to live in more beautiful surroundings."[117] She opted to spend the following weeks in Peking, knowing they would perhaps be her last, before joining Ivor in August for a period of mountain climbing in America. Before leaving China she met with W. H. Auden and Christopher Isherwood, who were traveling through the country in the process of writing *Journey to a War*. They were disappointed to have missed Richards, who was discovering attractions in America that they would pursue themselves in the following year.[118]

IV

July 7, 1938, marked the first anniversary of the Japanese invasion. By then the Orthological Institute of China had been placed on an entirely new footing. With another year's funding assured from the Rockefeller Foundation, Richards drafted a budget for 1937–38 that took account of the new circumstances wrought by the war. Due to the interruption of combat, the Orthological Institute had spent just over half of its $29,000 grant from the previous year. Richards now proposed that the remaining balance be applied in two areas. In the North, Bob Winter and Shui would supervise the project at the Ecole de Hautes Etudes in Tientsin, seeing to it that the Primer and Teacher's Handbook be published in Peking following Richards's departure. In the South, Richards appropriated $600 for the transfer of the Institute to Kunming, which was now to be headed by Arthur Pollard-Urquhart, a close friend and long-time member of the Western Languages faculty at Tsing Hua. It was Pollard-Urquhart who had first invited Richards to lecture at the University in 1929; his familiarity with both Richards's work and the Tsing Hua faculty made him an ideal representative for Basic in Yunnan. Chao and Wu were to join him in Kunming, where Education Commissioner Kung was ready to extend to Basic his official support. The move to Kunming represented a decision on Richards's part to link the fortunes of Basic with those of Yunnan, which was rapidly becoming the most important province of China with a steady stream of refugees from the war-torn regions of the country. Over the next five years the Institute would continue its work in the province in the face of bombings, political complications and a constant shortage of staff and resources.

During this period Basic's future in peacetime China became almost wholly dependent upon its position in wartime Kunming.

Pollard-Urquhart arrived in Kunming with Chao and Wu Fuheng on August 25, 1938, just three months after Richards's return to the United States. The situation in the town was chaotic. An estimated 60,000 refugees from the North and Central regions of China relocated to Kunming over 1937 and 1938. The sheer number of arrivals made overcrowding a problem. "Owing to the fact that the population has been doubled in the last few months it is extremely difficult to find any place to live in," Pollard-Urquhart explained to Stevens.[119] With the opening of the Burma Road in December, stretching 715 miles from Rangoon to Kunming, the town assumed an even greater importance as the terminus of the main artery for wartime supplies entering China. Amidst this confusion Wu, Chao and Pollard-Urquhart received a warm welcome from Commissioner Kung, who, just four days after their arrival, promised to recommend the Institute's work to all the middle schools of the province. Kung impressed Pollard-Urquhart, as he had Richards, as an exceptionally intelligent and far-seeing supporter. He showed a keen grasp of the problems facing Basic's spread in the province, warning Pollard-Urquhart that Basic work would "have to go very carefully so as not to antagonize the teachers who are really frightened by new ideas and are suspicious of foreign methods." In addition, Kung was known to be, along with the owner of the Yunnan Provincial Bank and the Governor, Long Yun, one of the most powerful men in the province. The support of an official of Kung's stature boded well for the success of the Basic enterprise in Yunnan. In a report to the Foundation in April dealing with "the possibilities of the future," Pollard-Urquhart wrote of Kung:

> . . . in fact he is the brains behind the small committee that governs Yunnan and is probably responsible for the civil administration of the province. He is keenly anxious to reform the whole educational system and is under no illusion about the poor quality of the teaching. He is urged on in his desire to improve education by the sarcastic remarks that have been made about it by the many newcomers who have arrived in Kunming during the last year. He is backed up in his reforms by the governor.[120]

His assessment points out the tense relationship that existed between native Yunnanese officials and the newly arrived Northern refugees, a situation that would greatly affect the Institute's policy in the region. Three of China's most prestigious universities, Peking National (or Pei Ta), Tsing Hua and Nan K'ai, combined in 1938 to form a single Consolidated University (Lien Ta), intending to begin classes in Kunming in December. Its students and faculty, nearly all refugees from Peking, adopted an offensively superior attitude to the local Yunnanese officials, who in turn obstructed their settlement in the province. As late as September, construction of the necessary buildings for the new University was still not underway due to official stonewalling on the part of the Yunnanese. The strained relationship between the two factions—openly friendly but plagued by the "air of superiority that all the intellectuals have shown toward Yunnan and the Yunnanese"—placed the Institute in an awkward position.[121] On the one hand, Pollard-Urquhart and his associates were in Kunming by invitation of Yunnan's Commissioner of Education and thus received better treatment than the Consolidated University; on the other they had strong ties with the Northern academic community and were reluctant to alienate those intellectuals who might support Basic after the war. Pollard-Urquhart quickly realized that the Institute would have to steer a diplomatic course between both camps.

The first weeks in Kunming, however, were propitious. Kung soon bolstered his support of Basic by suggesting that the Institute begin demonstration classes in three local middle schools. Given the size of its staff Pollard-Urquhart feared that the undertaking might be too ambitious, but ultimately he agreed. A number of other middle schools also asked for introductory Basic trials in the first weeks, an opportunity which the Institute had to refuse. In Peking, Winter and Shui succeeded in publishing in October the 427-page *First Book of English for Chinese Learners*, a middle school primer for introductory language instruction. The Hautes Etudes adopted it immediately, while Yenching University agreed to use it in their middle schools in the near future.[122]

By this time Richards was lecturing once again at Cambridge, after spending the better part of the summer in conference with Rockefeller officials in New York and Boston. With the Institute under the joint leadership of Winter and Pollard-Urquhart and its support secure for another year, an immediate return to China seemed less pressing than it had before his departure. In addition, the Rockefeller

Foundation was now considering plans for an Institute of Linguistic Studies to be headed by Richards in the United States. In preparation, Richards spent most of August visiting language classes for foreign speakers in Boston, acquainting himself with the challenges of teaching English to recent immigrants. With a major commitment to Basic in America under discussion, Richards opted to return to Cambridge for the academic year until receiving a definite offer. His growing interest in other fields for Basic, however, in no way dampened his enthusiasm for the program in China. Through regular reports from Winter and Pollard-Urquhart he kept in close touch with local developments, and in his correspondence with Stevens he continued to argue for the importance of the Far Eastern work. But with Pollard-Urquhart himself admitting that "the best thing we can do is to stay on here doing what we can and then hope to be able to carry on our program more successfully when the war comes to an end," Richards's attention naturally shifted to other areas until a greater opportunity presented itself in China.[123]

Certainly the war showed no signs of abating. On October 21, 1938, the Japanese occupied the key port city of Canton; four days later, they captured the critical tri-city area of Wuhan after nearly a year of protracted fighting. With the Nationalist government in retreat at Chunking and the Communists entrenched in the central provinces around Yan'an, Japan gained virtually uncontested control of the Chinese coast from Canton to the Korean border. In the same month Richards received word that Kunming had suffered its first air raid. The Institute's activities after a single month in the province were immediately thrown into disarray. "Classes were being taught, meetings with the Commissioner, attempts to contact middle school teachers. All interrupted," Pollard-Urquhart reported tersely.[124] Owing to air raid preparations in late September, only twenty people turned out for a reception to which the Institute had invited all of the English teachers in Kunming. The first bombing on September 28 destroyed several buildings of the local Normal School which were to have housed professors and students from Tsing Hua. Regular air raids now became a standard feature of life in Kunming, severely hampering the Institute's work. As many of the middle schools evacuated to the surrounding countryside, its efforts were spread over an increasingly wide radius. By November 1 the staff was running demonstration classes at three middle schools ranging six, twelve and twenty miles outside of the city, "situated," Pollar-Urquhart reported, "in small temples with the poorest accommodation and so teaching is not easy."[125] At the end of October J. B. Grant, a Rockefeller official with the Foundation's Shanghai office, visited Kunming and confirmed Pollard-Urquhart's view that although the Institute was making adequate progress, the operation had become a "conservation program" at best.[126]

Ironically, as the Japanese bombings slowed Basic's progress in Kunming, conditions were proving more favorable in the occupied North. In December Winter conveyed the remarkable news that the Ministry of Education for the new Provincial Government of the Republic of China, a body established by the Japanese for governing the area, had expressed an interest in using the Institute's *First Book of English* for their middle schools. "The reason given," he explained, "was that, as the time allotted to English in these schools has been cut down to about one third in favor of Japanese, the methods of teaching English should be improved to compensate for this loss of hours." Its supporters had always maintained that Basic shortened the time needed to learn English; that it should be put to such a purpose was further proof of the unforeseen political ends Basic could serve. Even more outrageously, a Secretary of the Japanese Embassy sent Winter a note of congratulations on the completion of the Primer, along with an unofficial suggestion that the Japanese might employ Basic for a similar purpose.[127] Despite the Institute's lack of formal political allegiance Winter was appalled, criticizing the Institute for being "entirely passive in this matter." The Japanese interest in Basic was more surprising in light of their recent blockade of the Foreign Concession areas in Tientsin, indicating a mounting hostility toward the European nations. As the Hautes Etudes lie outside of the British Concession, the blockade did not directly affect Shui's and Winter's work in Tientsin. But coupled with the recent inquiries about the *First Book of English*, it suggested that the Basic program in the North would not continue without interference for much longer.

Through the months that followed in 1939, the Institute staff in Kunming found itself increasingly dependent upon Kung's patronage. Despite Pollard-Urquhart's resolve to stay clear of the animosity between the universities and the Yunnanese, circumstances pushed him closer to the Commissioner's camp as the year progressed. He was frustrated to find that "trying to work independently of the

Commissioner with the Private schools and the University is much more difficult and does not lead anywhere." In February he received only seven responses from forty notices sent out for an Institute-organized Winter Teacher's Conference. While some resistance could be chalked up to political tensions in Yunnan, Pollard-Urquhart also cited the same academic snobbery toward Basic that Jameson had complained of in 1933. As he told Stevens,

> I find with all the University people that they have an idea we are trying to put something over on them, that we wish them to give up their knowledge of English and boil it down to 850 words. Our answer must be that we have nothing to do with the Universities, but that we are trying to make a basis of sound teaching so as to avoid the abominably bad English that is all the students can show when they reach the Universities.[128]

It was exactly this hostility on the part of the universities that originally led Richards to concentrate on getting Basic into the middle schools. Given this kind of academic reception, Pollard-Urquhart not surprisingly came to regard Kung in an ever more favorable light. In contrast to the university faculty, he believed, the Commissioner was "working for the Province, with no superior attitude towards the local people, which has been the fault of the visiting Universities." Isolation also yoked the Institute more firmly to the local authorities. The Nationalist government, now located 300 miles to the north and east in Chungking, was in no position to offer support or to continue the work it had initiated in 1937. As Pollard-Urquhart informed the Foundation in an April report:

> The Ministry of Education is too taken up with the worries of the situation caused by the war to have time to think about furthering a new system of teaching English. So for the time being and probably for the duration of the war we should be content with our present programme of working with the Local Commissioner and trying to push our system in the Province which has so much promise for the future.[129]

To carry out this policy, he began a series of tours to the more distant regions of Yunnan in order to help Basic take root in the province. By the spring he had succeeded in persuading four schools—Ta-Li, Shin-Ping, I Liang and Chu Ching—to adopt the recently published First Book of English in their English courses.[130] In March Kung wrote to Richards vouching for Basic's advances in the region:

> Since the opening of the Institute there has been great progress in many ways. The principals of the schools where the Institute has been con-

ducting experimental classes have all sent in reports of the success of the work and their hope is that it may be continued. The winter school for teachers held here last month was of great help to those teachers who attended it as they were able to receive instruction in scientific methods of teaching and were also introduced to better textbooks. I have also learned with pleasure that the middle schools of Ta Li, Shin-Ping, I Liang and Chu Ching have adopted your text. I hope that in a few years time your work will be extended all over the province.[131]

While Kung's assessment was encouraging, it also masked some important obstacles. His letter makes no mention of the hostility to Basic on the part of the universities, nor does he record the disappointing turnout for the Institute's Teaching Conference in February. Pollard-Urquhart also faced the daunting task of working with Chinese officialdom, which he found "too often content with having passed a resolution and then imagine that the will has become an act." He complained that the local Ministry of Education "passes a list of excellent rules governing education . . . but little care is taken to see whether the rules are carried out or not. Much too much emphasis is put on the showy and useless side such as putting the students into soldier's uniforms and dressing the girls to look like boys, and then resting content with public defence." The Commissioner, however, proved an exception to the rule: "Mr. Kung is quite aware of the hollowness of this system, and as far as possible wants to put things right." So long as Basic formed a part of that process, Pollard-Urquhart was optimistic about Kung's desire for reform. After nearly eight months of working in the province, the Basic presence in Yunnan seemed solid. Pollard-Urquhart told the Foundation:

> One has to be careful with the Chinese to distinguish what is merely politeness from what is truth, and I think that when we first came we were very much on trial; but by a certain humility on our part coupled with definite results in teaching I think that now the Commissioner of Education is wholly for us. He is flattered to have us work for him, and when he attended the Education Conference last week in Chungking he was able to show that he was the only commissioner who was actively working for the improvement of English in his province by putting forward a single system.[132]

With the situation as promising as wartime conditions would allow, Foundation officials agreed in April to fund the enterprise for another year. With a surplus of $3,000 from the 1939 budget and an additional $2,512 of unused principal from the appropriation for 1937–38, support was extended through June of 1940 with no new expenditure required.

The most significant challenges to the Institute over the next year came not from Chinese or Foundation resistance, but rather from internal problems within the staff. In February 1940 Chao-chao Hsin, who had been with the Institute for over four years, was dismissed. Already in October 1938, some two months after the move to Kunming, Richards had informed Stevens:

> Chao Chao-hsing has, I gather, gone to pieces a little on arriving in Yunnan. He did well in Tientsin, but that seems to have been (as so often in China) a matter of personal loyalty. He has been wanting to take on a job (full time) in the University of Yunnan and I should not be surprised to hear that he has left the Institute.[133]

Pollard-Urquhart felt that Chao had come to Kunming under false pretenses. "After paying the fare for Mr. Chao, his wife, and mounds of luggage," he explained later to Stevens, "I found that he had secretly arranged for a job with the Yunnan University. He imagined I would never know, or he expected that I would let him carry on with us as well." In fact Chao did continue at the Institute through the spring of 1939, although Pollard-Urquhart later claimed that "he did no work for us, but caused us a lot of trouble by refusing to cooperate in our plans or do any teaching."[134] But with a heavy schedule of demonstration classes and teacher training, the Institute could not afford to lose such a highly trained member of its staff. When Pollard-Urquhart left for England in March for two months following his mother's death, Chao was left in nominal charge of the Institute's affairs. Pollard-Urquhart returned in May to learn that during his absence Chao had only reported at the Institute to collect his salary.[135] Soon after he was officially dismissed.

Chao's "defection" exposed one of the Basic program's more damaging weaknesses. For all of its efforts to recruit teachers and cultivate official Chinese support, in five years the Institute had managed to train only four full-time Chinese members. Richards was eager to develop a more permanent Chinese staff for the Institute, one that could take over the operation when the Basic texts were complete. In the spring of 1940 he secured a fellowship for Wu Fu-heng to work on Basic in the United States, and his expectations for Shui remained high. But neither one was given a full-time leadership position within the Institute. In part this was due to limited resources, which precluded a large staff, and in part to the qualifications of Winter, Pollard-Urquhart and Jameson, all of whom had distinguished teaching records in China going back to the 1920's. Nevertheless, the failure to find more Chinese either willing or competent to assume equal status with the Western members of the enterprise meant that Basic would remain a foreign presence in China. Without the greater participation of the Chinese themselves, it was open to the same hostility that had marked earlier "progressive" missionary efforts. That the Institute suffered from this stigma is suggested by a letter from Pollard-Urquhart to Stevens in August, describing a prevalent attitude at the Institute's summer teaching session for 1939:

> One professor opened the ceremony of the Summer Session with: "It is a shame for us that we should be teaching you English and a shame that you should be learning it. If China was a great country there would be no need for the Chinese to learn a foreign language.[136]

Richards was unlikely to be sympathetic to this kind of nationalist sentiment, as it typified exactly the narrow perspective that an international Basic English was meant to correct. But a larger Chinese presence on the staff would have given the Institute an adequate rejoinder to such criticism. As it was, Richards and his colleagues were unable to respond to this kind of attack except as an instance of ignorance to be overcome by the values of rationality and empiricism that Basic represented. Whatever Chao's particular reasons for leaving, his departure highlights the distance that could so often open up between Westerners and Chinese.

A circumstance more immediately damaging than Chao's dismissal was the serious misunderstanding that arose over a Western member of the staff in 1940. Bob Winter's long disappearance in the summer of 1940 temporarily shook the Rockefeller Foundation's faith in the Basic project altogether. The incident began in January, when Winter arrived from Tientsin to join the Institute at Kunming. The work he had undertaken with Shui in the North was officially over. With the completion of the *Second Book of English* (which Richards pronounced "ingenious but sensible"[137]) in March 1939 and the end of the association with the Hautes Etudes, Winter undertook to transport the published texts through Japanese lines to Kunming. In January 1940, according to Pollard-Urquhart, he "arrived [in Kunming] all of a sudden by air from Chungking and went away just as suddenly" after only two weeks in the town.[138] He left on the pretext of securing the passage of the Basic texts which had arrived in Hong Kong. With the bombing of the Haiphong-Kunming rail line connecting Yunnan to the coast, most goods coming into Kunming had to be brought via Rangoon on the Burma Road. Winter hoped to use his connections with the transport authorities in Chungking to ensure that the books traveled directly from Hong Kong.[139] From Chunking, however, he returned unexpectedly to Peking in April, failing to report at the Foundation's Shanghai office when he passed through the city en route. Two months later Pollard-Urquhart received word that Winter was arranging for the printing of more primers in Peking, with the assurance that both the Marist brothers and Yenching University (now settled in Shanghai) were using Basic texts.[140] Until August Winter was entirely out of touch with the Institute, though he continued to draw his salary according to the terms of the grant.

Winter's disappearance came at a particularly inopportune time, just as Richards and Pollard-Urquhart were making their case to the Rockefeller Foundation for a renewal of the grant. On January 31 Richards apprised Stevens of the Institute's accomplishments, along with new developments that improved their future prospects. By now the reliance on Commissioner Kung was nearly total and their faith in making an example of Yunnan for peacetime China had attained the status of official policy. "Only through cooperation with the Provincial Education authorities can anything solid be done," he informed Stevens:

> The heart of the whole problem now is teacher training. All sorts of local obstacles and vested interests in the English and Education Departments of the Universities prevent any satisfactory training for the teaching of English being given by them. What is needed now is a finished demonstration of how teachers may be equipped to give satisfactory instruction. The texts are ready: Shui, Wu, Winter and Pollard make an excellent team to carry out the demonstrations.[141]

Aiding Richards's case was a recent promise from Kung to fund a Teacher's Training Institute for the province, to be staffed by the Orthological Institute with facilities and student stipends paid for by the local Ministry of Education. Kung's commitment was the first tangible sign of *Chinese* government support since the Nationalist Ministry of Education's Committee on English Teaching in the summer of 1937, and Richards was anxious to remind Stevens of this link:

It will be recalled that, just before the Japanese hostilities began, the Ministry of Education of the Central Government accepted all the fundamental principles which the work of this Teachers' Institute would be continuing. Relations between the Central Government and the Yunnan Provincial Government have lately been markedly improving. . . . Thus a demonstration in Yunnan may reasonably be regarded as a measure which, when the time comes for a renewal of the Central Government's active interest in English teaching throughout China, would bear fruit far beyond the confines of Yunnan.[142]

He concluded by pointing out that a commitment of $9,600 for 1940–41 "should be amply sufficient to do properly a piece of work which might well be decisive for the future of teaching in the Far East." Pollard-Urquhart also assured the Foundation that in spite of brutal conditions in Kunming, where "classes have been held in rooms where the students sleep," good results were reported in those schools where Basic was used.[143] Without an additional grant the previous years' work in China seemed likely to go to waste at a moment when the Chinese themselves were showing a renewed commitment to Basic. In April 1940 Foundation officials elected to grant the Orthological Institute additional funds through June 1941, their first new investment in the project since 1937. The official minutes show that Kung's recent actions weighed heavily in their decision:

> The Commissioner of Education of the Province is favorable to immediate establishment of a training school for teachers of English, anticipating that this measure will greatly improve the work of young people in his province as compared with the work of the more cosmopolitan youth from the coastal area. Hundreds of students from the eastern part of China are being admitted to the national and provincial universities near Kunming in contrast from a few score from Yunnan able to pass the examinations. Although this is not the vital cause for further aid to the training program of the Institute, it is a means of energizing the program immediately and effectively.[144]

"In many respects," the report concluded, "the work is starting from a new beginning, but the prepared texts and experienced workers will yield more rapid returns on effort than during the first period." $9,600 was granted for the year, with the expectation of further disbursements over the next two to three years.

This new appropriation drew the attention of M. C. Balfour, a medical official for the Foundation in Shanghai, who began to question the Institute's achievements. In a letter to Stevens on June 14, he expressed concern that $9,600 "is considerably more than [the Institute] can reasonably use," pointing out that "by comparison, several complete medical schools in Southwest China are operating, inadequately to be sure, on budgets no larger than the equivalent in local currency."[145] The growing dependence on Kung also concerned Balfour. He notes that "local interest in the project seems to be limited to the Commissioner of Education who is said to be favorable. His nearly fatal illness last winter caused some concern." After highlighting the narrow base of the Institute's support in Yunnan, Balfour cites Winter's absence as further cause to doubt the integrity of the Basic project. "I believe," he writes archly, "that the activities of the Institute were terminated in North China last summer, but the only period during which Mr. Winter has been in Yunnan was for about six weeks in January–February." In conclusion, Balfour cautions Stevens that "although this project is technically outside my domain, I may express the frank opinion that the situation is somewhat less glorious than Dr. Richards's letters might lead you to believe. I wonder if you will not wish to have an impartial review or survey before the end of the present grant."[146]

Stevens did not immediately act upon Balfour's suggestion of an independent review for the Kunming program. But in August he asked Richards to draft a new budget taking Balfour's reservations into account. Balfour suggested a modified disbursement of $1,800 per quarter, a reduction of $2,400 from the initial endowment. The cut, as Stevens explained, "is in part because Winter apparently has gone back to the North, primarily on personal business."[147] Richards in turn expressed his own uneasiness about "Winter's uncertain location and his silence." After five months without hearing from Winter, he was now prepared to remove him from the Institute roster:

> I gather now that he has probably let himself be absorbed in Central Government activities. In any case, I fear he must be accounted a loss to the project and should be crossed off the budget. It is a pity. He could have been very valuable in the training school—there are few better teachers anywhere—but as he gets older his craving for adventure seems to increase if anything.[148]

It was an unfortunate time to be losing staff. On June 11, Kung signed a contract with the Orthological Institute confirming the establishment of the Yunnan Provincial Teacher's Training College. The transaction "has not been easy," Pollard-Urquhart told Stevens soon after:

> for about a month he [Kung] was uncertain as to whether it could be done, as he feared opposition from the Universities and also the Ministry of Education. But now he is convinced that the Universities have no serious plans for the improvement of English teaching in the Province and is therefore prepared to let us take on the burden.[149]

Under the terms of the agreement, the Institute paid the salaries for the College's staff, while the Commissioner contributed grants for student teachers as well as partial running expenses over the next two years. Shui was appointed Dean. This was not the moment to jeopardize the project with doubts about the Institute's integrity.

In late September several delayed letters from Winter arrived in Kunming. He explained that he had spent the last months campaigning for Basic in the North, having persuaded "three chief educational institutions, Yenching, Catholic University, and the Marist Brothers, to adopt our books for their elementary English classes." Balfour remained doubtful: "The simple truth regarding Winter's stay in Peking from April to August, which was originally stated for personal reasons, is probably that he became 'fed-up' with the backwoods of Yunnan, and yearned for the more pleasant surroundings of Peking, which is understandable."[150] The fact that Winter had failed to visit the Foundation office in Shanghai on his way to Peking added weight to Balfour's suspicions. In October Balfour wrote to J. Leighton Stuart, President of Yenching University, to corroborate Winter's story. Stuart informed him that, contrary to Winter's recent claims, no Basic materials were being used in the English classes at Yenching. As he explained to Balfour:

> We had planned to experiment with Basic English in the beginning class of our primary and secondary practice schools but Miss T'an Pin-pin, who was to be in charge of it, was kept in New York for radio work in Basic English, and the necessary books seem to be unobtainable here.[151]

At the end of September Winter was officially dropped from the Institute payroll.

Pollard-Urquhart felt the loss deeply. With Chao and Winter off the project and Wu in the United States working with Richards, he and Shui were each consigned to teaching eighteen hours a week. In October he began petitioning to get Winter back onto the staff. "Bob has worked for Basic now for four years and he cannot be thrown over until you have heard from him what he has done in Peking."[152] At the same time he wrote to Stevens attesting to Winter's value to the Institute's work. He explained that Winter returned to Peking the previous spring "because he heard the Japanese were trying to get his house and garden. There was not much then for him to do here."[153] Now the Institute needed his help badly. On September 9 the Yunnan Provincial Training School officially opened with an entering class of fifty students, its buildings and furniture paid for by the Commissioner. The Institute had also recently assumed English teaching responsibilities for the Ch'u Shih School in Kunming, one of the largest and most prestigious middle schools in the province with more than six hundred students. In addition, their involvement with the Jun Jui and Technical Schools was continuing into its third year, though Pollard-Urquhart noted that "not having Mr. Wu makes a difference, as I have not been able to get a teacher of his calibre to take his place, and so the teaching at Jun Jui will not be so good."[154] On a practical level the Institute simply could not afford to lose Winter, now on his way to Kunming via the Burma Road.

In the midst of this activity, Pollard-Urquhart died from an injury sustained during an air raid. His unexpected death was an event that endangered the entire Basic English project. Since the first Japanese bombing in September 1938, Kunming had been subjected to nearly constant attacks. After a lull during the winter of 1939–40, Japan continued the assault with fresh intensity throughout 1940. By the fall, the severity of the attacks had put the newly founded Teacher's College at risk. On October 4 Pollard-Urquhart informed Stevens:

> Since beginning to write this report it has become very evident that air raids and alarms are going to interfere with the school. We have just had a very bad raid when the centre of the city was bombed and the part round the school, though none of it fell into our courtyard. The Ch'u Shih school . . . got two bombs, but fortunately there were no people there. They are moving out to the country, which makes it more difficult for us to carry on their classes. Half our students have already left the city; but we are carrying on and at the same time we are trying to make arrangements to get some place which is nearer the country so that we may get out quicker. The students are anxious for the school to go on, and the best ones are staying with us. The Japanese occupation of Indo-China and the closing of the Burma Road have also made things more difficult, as now that there is hardly any gasoline I cannot visit other parts of the province to inspect the schools that are using our books. It is also impossible to get printing done, as there is no communication between here and Hong Kong except by air.[155]

Two days later, he was hit by a passing car during an air raid warning. He was hospitalized for a routine knee injury, but the wound became infected. He died from blood poisoning ten days later, at the age of forty-six. Services were held under the auspices of Tsing Hua University, where Pollard-Urquhart had taught as a Professor of English language and literature since 1923. Aside from the personal loss of "the oldest of all our friends in China," Richards realized that Pollard-Urquhart's death was also a serious blow to the Basic project in Kunming.[156] The Institute, he felt, under "extremely difficult conditions has been heavily dependent on his skill with people and understanding as a teacher and negotiator."[157] The matter of replacing Pollard-Urquhart became more urgent as the military situation continued to worsen. On November 2 Shui informed Balfour:

> The most pressing problem at present is housing. It is no longer possible to stay on in the town and hope to do good work. The Japanese have repeatedly bombed and machine-gunned us, coming sometimes at 7 in the morning. As we lost Mr. Pollard-Urquhart at the most critical moment, we missed the chance to get a place in the villages outside Kunming.[158]

If the Teacher's School found a new site quickly, Shui believed that classes for forty students could still be held. But with Winter in transit to Kunming on the Burma Road and Pollard-Urquhart dead, Basic prospects in China were at their lowest ebb.

V

On November 8 Bob Winter arrived in Kunming, where he received news simultaneously of his termination and Pollard-Urquhart's death. He immediately wrote Balfour in Shanghai to justify his eight-month silence, arguing variously that his letters had been lost, that Pollard-Urquhart's reports during 1940 had tacitly incorporated his own from Peking, and that he had been involved with wartime work in the North. Balfour was not persuaded. Regarding Winter's excuses as "a matter of self-justification," he informed Stevens soon after that he had "not considered it useful to enter into any discussion about the past with him. Nothing was heard from him from April to November, 1940, and as far as I know, Mr. Pollard-Urquhart received one letter during that time."[159] Given recent events in Kunming, however, the Foundation had little choice but to restore Winter to the project. In fact, he now seemed the most likely candidate for Director.

As Richards explained to Stevens: "Shui, I feel, for all his brilliance hasn't quite the stability to be trusted with full powers. He doesn't get on well with people."[160] On December 17, less than three months after his dismissal, Winter assumed the leadership of the Orthological Institute in Kunming.

He was taking the post during one of the most brutal phases of the war in Yunnan. "All of the institutions have been somewhat shaken by the recent bombings," Winter wrote to the Foundation upon his arrival. "It is not easy even to think rationally when one is crouching for hours every day in muddy ditches outside the town."[161] In January 1941 both Winter and Pollard-Urquhart (posthumously) received certificates of the Second Class Order of Merit from the Chinese government "in recognition of their more than fifteen years' service to Chinese education."[162] In the same month Winter typed a report for the Foundation in a Chinese cemetery during an air raid, feverish with typhus contracted from a rat bite. Thieves had recently looted his room during an evacuation, taking nearly all the possessions he had brought with him on the long trek across the Burma Road. Eclipsing the personal loss for Winter was the scale of death and suffering in Kunming. "I know that this is only child's play compared to what is happening in Europe," he tartly informed the Foundation, "but for a tenderfoot like myself it is not pleasant to see stupefied women sitting like watch-dogs in the craters where their families were blown up."[163] These initial hardships foreshadowed the kind of challenges that Winter would face in Kunming over the next two-and-a-half years. Famine, inflation, and the continual threat of invasion made Basic's "holding operation" extremely precarious as the war progressed.

Miraculously, during this time Winter and Shui succeeded in keeping the Institute operating. By March 1942 the Yunnan Provincial Teacher School [established by the Institute in 1940] had a student body of sixty with seven staff members. Kung's support of the school continued despite the worsening military situation; with the exception of Winter's salary, by the end of the year the provincial Ministry of Education was funding the entire institution, including rent, administrative costs and student stipends. Both Richards and officials at the Rockefeller Foundation hoped that Kung's increasing support of the school would serve as a model for future Chinese-Western collaborations after the war. They were also becoming acutely aware of the political value of Basic's presence in postwar China. Writing to John G. Marshall of the Rockefeller Foundation in the wake of the Japanese attack on Pearl Harbor, Richards expressed a heightened understanding of the delicate political matrix in which Basic was now likely to be involved. The "fundamental fact" of the Chinese situation, he argues, "is of course unchanged: that issues which might even dwarf these that agitate us all today hang on the Sino-Anglamerican [sic] relations—whose bridge is English." The equation of language with cultural influence is familiar from Richards's earlier thought, but now, with the political developments of the war, it assumed a more explicit Anglo-American cast. He continues:

> Assuming, as we do, that this War comes out right, the next great struggle—and it won't be long delayed—may well be for the allegiance of China waged ideologically between Russia and us. In that, the place of English in Chinese education is obviously very crucial. In the Yunnan training school we have . . . a seed bed, small and harassed, but of great value if only as a token of American concern with the fundamentals of mutual understanding. There are bound to be proposals for educational aid to China as part of post-war reconstruction. The Yunnan project . . . has a good chance of developing them into a model institution with a significance quite incommensurate with its scale or cost.[164]

Richards's case for the importance of a "token" Anglo-American presence in postwar China helps to explain the Rockefeller Foundation's continuing interest in Basic despite the wartime hardships. On March 15, 1940, the Foundation appropriated $9,600 for the Institute over a three-year period ending on June 30, 1943, its most sustained commitment to Basic yet. In stating their reasons for maintaining support, Foundation officials advanced an argument similar to Richards's:

> It is clear that the future structure of China's educational program depends on the second language for schools and on the production of books in the languages commonly used in Chinese schools and colleges. Neither printing nor teaching in English will be recommended on a large scale unless the teaching staff in a provincial program has a ready control of English. The signs today are fairly discouraging except for the determination of a few Chinese and Americans to assist the provincial governments in their training schools. Yet the work begun by Dr. Richards seems to have the surest prospect of success, and the School in Yunnan, through its precedent in establishing joint responsibility with a provincial authority, would serve as a model for institutions of great effectiveness elsewhere.[165]

With the diminishing prospects for Western contact, the survival of the Basic project in China took on a consciously political shading in anticipation of the ideological struggles of the Cold War.

With the work in Kunming promising to become a factor in postwar politics, Richards began to solicit support for the Institute from government sources. Early in 1942 he looked into the possibility of funding from the Division of Cultural Relations of the U.S. State Department, and again in September told Stevens that he was still "trying to get Government or private interest in continuing the work in Kunming."[166] In October Marion de la Motte, Director of the Education Division at the British Council, wrote to the Rockefeller Foundation's London office expressing interest in the Orthological Institute. Its work had come to the Council's attention through E. R. Hughes, head of the Chinese Department at Oxford University, who had recently visited Kunming under the auspices of the Rhodes Trust. He found that "much useful experience has been gained from the results of [the Institute's] work," and suggested that the British Council look into the project. "As you know," La Motte wrote, "the Council is deeply interested in all matters which concern the teaching of English abroad, and we should therefore be most grateful if you could let us have as much information as possible about this experimental school, which has been doing such valuable research work in the field of the teaching of English and which, if it were to close down, would be a real blow to the training of the English teachers in China."[167] Ultimately these solicitations came to nothing; while the Orthological Institute received disbursements from the British Embassy and the British-Chinese Cultural Relations Committee in 1943, they were more on the order of wartime relief than a sustained commitment to the Institute's work, and the possibility of long-term interest vanished with mounting inflationary pressures later that year. But they demonstrate that Richards now saw the Basic investment in China changing in anticipation of the Cold War, and he was trying to put the work on a new footing.

Meanwhile in Kunming, Winter and Shui faced a number of extreme hardships as the war intensified. The series of bombings that began in the last months of Pollard-Urquhart's tenure continued through most of 1941 as the Japanese increased their efforts in Burma in an attempt to advance through China from the south. For most of the year Winter was virtually out of touch with Richards and the

Foundation due to the uncertainty of the mail; a Christmas card from Richards sent in November 1941 failed to arrive in Kunming until July of the following year. In mid-1942, when Winter was able to get mail through more regularly, he painted a harrowing picture of wartime conditions in the town:

> With the fall of Burma and west Yunnan the whole Chinese population of those regions was dumped on our heads. Some have walked for two months, eating roots and grasses. When Pao Shan was bombed two months ago [June 1942] four thousand people were killed in the space of five minutes and the rest of the population started running in this direction. Refugees who were fortunate enough to get on trucks have told me that the road was so strewn with the dead and the dying that their skulls popped under the tires of the trucks racing along the road. They brought cholera with them. We have reduced the number of cases to about three hundred in Kunming proper, but the disease is spreading rapidly through the country districts, where there is no control. The streets are lined with refugees offering for sale the last garment which they can decently strip off their emaciated bodies. They are given a small amount of rice each day by the central government. The local government does nothing to help them.[168]

By August 1942, the military situation at least showed signs of temporary stability. "As you probably know," Winter informed Stevens, "the enemy is at Salween, about two hundred miles west of us. But, as they have been for two years at the Indo-Chinese border, which is also two hundred miles from Kunming, there seems to be no reason for alarm." With the recent arrival of the American Expeditionary Force in the town, evacuees were beginning to return from the countryside. During this time Kung devoted a generous amount to the repair of Institute buildings damaged in the bombing, ensuring that Shui, Winter and the staff would "have our own school and not have to occupy borrowed buildings." Although only twelve schools in the province still included English in their curriculum, the Institute was now responsible for training all of the English teachers in Yunnan.

Internal conditions in the province, however, remained precarious. As the Japanese attacks abated, the region suffered from an astronomical rate of inflation. "Our work," Winter reported in August 1942, "has been very much less interfered with than during the previous year. Now our problem is the high cost of living, which has reached something like three times New York prices, and is still going up." As a result, "I don't suppose that anyone connected with the schools has tasted meat for the last six months. . . . Food prices are about ten times what they were when I got here."[169] By the year's end inflationary pressures had reached catastrophic proportions. "We are almost at the breaking point because of prices," Winter explained to Richards in November:

> In the university the babies which have been born in the last six months are dying of malnutrition. . . . Everyone who can has cleared out. Perkins—American Consul—had to be sent home. The new one, Ludden, whom you may have known in Peking is tougher, and may be able to stick it out.[170]

In a letter to Stevens he added:

> I suppose there is no need for me to enlarge upon the difficult conditions under which we are working. We are crowded, underfed; servants, students and faculty are all mixed up together and we have to climb over the ruins to get in and out of the school. . . . We used to live in terror of the constant bombing. Now I pray for the town to be bombed so that the prices will come down.[171]

When a British Parliamentary Mission toured Kunming in December, they were not permitted to visit the Institute's office "because it is in the midst of a heap of ruins, and the stupid local authorities only wanted them to see the smart parts of the town."[172] A letter to the foundation from John K. Fairbank, the distinguished Harvard Sinologist then serving at the American Embassy in Kunming, describes Winter's life at this period:

> In air raids his clothes have been completely stolen twice and he now has a pair of monkeys in the yard, one of whom is a fierce biting beast and would have to be shot by an intruder. He has a courtyard full of flowers and a bookcase full of books, and knows all the ins and outs of local folklore and gossip. . . . [He sees] something of the Tsing Hua faculty, who of course esteem Winter; you remember his single-minded defense of the University against the Japs. But aside from them and the consulate, life is pretty lonely. . . . We are both amazed at his enthusiasm and morale; he is lively in thought and vigorous in comment and a godsend to the Tsing Hua group.[173]

In the face of these difficulties Winter was determined to continue work in Kunming, where he felt that Basic could still accomplish a great deal. By November 1942 Kung's subsidies to the Provincial Training College had actually increased from $250 to $350 monthly, a promising development for the future of English in the province, which now seemed the main justification for the venture. In addition Wu, now back in Kunming after a year in the United States with Richards, received an offer to take charge of all English teaching at Yunnan Provincial University. With Shui installed as Dean of the Provincial English College, Winter could write with some confidence at the end of 1942 that "it looks as if the school would be on its feet when I drop out next June."[174] Basic now seemed assured of independent Chinese support, with two of its most devoted members holding prominent administrative positions.

The advances seemed more remarkable given the rapidly declining situation of English elsewhere in China. At the same time that Kung increased his disbursements to the Institute, a Chinese faculty member of the Szechuan Provincial College of Education warned Richards:

> The stubborn fact is that English is visibly dwindling away in importance. . . . As the present condition is allowed to go on, English is sure, one day or another, to be wiped out from the curriculum, at first in junior middle schools, then in senior middle schools and finally in colleges. By the loss of such a link, such a medium, of culture and mutual understanding we should lose much, and the Anglo-Saxons should lose much too.[175]

The Director of the China Institute confirmed this report by informing the Foundation "that he had observed a striking decline in the ability of successive generations of Chinese students to speak and understand English."[176] In a letter to the Rockefeller Foundation in March 1942 Richards acknowledged the forbidding cultural climate:

> That there will be an immense decline in the number and competence of the Chinese who have some knowledge of English in the next generation is beyond a doubt. The channel for China's communications with the rest of the world through English has been narrowed down. Chinese education has struggled to maintain itself, but much has had to be sacrificed in the interests of the rest, and a chief sacrifice has been elementary instruction in English.[177]

The loss of linguistic ties, Richards argued, would severely damage future relations between China and the West. He realized that a one-sided effort on the part of Western scholars to understand the Chinese would not be an acceptable substitute because

> They cannot enter into—and take a natural part in—the viewing from Chinese standpoints of the Western World, its science, its technics, its

economics, its history, its political theory, its law, its literature, its philosophy. They can have only a minor place in the historically unparalleled effort which China is making to assimilate the achievements of one half of the world's intellect to the other. And it is plain that their share in the designing and the conduct of China's educational system, her postwar reconstruction, her internal and international policies must and should be slight. All that is China's business. Our contribution is to do what we can to see that in all this China's access to Western facts and ideas is as clear and open as possible.[178]

With the future of Anglo-Chinese relations at stake, Richards believed it was critical for the Institute to expand its activities. In October 1942 he outlined an ambitious plan for the future:

> I feel that the School [in Kunming] should grow, should spread to Szechuan where a daughter school should be established. Its publications should be extended. There are many directions—including use of the visual aids to English teaching which we are working on here—in which the School could develop. It already has Government and Provincial standing and support. It has been a point at which British, Chinese and Americans have already worked successfully together for years on the teaching of English. . . . With this background and these possibilities of growth before it the School seems to me to have great possibilities both as an actual agency in education and as a symbol of cultural cooperation.[179]

But by early 1943 the astronomical rate of inflation in Kunming precluded even a symbolic show of support. In February 1943 the cost of maintaining the Institute's work soared from roughly $350 per month before the inflation to $1,350, a nearly fourfold increase. Under this kind of pressure, Foundation officials deemed in April 1943 that "the high cost of living in West China and the poor rate of exchange led to a decision that further support for the work of the Institute at present could hardly be useful."[180] They decided to bring Winter back to the United States for consultation about the situation in Kunming while considering what provision to make for the future. They also felt, understandably, that Winter deserved a respite from Yunnan "after the severe hardship which he has gone through since the outbreak of the war in China."[181]

Richards agreed with the plan to bring Winter to the United States, though he insisted that the Foundation agree to help him return to China when the consultation was over. "China is his place," he contended, "and his future should be there. He is too restless a person to settle down into retirement away from all his fantastic interests."[182] Winter himself had doubts about returning, feeling, as he told John Fairbank, "that I am best fitted to do the thing that I am now doing, and I don't really want to go home."[183] But with the future of the Basic program in jeopardy, he finally agreed to go. Winter left China in July, arriving in Los Angeles after a short stay in India delivering Basic Army manuals to Chinese soldiers, on October 26. By November he was in New York consulting with Foundation officials.

In deciding whether or not to continue their program in China, the Rockefeller Foundation solicited an independent report on the Institute's situation. William Sloane, an official with the American Information Service at the U.S. Embassy in Kunming, visited the Provincial English Teacher's College at the Foundation's request in November 1943, at about the time of Winter's arrival in New York. Sloane's report is one of the only assessments of Basic in Kunming to come from an observer outside of the Institute itself. As such, his rather guarded estimation balances some of Richards's and Winter's more optimistic pronouncements to give a complete picture of the Institute's wartime operations in Kunming. Sloane shared Richards's sense of the declining importance of English in China's future. On November 21 he wrote to Stevens:

> The general English teaching program in China, as you know, is deteriorating, and the present government policy of speaking Chinese on all possible occasions has gone so far that a recent scientific meeting was ordered to be wholly conducted in Chinese with the result that most of the scholars got nothing out of it at all.[184]

Given the shrinking scope for English, Sloane was baffled by Commissioner Kung's continued support of the English Teacher's Training School. "I have not been able to find out why this little Institute has been able to secure its pittance from the Yunnan coffers," he told Stevens in a report of December 4. While he found Kung himself to be "a man of refinement and some apparent distinction," Sloane was more willing than the members of the Institute to attribute his aid to self-interest. Holding that "the politics of this province is about on a par with the morals of Mata Hari," he surmised that the source of the Commissioner's interest lay in the tension between the Universities and the native Yunnanese:

> The out-of-town colleges are quite contemptuous of Yunnanese educational standards and try to keep the number of Yunnanese pupils as low

as they can. By taking in eighty percent of the local students, the English teachers' college tops the treasury, or perhaps vice-versa.[185]

Sloane had no evidence for this charge; it depended more on his sense of Chinese politics than on concrete fact. But it indicates the skepticism he was inclined to bring to his assessment of Basic's success in the war-torn province.

Sloane found the Institute itself "optically if not biologically clean," located "in a section of the city chiefly notable for its thieves' market." "There is an air of effective work about this little place," he wrote Stevens. The compound, consisting of four classrooms, a dormitory, a library and an office for Shui, enjoyed better facilities than those of the Consolidated Universities. Shui, now the Director in Winter's absence, was overworked but "cheerful, energetic and determined." Sloane felt that the curriculum at the teachers' school was unexceptionable:

> It uses Basic English in the first year and part of the second, but seeks to broaden out into full English in the Junior and Senior or third-year work. About eight or ten English courses are taught, including "Practical English," English Poetry, Reading English, Grammar, Written English, Composition, etc. I have no notion at all of how good the teaching job really is. But if I were a local Rotarian—and the Rotary is quite a social force in Kunming—I would sponsor a campaign to raise funds for this school and increase its output for merely commercial reasons.[186]

Nor did he find fault with the leadership of Shui and Wu, an important point for the Foundation given the fact that they represented the Institute's first Chinese directors, a goal toward which the Rockefeller had been working since the project's inception. In his interviews with them, "they stressed that their Yunnanese connections were done with their eyes open, that Yunnan was a good test-tube, and that they had had excellent cooperation from the Yunnan education people. They added that they were freer to work in a back-country province like this one. This I can tell you is all too true."

But in addition to the isolation of Yunnan, Sloane was dismayed by the small size of the school. He found that the teachers' college was able to accommodate no more than fifty students per year, turning away an equal number of applicants annually. The staff struggled to handle even this small number, with Shui maintaining a teaching schedule of eighteen hours a week in addition to his administrative work as principal. Wu, now serving as Dean, shouldered an equally exacting routine. Their workload severely limited the Institute's achievements. Sloane gave Stevens a sobering description of the school's accomplishments thus far:

> Fifteen graduates last year [1942]. Seven are teaching English, but three are in the school itself. Another is tutoring, and a fifth is teaching English in the army. So, actually only two graduates are actually [sic] teaching English in Chinese schools. They are both in Yunnan middle schools. Dr. Shui denies that English teaching has declined as a result of the war. He feels that the Middle School is soon enough to begin English anyhow, and cites his own personal history. All I can say is that now that the government requires Mandarin, English has necessarily declined as a secondary language. Dr. Shui has no comment on this.[187]

If Richards planned to make a "seedbed" of Yunnan, two graduates in nearly two years was a worrying rate of growth. While Sloane approved of the leadership and direction of the Institute's work, he dismissed its potential for assuming any kind of national importance in China:

> On my side I told [Shui and Wu] that I could not speak for all the R[ockefeller] F[oundation], but that I doubted what support they could hope to get from anybody unless they could show that they had a plan for a future of at least regional and preferably national significance. I pointed out that American philanthropy could not keep small cultural enterprises going merely for their own sake and that bitter experience had taught Americans that institutions over here could be subsidized for decades without becoming either self-supporting or significant to China as a whole. Both men assented to this, quite fervently and have agreed to forward you their plan for making the enterprise a bit more important.[188]

Ultimately, Sloane recommended that the Rockefeller Foundation continue its support for the Institute on some level. He advised that a stricter plan of expansion be drafted, and that further subsidies be linked to the Institute's progress: "funds for building constructively should be available, but not funds merely to buy twigs for a dying fire." But otherwise he felt that the Institute was in "able, impressive" hands under Wu and Shui, and that their program was "right in advocating the usefulness of English, not its literary beauties." Still, Sloane's cautious optimism must have come as a surprise to Stevens after Richards's and Winter's more exuberant assurances. By all accounts the future of English in China was in serious jeopardy, and this at a time when its political importance was most apparent. But Sloane's report suggested that the Institute's work in Yunnan was less likely than ever to turn the tide.

In the event, Winter's return to the United States signaled the end of the Rockefeller Foundation's involvement with Basic English in China. During its engagement with the project from February 1936 to June 1943 the Foundation had spent a total of $53,600 in support of the Orthological Institute of China, exclusive of various travel stipends for Richards, Jameson, Winter and Wu. Over that time Basic had stirred academic debate, inspired educational reform on a national level, and finally subsided to a token presence in an isolated rural province. Ultimately, even Sloane's cautious hopes for the Institute turned out to be misplaced. Following the Japanese surrender in August 1945, civil war between the Nationalists and the Communists immediately broke out in China, resulting in a four-year struggle for control of the nation. When the Communists took power in 1949, the relationship between China and the West was placed on an entirely new footing. Richards's original ambitions for English in China became ideologically suspect, seen as part of a long history of Western imperial presence in the country that the Communists firmly condemned. As the isolation between China and the Western nations increased, the time, effort and resources devoted to Basic since 1933 seemed increasingly like a lost investment.

Ironically, the coda to the Rockefeller Foundation's involvement with Basic in China came with a final disbursement to Bob Winter. On June 16, 1944, the Foundation made a direct grant to Tsing Hua University "toward development of its program of teaching in humanities under the direction of Winter, for the period ending June 30, 1946." After a year in the United States at the Foundation's expense, Winter was eager to return to his beloved university. The Foundation agreed to endow his appointment as "it was believed that such work would maintain instruction in the humanities at a high level which was especially needed at that time in China."[189] On October 17, 1947, a further appropriation of $20,000 was made to Tsing Hua for the purpose of maintaining Winter's work over a five-year period ending on December 1, 1952. An addenda to the 1943 report explains the Foundation's interest in continuing Winter's work:

> Political and economic disorder in China make difficult the initiation there of long-range new projects in the humanities on a sound basis. . . .

But the seriousness of the situation increases the importance of maintaining China's few cases of free speech and humanistic thought. Of these Tsing Hua is of the most importance.[190]

Well before the end of the grant, however, even such limited aims became difficult. On January 31, 1949, Communist soldiers occupied Peking, signaling the beginning of Communist rule. Winter, who had turned sixty-two the previous day, opted to stay with the university where he had taught for more than twenty-five years. In one of his last communications with the Rockefeller Foundation, he offered reasons for his decision in terms that might serve as an epigraph for the entire Basic project in China:

I want to take advantage of this letter to thank you for all the really saintly patience you have shown for my vagaries. I hope to go on as I have done, scolding the Communists when I think they are wrong, trying to establish communication for them with the great Western tradition and with other peoples, so that they may enlarge the meaning and possibility of their own great civilization and use objective judgements based on exact evidence; in other words, help them to find their way in the confused world which faces them. And when the iron curtain rolls up, I hope to have many interesting things to tell you.[191]

7   Empires of the Future

*Communist China and the
Cold War, 1950-1951*

I

On September 6, 1943, in the midst of the Second World War, Winston Churchill delivered a speech at Harvard University on the subject of Anglo-American unity. His theme was the global power and responsibility that Britain and the United States were certain to bear in the future. "It must be world anarchy or world order," Churchill warned his audience at Sanders Theater. "Throughout all this ordeal and struggle which is characteristic of our age, you will find in the British Commonwealth and Empire good comrades to whom you are united by other ties besides those of State policy and public need."[1] Foremost among such ties was that of a shared language. Along with a "marked regard for fair play, . . . a stern sentiment of impartial justice, and above all the love of personal freedom," Churchill cited the common inheritance of English as one of the most important elements uniting Britons and Americans in the coming world order. "I like to think," he told his audience,

> of British and Americans moving about freely over each other's wide estates with hardly a sense of being foreigners to one another. But I do not see why we should not try to spread our common language even more widely throughout the globe and, without seeking selfish advantage over any, possess ourselves of this invaluable amenity and birthright.[2]

In sketching out the global destiny of the English-speaking peoples, Churchill cited Basic English for special commendation. He praised the work of the Harvard Commission on English Language Studies in spreading Basic English—the invention, as he pointed out, of "two Englishmen"—to Latin America. Addressing the proponents of Basic as "the head-stream of what might be a mighty fertilizing and health-giving river," Churchill imagined the "grand convenience" of a future in which English-speakers would "be able to move freely about the world, and be able to find a medium, albeit primitive, of intercourse and understanding." The benefits of linguistic hegemony, however, would not belong to the Anglophone nations alone. "Might it not also be an advantage," he asked, "to many races, and an aid to the building-up of our new structure for preserving peace? . . . Such plans offer far better prizes than taking away other people's provinces or lands or grinding them down in exploitation." Exactly what those prizes were Churchill left undefined. But to drive the point home, he concluded with a phrase that seemed to link the ascendancy of the English language with the ominous legacy of Britain's imperial past. "The empires of the future," he assured his audience, "are the empires of the mind."[3]

As the head of Harvard's Commission on English Language Studies, Richards felt the repercussions of the Prime Minister's remarks almost immediately: "the waves from Churchill's speech and mounting into my once placid and sometimes lucid lagoon till reflexion seems something only for the angels and the blest!" he lamented to a colleague at Magdalene College in November.[4] The resulting publicity gave a great boost to the Basic movement in the United States. On October 18, less than five weeks after the Harvard speech, *Life* magazine published an article on Richards and Basic "which doesn't give a bad idea," he proudly informed a friend, "of what we're trying to do."[5] One outcome of the attention was that the Chinese Air Force, then training in the Arizona desert, adopted Basic as a part of their instruction course. The irony that Basic, originally conceived as an instrument of world peace, should be used to train soldiers for combat was apparently lost on Richards in the resulting excitement. "Endless developments on all levels," he reported at the end of November 1943. "It may really I think help to win the peace."[6]

In retrospect, Churchill's Harvard speech was a mixed blessing for Richards's cause. William Empson later called the Prime Minister's support "the kiss of death" for Basic; a rhetorical flourish "that gave just what he wanted for his speech, breadth of post-war vision and co-operation between our two countries" without the practical measures needed to effect it.[7] Although both Churchill and Roosevelt looked into the possibility of state support for Basic, the attempts ultimately yielded nothing; in 1944 the British government committee responsible for reporting on the issue determined, with Churchill's confirmation, "that the government could not support any one method of learning English."[8] Moreover, as Empson realized, the real power to implement Basic globally belonged to the foreign governments that might adopt it, not to officials in Washington or London.[9] In this respect Churchill's speech was positively damaging to the Basic cause. As John Paul Russo points out, "the retreat from colonialism induced a tremendous feeling of guilt that extended to any official promotion of Basic English."[10] By annexing Basic to his vision of a post-war Anglophone world order, Churchill created the lasting suspicion that Basic was a less-than-disinterested instrument of global American hegemony. The more adverse effects of the Harvard speech were apparent to the Richardses even at the time. As Dorothea informed her brother-in-law in November:

> You have no idea how many people you have to watch out for. All sorts of French Canadians with different slants from extreme Nationalism who see nothing in Basic but [an effort] to deprive them of their own language. Then the Latin Americans fear U.S. cultural aggression and want Spanish to be the world language. Others are afraid of an Anglo-American bloc and linguistic imperialism. Then there are our friends the comrades [the Communists] who think—because Churchill was in favour of it—they must damn it.[11]

As with the growing politicization of English in China during the final years of the war, the differing responses to Churchill's speech indicated the ways in which Basic was to be swept up into the diplomatic tensions of the Cold War.

Seven years after the Harvard speech, Richards was given a unique opportunity to reflect upon the aptness of Churchill's characterization of "the empires of the future." In January 1950 C. W. Luh, President of Yenching University in Peking, invited the Richardses to spend their Spring sabbatical in China. The invitation came at a crossroads in the nation's history. On January 31, 1949, Nationalist troops had surrendered Peking to the Communists, marking the final stage of a violent civil conflict that had begun with the Japanese surrender in August 1945. In October, just two months before President Luh's invitation, Mao Tse Tung had declared the founding of the People's Republic of China, re-designating Peking as its capital. The impact this change would have on Chinese life was still uncertain. Luh assured the Richardses that they would have no trouble entering the country, as Yenching had been recently appointed the headquarters of English teaching in China.[12] Eager to explore the possibilities for Basic under the new regime, the couple sailed for Hong Kong in March 1950. Over the next four months, they were deeply impressed with the energy, efficiency and relative tolerance of the Communist "revolution." "There seems no shadow of doubt," Richards wrote home buoyantly, "that it is enabling great things to be done, and that corruption has been banished as never!"[13] He was particularly surprised by the new regime's apparent mildness in dealing with its former opponents. Describing the absence of coercion in favor of more suasive forms of "re-education," Richards declared that "it nearly makes me join a confession myself. If the Empires of the Future are the Empires of the Mind I know who's going to win through."[14]

Richards's ironic turn of Churchill's phrase indicates his continuing faith in international communication and understanding despite the political obstacles they faced after the Second World War. That he should use an assertion of Anglo-American power to praise Communist China suggests the mediating role that Richards hoped to play as the world resolved itself into the polarities of Communist and capitalist. His enthusiasm for the People's Government, which he continued to endorse upon his return to the United States despite the advent of the Korean War, reflected Richards's belief that the Communists were making the kind of changes that he felt were needed in China. But it was also in part a reaction to the growing political hostilities of the Cold War, which he saw as inimical to his vision for world peace through language. Once again, China served as a means for Richards to articulate his hopes for the future and to criticize attitudes prevalent in the West. His frustration at the ideological divisions of the Cold War assumed at times a critical tone reminiscent of Lowes Dickinson's in *Letters to John Chinaman*. Richards's experience in Communist China demonstrates the challenges he faced in preserving his own notion of an "empire of the mind"—a world unity based on rational consensus, education and mutual understanding— as the less benign regimes of the Communist and capitalist blocs threatened to fracture the globe.

II

Since his departure from China in October 1938, Richards had devoted himself almost continuously to the promotion of Basic English.
After resuming his teaching obligations at Cambridge University for
the winter and spring of 1939, he sought to return to the United
States with the outbreak of the European war. After consultation with
Foreign Office officials in London, it was determined that his most effective wartime service would be to promote the British cause in the
United States, which was still officially neutral. In September Richards explained to D. H. Stevens at the Rockefeller Foundation:

> As you'll imagine I am to combine normal work with being as useful to
> the British Cause as I know how. I think the aspects of the British cause I
> can represent are aspects of wider causes still and I am counting from a
> lot of advice from you on that. A big piece of bold, quick thinking any-
> how will be needed if this war isn't to lead to an even messier place, and
> we are hoping you in America will do a large part of it.[15]

Richards was also eager to resume his Basic work. In March 1939, the
Rockefeller Foundation awarded a $50,000 grant to be extended over
a five-year period for Basic activities in North and South America.
The grant was to be administered through Harvard University,
where Richards was appointed to the position of university lecturer
while also serving as the chair of the newly formed Harvard Committee on Communication. In addition, the grant provided funds for a
separate Orthological Committee, also under Richards's direction, affiliated with Ogden's Orthological Institute in London. Under the
terms of the grant, Richards and his colleagues were to undertake research on adapting Basic for Latin America as well as integrating Basic into courses for recent immigrants to the United States. Some of
the projects initiated in the first years of the grant included the development of radio courses in English for South America, publication of
a series of primers in Basic aimed at literate aliens and at the illiterate
poor in the United States, and the production of a series of introductory phonograph records on English.[16]

Richards also took a great interest in the possibilities of visual
media for introducing new audiences to Basic. He spent the summer
of 1942 at the Disney studios in California working with artists to develop a series of short films presenting English vocabulary through
pictures. The experience pointed the way to Richards's later design of

English Through Pictures, which relied almost exclusively on schematic illustrations to convey the Basic word list. The advantage of a pictorial approach to language instruction, which increasingly became the focus of Richards's work in the 1950's and 1960's, was that it allowed for self-teaching, permitting students to learn English on their own without the ideological interference of governments or classrooms. In addition to Basic translations of classic Western texts like Plato's *Republic* and the *Iliad*, which also absorbed his attention in these years, teaching English through pictures represented Richards's efforts to advance his cause in the face of the mounting political tension of the Cold War.

Despite the improving opportunities for Basic in the United States, the Richardses found the transition to their new home difficult. "We don't like feeling like exiles and we fear we will feel like exiles still when we get back," Richards confided to a Magdalene colleague in December 1941.[17] Aside from nostalgia for friends and acquaintances in Cambridge, the attitudes of their American hosts occasionally made adjustment difficult. The couple were deeply disturbed by America's wartime neutrality. "People here [are] utterly unconscious that London is being smashed to dust," Dorothea recorded on New Year's Eve, 1940. "IAR [Richards] so angry he could hardly speak."[18] Through radio broadcasts, letters to publications such as *Time* and his work on behalf of the Harvard Defense of America Committee—a strongly pro-British organization for which he translated several documents into Basic—Richards canvassed strenuously for American intervention in the war. One of his more oblique efforts at propaganda resulted in a Basic version of Plato's *Republic*, which he intended for use in the schools as a war education measure; the discussion of Justice in Book One was, he felt, "right on the contemporary problem."[19] After the United States' entry into the war in December 1941, Richards began privately to express concern with the onset of the "American century." "[It is] perfectly clear," he wrote in May 1942, five months after the declaration of war, "that most Americans see this moment as a godgiven one for taking over through educational and economic Imperialism and the Basic English which they regard as mismanaged by the old school tie."[20] As a Briton, he felt the negative consequences of such developments acutely. "Britain symbolically represents all that America aspires to escape from," he wrote to George Sansom in December 1942, "and whatever we do or don't do I fear we will retain the role."[21] The rising American dominance in world affairs concerned him deeply in the following years, an anxiety he would find confirmed by U.S. policy toward China in the Korean conflict in 1950–51.

In addition to his misgivings about developments in the United States, Richards also began to have doubts about his partnership with C. K. Ogden. Ogden's intransigence in accepting modifications to Basic had been a source of friction between the two for some time. With Richards's departure for the United States tensions heightened. Ogden, mired in negotiations with British governmental agencies in London, became increasingly hostile to Richards's work in North America. When the Richardses visited London in the summer of 1946, their first trip to Britain in seven years, Ogden treated them with marked antagonism. He found the "March of Time" films developed with the Disney studios "most awkward, embarrassing and useless," reminding Richards that he himself had "put twenty years into designing and making films which would get round the teacher so that a thing which has only taken five years [is] no good." More generally, Richards found him "determined to keep American products out of England."[22] By 1947 Ogden seemed to have become a liability to the Basic movement internationally. Richards had come to feel that Ogden does not "want anyone to do anything with [Basic] except himself, and yet—for one reason or another—he does not get anything done."[23] His insistence on retaining control of the copyright severely hindered efforts to publish Basic materials worldwide, while a growing obsession with the distribution of profits threatened to compromise the movement's integrity. In 1948, under pressure from the Trustees of the Basic English Foundation in London, Ogden retired from his position as General Director and ceded leadership to John Muir. By this time Richards had effectively separated his activities from those of the group in London. But the rift signaled the end of efforts to coordinate Basic internationally and contributed to its eventual demise.

By 1949, however, as the Richardses again considered returning to China, the prospects for Basic were still encouraging. With the continuing support of the Rockefeller Foundation, both the Harvard Commission on English Language Studies and the Orthological Institute, now operating under the name of English Language Research, were involved in an impressive array of Basic activities, ranging from the publication of *English Self-Taught through Pictures* to the development of instructional records, broadcast materials and films.[24] In the summer of 1949, anticipating a sabbatical for the following spring, Richards began to inquire about the possibility of a visit to China. His former pupil, William Empson, had recently returned to the country under the auspices of the British Council, where he taught English literature at the Peking National University (Pei Ta). In July 1949 Empson responded encouragingly to Richards's inquiries: "I told one or two people in the universities there was a possibility you might come over here from Harvard in a Sabbatical year, and they were extremely eager that you should do it as soon as possible."[25] He also offered a mildly optimistic prognosis for the current status of English in China. Despite the Communist occupation of Peking in January, Empson reported that "the position in the universities about English seems to be that a great deal of discussing is going on but hardly anything has been decided. It is clear however that they are going to go on teaching English."[26] With Empson at Pei Ta, Bob Winter still teaching at Tsing Hua and Chao Chao Hsin, who had worked closely with the Orthological Institute of China until his sudden departure in 1940, heading the Tsing Hua Western Languages Department, Richards's academic connections in China were still strong. In January 1950 he felt confident enough about the prospect of entering China to tell a friend: "As to our [sabbatical] decision it is Japan and China—if the strings we are pulling to get to Peking don't break. We are daily expecting to get word one way or another and count on sailing anyhow [the] first week in February."[27]

In mid-January the Richardses received word from C. W. Luh, President of Yenching University in Peking, that he foresaw no problems with their entry into China and offered a visiting lectureship at Yenching. Newly appointed by the Communist government as the national center for English studies, Yenching was the ideal location for Richards to survey the current linguistic situation. But the exact diplomatic status of the Richardses in China promised to be as hazy as that of the future of English. Relations between the Western nations and the People's Republic of China were still largely undefined. In April 1949, immediately following the Communist victories in North China, the British frigate *Amethyst* attempted to enter Nanking in order to evacuate British civilians. Communist troops opened fire on the vessel, killing 17 crew members and wounding another 20. Although the ship was eventually rescued, the incident signaled the new regime's intolerance of Western military interference in Chinese affairs. In January 1950, less than three months before the couple's departure, Dorothea reported that the "exact status [of the] British recognition of the Communists remains cloudy."[28] Foreign Minister Chou En Lai expressed a willingness to exchange diplomatic representatives with Britain pending further talks, a gesture widely seen as a maneuver to re-negotiate the Sino-British treaties that gave Britain so many rights in the country.

Relations with the United States were in much worse repair. Continuing support for the Kuomintang precluded diplomatic recognition of the People's Republic of China, whose recent victories in the North had been over Nationalist troops armed with American tanks and planes. In January the Richardses also received word of the first confiscations of American property in Peking.[29] Despite their diplomatic ambiguity, the couple booked a passage to Hong Kong in February. They were reassured of the relative stability of conditions in China by Lucius Porter, an old missionary friend from Yenching who had contributed to the translation in *Mencius on the Mind*. Porter visited Harvard during a round of sermons and talks on the new regime in January. He informed the Richardses that in spite of "requests for more classes in economics [and] social science on Marxist lines," the Communists had otherwise not interfered with the Yenching faculty or curriculum.[30] Armed with Porter's assurances and eager to see the new People's Republic for themselves, the couple sailed for Hong Kong on February 9, 1950.

Richards used the three-weeks passage to translate parts of the *Iliad* into Basic.[31] Like his recent version of Plato's *Republic*, the *Iliad* translation demonstrated Basic's ability to present complex texts in a simplified form, thus making Western ideas accessible to a wider, non-Western audience. It also signaled what Richards himself saw as perhaps the final opportunity to establish Basic in China. "I'm trying to turn out a Simplified *Iliad* and gazing at shelf fulls of instructive books on everything I've brought along," he wrote to James Wood. "I can at least leave them for China to misunderstand if I don't find time to open them."[32] As he had during the war years, Richards found solace in the uncertainties of China's present by planning for its future. On his arrival in Hong Kong on March 1, however, he found the city swarming with rumor and conjecture about the current situation. The city was "crammed with refugees from all over China," with housing scarce and prices alarmingly high.[33] Fortunately the Richardses were able to find lodging in the home of an officer in the U.S. Consulate, located on the Peak in Hong Kong's Central district and offering "unbelievable fairyland landscapes stretching out 1,000 feet below on all sides."[34] Their entry to the mainland still in doubt, Richards cabled Yenching. Even with an invitation from Yenching, the situation was precarious. "We have a better chance than anyone with Yenching backing," Dorothea wrote to her brother-in-law, "but there is no certainty. If we don't hear shortly we shall have to make different plans."[35] As the days stretched to weeks, they contemplated visits to India and the Philippines along with the offer of a two-month position as Educational Advisor to the British Liaison Mission in Japan.[36] In the meantime, they awaited official word on their entry status. "The Communists have tightened up a lot," Dorothea complained, "and they have a technique of saying 'yes' but actually doing nothing about the necessary permit."[37] As a result most of March was lost to administrative delay.

While the Communist bureaucracy temporized, the Richardses gathered what news they could on the situation in China from recent refugees. One of the most troubling reports concerned a famine that was said to be causing great hardship. "There are gloomy tales of country people pouring into cities everywhere to find, as a rule, no help," Richards wrote home.[38] In the wake of the victory over Chiang Kai-shek, the Communists were now reported to be facing sporadic peasant revolts due to famine. Equally distressing to the Richardses were reports of the growing Soviet influence in China, which had dire implications for the future of English in the country. "All the Peking hotels are being filled with Russians," Dorothea reported. "Many people think Russia will be taking precedence over English from now on."[39] Hilda Hague, a friend from the earliest Peking days who had recently fled the mainland, warned Dorothea there was "no hope of any further English teachers being admitted" to China.[40] Through Peter Gonllard, an associate of the American anthropologist Joseph Rock whom the Richardses had met during their Himalayan sojourn of 1938, they heard of Rock's difficult escape from Communist China with the aid of General Claire Lee Chennault, commander of the Flying Tigers, and of his conviction that an American war with China was imminent.[41]

From others in Hong Kong the couple heard of the indoctrination schools recently established by the new regime for the political re-education of the populace. An Anglican schoolteacher lately expelled from Peking told them of being denounced for reprimanding a student in a trial in which she had been allowed no witnesses and was threatened with a sentence in a concentration camp if she failed to apologize.[42] "It's a puzzling life," Richards wrote his brother, "listening to so many people and passing from what angle of their own or others interests they are talking."[43]

On March 20, nearly three weeks after their arrival in Hong Kong, the Richardses resigned themselves to the opinion of their friends that "we wouldn't now get permission for Peking."[44] Two days later, they received word that the People's Government had issued entry permits to Peking via Tientsin. Five days later, they were en route to the mainland, anxious to experience for themselves the recent changes: "It is certainly going to be absorbingly interesting," Richards wrote on the eve of his departure.[45]

III

On April 3, 1950, the Richardses entered the mainland Chinese port of Tientsin. After a thorough search of their belongings, they were directed to the Foreign Affairs Office, now hung with large portraits of Mao and Stalin, where they applied for separate travel permits to Peking. Tientsin, with its banners of Mao and the Communist hammer and sickle and its "shop windows criss-crossed with paper against bombing raids of imperialist Americans," offered a grim introduction to the new China.[46] On the 6th they arrived in Peking. Although the Hotel de Wagon Lits, a familiar landmark from their previous visits, was now "shabby [and] full of [Russian] comrades," they were soon reassured by a new spirit of energy and efficiency that seemed to animate many of the Chinese with whom they came into contact.[47] In contrast to the squalor and official corruption that had distressed the Richardses under the Kuomintang, the Communists were bringing tangible improvements to Peking. "All seems astonishingly like it used to be," Richards noted,

> except that good things are being seriously undertaken and put through. For example and consciously symbolic the drainage and water supplies of Peking are being thoroughly cleaned out and put into proper repair

> for the first time in living memory. It is all rather inspiring. People of al-
> most every angle of opinion agree that a big surge of energy has been
> released in the people and turned to good effect on much-needed tasks
> and that corruption is non-existent.[48]

The change seemed one of spirit as much as science. Despite the official punctiliousness over permits, the Richardses found soldiers and
police alike to be "remarkably gentle, polite and helpful while me-
ticulously carrying out their orders. . . . They have special instruc-
tions as to their dealings with foreigners and in spite of very deep
and strong feelings about Americans (based on bombings and supplies to Formosa etc. and a lot that people in America don't hear
about) the behaviour to people like ourselves is really a model."[49] The
civilian populace also impressed the couple as "friendly and jolly as
ever"[50]—"never was there a people," Richards informed the Master
of Magdalene College, "from whom one gets better change for a
smile."[51] At the Temple of Heaven, a former imperial palace "now
thronged with Chinese sight-seers like Hampton Court," they met
with a group of young men offering to share their breakfast.[52] After a
month of exposure to conflicting reports in Hong Kong, the Richardses were relieved to see the country in such good order. "Compared
to the fantastic fears which are widespread in America," the couple
wrote to Western friends, "seeing things here is a soothing experience."[53]

On April 6 the Richardses visited Bob Winter, still teaching in the
Western Languages and Literature Department at Tsing Hua. He was
housed comfortably in his own bungalow and garden, which the government insisted that he keep "in recognition of services."[54] Having
witnessed the Kuomintang's brutal purges of the universities during
the civil war, Winter was an ardent supporter of the new regime. The
Richardses soon came to share his admiration for the integrity of the
Communist leadership. They assured friends at home that

> Mao Tse Tung and his associates live like the peasant, work 16 hours a
> day, carry a load of responsibility which daunts all of their subordinates,
> go in for self criticism (which seems the queer key to it all) as much as
> any and do their best to keep track of excessive zeal of new converts. The
> whole thing advances as a task in Education by which all are to be led in
> time to conversion.[55]

To some degree the new democratic spirit diminished Peking's former charms. The Llama Miao, the Richardses' former temple home,

was now subdivided into accommodations for the Tsing Hua business staff and their families where, as Dorothea lamented, "laundry, piles of coal balls, bricks [and] rubbish, give the sad look of a tenement which is inevitable."[56] The couple was also barred from wander in the Peking hills, one of their chief pleasures, by a regulation requiring foreigners to stay within eight miles of the city. But in many respects they found life in China much as they had left it in 1938. At Yenching they lodged in the house of a former Manchu prince, overlooking a stunning garden replete with pond, willows and an ornamental bridge.[57] For their weekly excursions to Peking, they had the loan of a house in a former Palace Temple located in the ancient city center. With old friends like Bob Winter, William Empson, Grace Boynton, Bob Drummond and Hilda Holland still in and around Peking, the Richardses resumed the congenial round of dinners and cocktail parties characteristic of Chinese academic life. The majority of their Peking acquaintances, like so many they spoke with during their first weeks back in China, were on the whole deeply sympathetic to the Communist management of the revolution. T. C. Chao, Dean of Religion at Yenching, went so far as to suggest an affinity "between new materialist doctrines and ancient Chinese nature worship."[58] On May 1 the Richardses witnessed the May Day processions in Red Square—"the space," wrote Dorothea, "which we remember as all flower beds and shrubs which has been cleared to permit of enormous assemblies of people."[59] Despite heavy rains, 200,000 gathered to watch a parade of "many thousands, some drowned as rats, struggling with great red banners and huge portraits of Marx, Engels, Stalin, Lenin and Mao."[60] Although oversized portraits of Marx and Lenin hung from the gates of the Forbidden City, the colorful display of silk banners, paper lanterns and traditional rice-scattering folk dancers confirmed the Richardses' impression that the revolution had released a new spirit in China "after a period of blackest inefficiency."[61] "Altogether," Richards assured a friend after his first weeks in the country, "though there is plenty to *think* about there is little to worry over."[62]

By far the most troubling development in the Richardses' view was the ideological conformity now required at the universities. Organized indoctrination of lectures and discussions took up a considerable amount of time under the new regime, as students and faculty alike were compelled to join small Party-led groups which pressured them to modify their views to suit the new political orthodoxy. While uncomfortable with the policy of indoctrination, Richards tried to put as positive a construction upon it as possible. He described the process for a friend at home as follows:

> In the educational institution you join a group of five or six led by a party member who submits himself to all the proceedings you are submitted to. You come out of this series of Oxford grouper confessions and spiritual exercises as a rule, a dependable supporter of the regime— much aware that Mao Tze Tung himself has done more 'confessing' than any other man in the party. In fact this is a tremendous religious movement (comparable to Islam) and in many ways full of hope, especially for the East.[63]

Nevertheless, Richards felt misgivings about the overpowering demand for conformity. "Interference with regular studies is, of course, considerable," he admitted, noting that "there is anxiety for some that *in time* they may be expected to change their views more than they will find easy." But for the moment, while "wide allowances seem to be given in the matter of tempo," the government "conversion" policy seemed relatively benign.[64] In light of the massive improvements underway in China, Richards felt that the excessive doctrinal zeal was infinitely preferable to the recent atrocities of the Kuomintang. "If there is not [as] much freedom of thought as one would wish," he explained in one letter, "there is a fine absence (complete we believe) of the horrors of arrest, torture, etc. which blackened the [Kuomintang] regime."[65] To Richards, political conformity seemed a small price to pay for the profound investment being made in China's future.

Contributing to Richards's stand on political indoctrination was his conviction that the People's Republic was acting independently of the Soviet Union. Since the beginning of Soviet aid to China in the Second World War, observers had feared an increasing Russian influence in Far Eastern affairs. With the Communist victory in 1949, predictions of a Sino-Soviet ideological bloc seemed likely to become a reality. Refugees in Hong Kong reported a strong Soviet presence in China, with Russian advisors and military officers swarming the major cities. Richards was anxious to put fears of a new Russian ascendancy in China to rest. "The Russians," he informed colleagues at home, "of whom there are more and more daily in China, are under quite as much restriction as other foreigners. . . . They are not allowed to mix with Chinese—other than their technical colleagues."[66] Despite the overtly Marxist ideology of the Maoist regime, Richards felt that the revolution in China at bottom had more to do with local conditions than with international Communism. "On the big question," he wrote,

> I have a strong feeling from those in and those near the highest people that this is going to be a thoroughly Chinese job—taking its inspirations, its slogans, its organization, its methodology and even its philosophy from Marxism but remaining in the actual working out and human behavior side very traditional, with perhaps some return to older Chinese modes.[67]

While "confident that history is on the side of . . . MarxLeninism" in China, he was relieved to find it "interpreted about as strictly as no doubt we interpret Lao Tze."[68]

Richards tended to see the Communist reconstruction in moral rather than political terms. Along with the "Oxford grouper" techniques employed in the universities and the "million penitent scale" of Communist conversions among the populace, he recognized in the widespread admiration for Mao an essentially religious impulse.[69] "Fundamentally," he wrote, "this is a religious movement under a leader who seems to impress everyone like a saint should."[70] In another letter he reported that the revolution was being effected "by the same means used by the Pilgrim Fathers—mutual moral suasions."[71] By downplaying the political content of the Communist revolution, Richards was able to support the work of the new regime without necessarily endorsing its ideology. Explaining China's revolution in religious terms also extended the hope of future contact between China and the Western nations. Aside from the threat to English, which would almost certainly be eclipsed by Russian under a close Soviet alliance, the prospect of a Sino-Soviet axis based on shared political ideology and a mutual hostility toward the West threatened the entire international vision upon which Basic English depended. By distancing the Chinese from the Soviets, Richards was free to envision China as a middle ground between the emergent Russian and American spheres of influence. "I am inclined the think," he assured friends at home, "that there is as little risk of China becoming a Russian satellite as there is of Britain becoming an American."[72] The comparison is a telling one, as it reveals Richards's fear that both Britain and China would become victims of the growing fracture between the Soviet and American allies, whom he regarded unequivocally as "two companies of madmen apparently determined to destroy us all."[73] By asserting China's independence from the Soviets, Richards allowed for the possibility of a third term in the bifurcation of world politics; seeing the revolution in moral terms made the People's Republic seem an alternative to the ideological frictions of the Cold War. His view of the political situation depended upon a wider dissatisfaction with postwar global developments, which helps to explain his willingness to overlook some of the more coercive aspects of the Communist regime. "Politics" in China, he assured a friend, "has now become evangelistic and heartsearching and is now the key to betterment. It is all most moral and uplifting. Only the old Liberal in me sighs and wonders at times."[74]

The "old Liberal" in Richards was much in evidence in the lectures he delivered to the students and faculty at Yenching. In addition to talks on Communication Theory and Techniques of Mass Instruction, he spoke on such venerable Western authors as Shakespeare, Homer, Coleridge, Keats and Plato. Although the audience for his first "Theory of Communication" lecture overcrowded the room, later groups tended to be small, at times consisting almost exclusively of staff and former graduates.[75] After one thinly attended lecture, Dorothea complained that "the class doesn't seem to understand and didn't turn up. No curiosity about theory—or power of thought."[76] Chao-chao Hsin, a former colleague from the Orthological Institute who now headed the Western Languages and Literatures Department at Tsing Hua, explained that the best students had gone to work for the Party, leaving, in Dorothea's words, "only dullards . . . who aren't interested in anything." He also informed the Richardses of the growing emphasis on technical training in the universities. At Tsing Hua, nearly three-quarters of the students were now engineers;[77] by 1956 it would be incorporated into Peking National University as an exclusively technical school.[78] With the diminishing attention to literary studies, the Chinese seemed to be returning to the purely technical borrowing from the West that Richards had opposed in the Thirties.

Another cause for the disappointing response may have been the rising hostility toward the United States and the capitalist nations generally encouraged by the new regime. "Only two years ago," Dorothea noted, "students and everybody . . . were wildly enthusiastic about [the] U.S.A. All wanted to go there to study. Now they regard it as decadent, about to collapse."[79] At Pei Ta, where William Empson taught, a recent incident in which a female student accused an American G.I. of rape had deepened the prevalent tensions. Although the incident was widely regarded by the Richardses' Peking acquaintances as a trumped-up charge aimed at fueling anti-Western sentiment, it was emblematic of the perilous state of Chinese attitudes toward the West.[80] Richards experienced some of the mounting hostility first-hand. During one lecture, the Chinese artist Li Lao Chin stood up and shouted at Richards, "yammering cliches" about "dialectical materialism."[81] At a luncheon affair following Richards's lecture on "Socrates' Defense," Phyllis Liang and Liao Chin, academic acquaintances of the Richardses, began fulsomely praising developments in the Soviet Union. After Richards "flared up and said in England we had freedom of speech," Liang roundly denounced the value of Western literature for China—citing John Galsworthy and Aldous Huxley as examples—and expressed her preference for Marxism. When Richards mentioned Plato and Aristotle, Chin "got furious and said they have nothing to do with it." "Came away miserable," Dorothea recorded of the conclusion of the affair, "because IAR got offensive and so did they."[82]

Such incidents contrasted sharply with the respect accorded Richards in Peking academic circles prior to the war. Although the Richardses continued to credit the general friendliness they encountered in the face of ongoing American support for the Kuomintang, it was clear to them that Western influence in the country was likely to decline. "I would guess," Dorothea wrote home, "that Western powers are on the way out and are to have less and less part in the planned future."[83] Richards, too, admitted that "on the whole I doubt if Western powers (or Western studies) will have much place here for quite a while to come."[84] Although they continued to support the transformations taking place in China, they found it regrettable that it should rely upon anti-Western sentiment. "A lot that really needs doing is being done in China," Dorothea wrote, "but it's sad that the Japanese and all capitalist countries are being lumped together indiscriminately as Imperialist. It's not a matter that can be argued about at present."[85] That the revolution was to be "a thoroughly Chinese affair" was clearly a situation that cut both ways.

As if to confirm anti-Western feeling in China, on June 25, 1950, war erupted in Korea. The Richardses received word near the end of their stay that the North Korean army had crossed the thirty-eighth parallel into South Korea on June 26. President Truman's order to send American troops to Korea a few weeks later, backed by a UN pledge of assistance for South Korea, supported their worst fears about the declining role of the West in Chinese affairs. "I really can't see," Richards wrote immediately following the UN intervention,

> how Korea can't fail to turn the rest (what little remains) of Western activities out of China completely. That is, in my eyes, what it is all for. How completely the U.S. seems to forget that war is primarily psychological nowadays and everything the U.S. does from this angle [is to be] just [a] natural feed for propaganda only.[86]

The presence of American troops in Korea fed Chinese fears of an invasion. The United States, which failed to officially recognize the People's Republic of China and continued to support the Kuomintang, was now in a position to attack Peking, a fact the regime was quick to capitalize upon in galvanizing popular support. When the Richardses left Peking on July 30, however, hostilities were still confined to Korea. The couple prepared for their departure by drafting the extensive lists of their baggage, "down to the odd sock or the spare linen strap for the wrist watch," required by Communist officials.[87] They found "everyone very agreeable—in spite of all that has been happening in Korea," and left China with their favorable impression of the People's Republic intact.[88] On August 5, after "quite a voyage avoiding the Korean war," they arrived in Japan, where Richards was to spend a month as Education Advisor to the British Liaison Mission.[89] They found Japan "astonishingly unchanged" since the war, though proficiency in English had noticeably declined.[90] On September 9, after a month in Japan, they left for the United States, returning by plane through Alaska and Canada in time for Harvard's fall term.

Their four-month stay in the People's Republic was the last time the Richardses would see the country for nearly thirty years. On the night of their departure, Dorothea wrote that "China already seems ineffably remote—a kind of dream and Yenching a kind of inner enclosure with a peaceful far-off beauty very much belying the real strenuous strain of the place."[91] A continuing source of strain in the years ahead would be the deterioration of relations with the West, which was to severely restrict contact with China over the next decades. At the outbreak of the Korean War, Richards observed that "the poor planet seems to house two vast masses of madmen. Maybe it's like the poles of the magnet. Each requires the other?"[92] Events in the coming years would provide abundant evidence for his view.

IV

Once back at Harvard, the Richardses tracked developments in Korea with increasing dismay. In September 1950, China's covert support for the North Koreans brought them dangerously close to direct involvement in the conflict. When UN troops, led by General Douglas MacArthur, crossed into North Korea on October 7, the Chinese retaliated with a movement into the Korean peninsula. Massive infusions of Chinese soldiers into North Korea over the following weeks succeeded in stalling the UN advance; by December, the allied forces had been pushed back to the thirty-eighth parallel. "We are naturally very depressed," Dorothea wrote to Will Richards in late November, "at the thought of China getting into war with the U.S. How one wishes that Britain had the lead."[93] After four months in the People's Republic, the couple was acutely aware of the damage the conflict wrought on the Chinese perception of the West. "One of the troubles," Richards lamented, "is that no public figure here makes any attempt to imagine how the U.S. really appears to Peking eyes."[94] The failure to understand the situation in Korea from the Chinese perspective was to Richards's mind the chief cause of the crisis. Never did his notion of war as a product of misunderstanding seem more applicable. Particularly distressing was the display of American chauvinism that followed China's entry into the conflict. "Things happen quicker and quicker," Richards wrote to the Master of Magdalene College on December 5. "When we wrote this MacArthur was announcing his home by Christmas offensive. Now the American century seems to have come and gone in a lustre. The combination of all this power with so little discretion is alarming."[95] By December 10, with UN troops steadily retreating down the Korean peninsula, American opinion seemed "howling for the A-bombs to be dropped."[96] It was, to Richards's mind, an appalling repetition of the errors that had led to the First World War.

Richards did what he could to mitigate the consequences of the war by pleading for an understanding of conditions in China. "Washington and Peking," he felt, "seem to cherish two sets of delusions which match one another in stupidity, and for a long time now what each has done has looked as if it were designed to increase the others' suspicious fantasies and fears."[97] In speeches and letters throughout the winter of 1950–51 he tried to circumvent what he saw as a naïve ideological construct that pitted Communist against capitalist nations. In more imaginative moments he pictured a "vast neutral group forming pledged to do nothing to help either the U.S. or USSR bloc or join it in any fashion. India, Japan and Germany would make a fine widespread start—all resolved never to rearm and perhaps they'd get Italy and France and even [the] U.K. to join them."[98] A visit from Prime Minister Clement Attlee to the United States in December, in which Attlee pledged British support for the American efforts against international Communism, dimmed the hope of British participation in such a scheme. On a more local level, Richards spoke to the editors of *Life* and *Time* magazines in New York, explaining his experience in the People's Republic and asking them to stop their "anti-Chinese rabble-rousing."[99] He also delivered lectures on his view of the conflict at Wellseley, Harvard and Amherst throughout the winter. His speeches on behalf of the Chinese—"quite a delicate business in [the] present state of public opinion"—were actuated by a belief that a better understanding of conditions in the People's Republic would win the sympathy of most Americans for the Chinese cause.[100] He felt it was a tragic mistake that the United States, "which should be much nearer to understanding and sympathizing with what is taking place [in China,] should have got itself in this ridiculous false position."[101] It was a concrete instance of the breakdown in communication that Richards believed to be at the root of international conflict.

Two lectures that Richards delivered at this time convey a sense of his outrage at the American failure to understand the Chinese. The first is a draft for a speech dated December 12, written near the height of China's involvement in Korea. Richards opens with a passionate denunciation of the American diplomatic response to the war:

> U.S. policy risks itself and the rest of the Century for most of the planet through lack of imagination. There is nothing in the Committee lingo of the Truman-Attlee declaration to give ANYONE any lift—no fresh idea, no new perspective, no wider vision. Only the stale repetition of formulations which seem with each repetition increasingly insincere.[102]

He goes on to characterize the UN as "a gang of which the U.S. is the gang leader. It is no more than an attempt to disguise and reinforce the power drives of the U.S." American foreign policy, viewed from the perspective of other world nations, appears "sickening, vomitory hypocrisy." Actions which may look "harmless, correct and restrained enough" to American eyes, such as denying a UN seat to the People's Republic of China, contribute to an international image severely at odds with that the United States imagines its projects. American sloganeering about China sounds hypocritical not only to the Communist Chinese: he reminds his audience that "they sound so to the very many people who are neither Communist or anti-Communist and who are beginning to wonder whether they can dissociate themselves from both." The world "still admires almost everything about the Americans except their political chicanery and devices." But the military debacle in Korea "has suddenly made the Atlantic Powers team realize how closely their own fate is bound up with this inadequacy."[103]

Richards saw the United States' behavior toward China as symptomatic of the postwar shift in power that had diminished Britain's influence in international affairs. His distress over American influence abroad stemmed in part from the threat it posed to Basic by associating English—along with the Western tradition it was meant to disseminate—with the particular ideological agenda of the United States and its official allies. Like Churchill's speech at Harvard, which anticipated the spread of the English language with postwar Anglo-American power, the Korean War made it increasingly difficult for Richards to promote English as a disinterested instrument of modernization and international understanding. Given the extent of his efforts in China, where Basic had shown the most promise, it seems natural that his frustration over recent global developments should focus on American policy toward China. By presenting U.S. actions through Chinese eyes, Richards was able to express his own concerns about the current world situation. Just as his critical work in the Twenties had shaped his subsequent perception of China, the postwar threat to Richards's Basic ideals contributed to his sympathy for the new People's Republic.

Richards's rhetorical strategies in his speeches at this time often resemble those of his Cambridge predecessor, Lowes Dickinson, in *Letters from John Chinaman*. In a speech at Amherst in January 1951, he begins by asking Americans to consider the appeal of Communism for the Chinese:

> Why did the brains, knowledge and honesty of China swing to the Regime? Even men and women educated in the United States, the great lovers (formerly) of the United States? This is something very difficult to imagine, because if you *do* imagine it you will see that you would have felt *morally* bound to do the same.[104]

Contrasting the Kuomintang's record of arrest, torture and assassination with the "new possibility of pride" for China under the Communists, he describes the fear and resentment that the United States' support for Chiang Kai-shek aroused. To illustrate the point, Richards adopts the voice of his "personal Chinese friends in Peking"— the "voice of the articulate (ex-liberal, ex-friend of the U.S.), now ardent fellow-traveller" of the Communists in China. "'Suppose in 1776,' they used to say, 'when you were getting on with your own revolution, some outside power, Spain say, had come in, picked up the red-coats, and put them down re-equipped and re-trained, again and again, just where they could most embarrass General Washington. What would you have felt about that power?'" Richards answers the question with a firm Chinese condemnation of America's Far Eastern designs:

> We need to have our revolution . . . and we are pretty sure—in spite of all your Voice of America talk and U.N. pretences and the rest—that what you really want to do is to reestablish conditions under which you can make money out of China. We have heard your businessmen talking about Formosa becoming a bigger and safer Hong Kong, and about 're-activating the Civil War'. Can you blame us if we don't trust you? We have not heard a single one of your public leaders talk as if he were trying at all to imagine how we are thinking in China.[105]

In *Mencius on the Mind*, Richards argued for the possibility of comprehending a foreign intellectual tradition with his theory of Multiple Definition: the habit of imagining communicative intentions and expectations other than our own for the purpose of understanding a culture, as far as possible, within its own terms. In his lectures and speeches opposing the Korean War, he applies the same theory to international diplomacy; imagining American policy from a Chinese perspective is the first step to resolving the crisis. His response to the war points to the more difficult political realities that Richards was forced to confront as the British empire ceded precedence to the

American. "Ideas have power," he wrote in a letter of 1951, "if actions are made at all to correspond."[106] The American intervention in Korea, however, suggested that ideas—including Basic English—depended upon interests and powers quite different from any Richards was ready to approve. But if his outrage at American policy was in part due to this realization, his solution points to the consistency of his linguistic and political ideas. The ideological divisions that led to the conflict with China, like the nationalist hostilities of the First World War, were for Richards the product of ideas rather than economic, political or philosophical realities. Ideas, in turn, are instrumental: human artifacts, like the language that transmits them, to be shaped to human purposes and ends. The error of war—to Richards's mind inconceivable as a desired end—is no different in kind than the failure to construe a passage from Mencius. In both cases, error stems from the inability to recognize ideas as instruments, and so to grasp the purposes underlying them. Seeing the war with a sympathy for Chinese purposes would circumvent the propaganda and almost willful misunderstanding that Richards felt to be at the heart of the conflict. What he felt was most needed was a shift in perspective, an ability to see oneself through the adversary's eyes. The empires of the future were those of the mind because it was through this mental exercise—a global habit of Multiple Definition—that world problems were to be resolved. His political theory was thus a logical extension of his literary ideas since *The Meaning of Meaning*. The Korean War, involving the threat of atomic annihilation, was to Richards a vast example of the dangers involved when ideas are mistaken for ends rather than means: when the empires of the mind harden into less flexible realities.

Ultimately, the situation in Korea did not escalate into the atomic war that Richards feared. After Truman's dismissal of MacArthur in April 1951 for threatening to launch attacks within China, fighting continued in the region of the thirty-eighth parallel for another two years, culminating in the truce of July 1953. But in terms of the change in Chinese-Western relations, the conflict was every bit as devastating as Richards had imagined. By the war's end the vast majority of Westerners remaining in China were expelled; Bob Winter was the only one of the Richardses' friends to remain in Peking after 1951. The war in Korea also intensified political tensions that signaled the end of the Basic movement internationally. Though Richards continued his research into language-teaching techniques at Harvard for another twenty years, Basic no longer absorbed as much of his attention. According to John Paul Russo, the years 1951–52 marked "something close to a crisis" in Richards's career as he struggled with the decision to pursue Basic or return to issues of philosophy.[107] Without officially abandoning the Basic cause, he gradually shifted his interest to other areas. Basic English had been conceived in the mixed spirit of anger and optimism at Cambridge following the First World War. By the 1950's, it had come to seem a product of its time. In one sense, Basic had outgrown its purpose. Designed in part with the intention of helping countries like China to modernize and thus free themselves from a history of colonial dependence, Basic seemed less urgent as that independence came to be realized in the decades of decolonization. While the Chinese were far from completing the process of modernization, the Communist revolution signaled an intention to pursue it by other means. Richards would not have a chance to see the results for nearly thirty years.

8 ☞ Conclusion

In April 1979 Richards made his sixth, and final, trip to China at the age of eighty-six. In the wake of the Cultural Revolution, and after nearly thirty years of virtual isolation from the West, the People's Republic was beginning to extend a cautious welcome to foreign visitors. Signs of the thaw had become apparent to Richards in the previous year, when Chou Pei-yuan, president of Peking University, sent a present "as a token—and only as a token—of our gratitude" for his contributions to the school.[1] Shortly thereafter, he received word of a delegation of American teacher-training experts scheduled to visit Peking Normal University in the spring. Due to uncertain health, by March 1979 it seemed unlikely that Richards would be able to join the group. But a sudden improvement in his condition at the beginning of April prompted him to accept the invitation of a two-month national lecture tour across China. On May 3, 1979, he arrived in Peking for the first time since 1950.

The following day he witnessed celebrations for the sixtieth anniversary of the May Fourth Movement in China, commemorating the demonstrations against the signing of the Versailles Treaty in 1919. The occasion seemed an appropriate symbol of the hopes and frustrations that had formed the context of Richards's work in the country over the last fifty years. Later that day he met with Bob Winter, now ninety-three and "bubbling over with his pride of health and longevity," who was living at Peking University after enduring several difficult years during the Cultural Revolution.[2] Within three days of his arrival, however, Richards began to feel ill: weak and sleeping heavily for several hours a day, on May 6 he was taken to the Peking Union Medical College Hospital—the legacy of the Rockefeller Foundation—for treatment. Doctors there diagnosed him with a mild case of flu, and by the 9th he felt well enough to begin his tour. Three days later Richards flew to Kweilin, in southern China, where he delivered a lecture on language-teaching techniques to an assembly of two hundred teachers. A similar talk in Hanchow on the 19th drew a crowd of over seven hundred, with a majority watching from monitors in the classrooms due to the audience overflow.[3] After further lectures in Shanghai, Richards began to show symptoms of the dropsy that he had been diagnosed with in Cambridge. After five days in the hospital at Tsinan, he insisted on resuming his lecture schedule with a talk at Shantung University on the 29th. There, after "the most concentrated hour of ceaseless photography from all angles," he gave a talk on the politically sensitive topic of Plato's decidedly un-Marxist dialogues. His hosts were apparently unoffended, and the university president entertained him privately at his flat.[4] In over two weeks of lecturing, Richards was greeted at the Chinese universities with an impressive display of courtesy, attentiveness and the deep respect accorded to a visiting dignitary.

On June 5, while waiting in Tsingtao for a train to Peking, Richards suffered a collapse that left him delirious and incoherent. He was taken once again to the Peking Union Medical College Hospital for treatment, where doctors diagnosed the trouble as an after-effect of the dropsy treatment in Tsinan. His remaining lectures were canceled and doctors committed him to close observation. When his condition failed to improve after several weeks, it was decided that he be returned to England for further treatment. After a visit from Gong Wei of the Foreign Affairs Department at the Ministry of Education, who assured Dorothea of "how much they owed to Ivor over the years,"[5] he was flown to England accompanied by a Chinese doctor, nurse and interpreter, paid for by the Chinese as "a tribute for all IAR has done in the past."[6] Seven weeks after his return, still incoherent and weakened by pneumonia, Richards died on September 7, 1979, three months after his initial collapse in Tsingtao. The trip to China had been, literally, the final undertaking of his life.

Over a span of fifty years, Richards had devoted a significant portion of his thought and career to improving education in China. From his visiting professorship at Tsing Hua in 1929 to his work on behalf of Basic English culminating in the lectures of 1979, he consistently regarded China as the most opportune place to put his ideas about language, communication and peace into action. During that time, his project engaged some of the most important historical changes of the century: the transformation of China from an imperial dependency to an autonomous world power; the eclipse of Britain by the United States as the major influence in global affairs; the bifurcation of world politics following the Second World War; the dismantling of the former European empires and the concomitant rise of English as the century's *lingua franca*. Richards's experience in China is historically significant for reflecting these developments, and its interpretation involves several contemporary questions about the nexus of culture, language and power. Was Basic English in fact the means to international communication and world peace that Richards envisioned? Or was his project, rooted in the values and concerns of interwar Cambridge, essentially a product of its time, providing insight into a particular moment in Britain's cultural history? Or, finally, was the Basic experiment in China a subtle but powerful act of imperialism? Did Basic English, with its assumptions about rationality and the superiority of Western science, participate in that system of cultural production—mapping, naming, institution-building and narrative fashioning—that Edward Said identifies as "a Western style for dominating, restructuring and having authority over" foreign cultures?[7] In short, how does Richards's encounter with China add to our understanding of the relationship between culture and imperialism?

In approaching these questions, it is important to appreciate the ways in which the imperial situation was complicated and transformed over the course of Richards's career. From the coercive intervention and direct appropriation of resources characteristic of the nineteenth-century European empires, the imperial relationship has shifted increasingly to a less explicit—if equally contested—struggle for linguistic, political and cultural influence in former colonial territories. In recognizing the connections between language and the cultural assumptions it carries, and in applying these insights systematically in China, Richards was one of the first to consider the implications of this shift. If Basic English was in fact a part of the imperial process, a means of ordering and controlling knowledge to suit Western purposes, the territory at stake had become one of language as much as land, moving beyond national borders to involve the circulation of ideas and information—an "empire of the mind." The significance of Richards's project in China lies in the questions it raises about our understanding of this development.

It was Winston Churchill who first characterized the "empires of the future [as] the empires of the mind" in his Harvard speech of 1943. As Churchill understood the phrase, the "empires of the future" were those in which the English-speaking peoples would preserve their former imperial privileges through the advantage of a dominant world language. Significantly, he recognized Basic English as a potential instrument in this process. If Richards's own aspirations for Basic were not as explicitly political as Churchill's, he certainly attributed a similar importance to the global dissemination of English. In a 1968 interview with B. A. Boucher and John Paul Russo, Richards described his intentions for Basic as follows:

> I think we have a better way of teaching English, but while you're teaching beginning English, you might as well teach everything else. That is to say, a world position, what's needed for living, a philosophy of religion, how to find things out, and the whole works—mental and moral seed for the planet. In this way the two-thirds of the planet that doesn't yet know how to read and write would learn in learning how to read and write English, the things that would help them in their answers to 'Where should man go?'[8]

That the "mental and moral seed of the planet" should emanate from the English language, and that it should provide information for two-thirds of the planet on "what's needed for living" are assumptions that share many affinities with Churchill's. In both cases, the superiority of English and the values it carries are taken for granted. It is something that others need; teaching English is a means for teaching "a world position" that is assumed to have an inherent value for the rest of the planet. In this respect Richards's expectations for Basic mirror Churchill's hopes for an Anglo-American world order. The recent understanding of empire as a system of knowledge—a constellation of institutions, assumptions and cultural practices that enable the exercise of authority—would therefore seem to embrace his work in China as a prop to the values underpinning the imperial enterprise. Seen in this light, Basic appears as an assertion of Western superiority aimed at framing world problems in the language of the colonizer.

But this interpretation neglects some important differences that set Richards's efforts apart from Churchill's imperial ambitions. Basic English was, of course, a product of its particular time and place. It was informed by conceptions of rationality, freedom, progress and subjectivity that bear the marks of Richards's own cultural tradition.

And a salient feature of that tradition was a history of imperial rule. The fact that Richards was invited to teach at a Chinese university, that the Chinese were interested in adopting English and that institutions like the Rockefeller Foundation were willing to fund his plans all depended in various ways upon the legacy of empire. But to label Richards's project "imperialist" because of these circumstances misses some of the complexities of his experience in China. Richards's interest in Basic stemmed from a disappointment with developments in the West. Grounded in a profound distrust of the nationalist ambitions and divisions that had led to the First World War, Basic was not intended to elevate an inferior race but rather to preserve the Chinese from the excesses of Western "progress." For Richards, a Basic success in China meant the beginning of remedial processes equally necessary in the West, leading ultimately to a situation in which divisions such as East and West, like those of Communist and capitalist, would be recognized as products of language rather than fixed realities. This helps to explain Richards's disagreement with T. S. Eliot on the value of studying a foreign tradition, his insistence on the need for communication between China and the West, his sympathy for Communist China and his cynicism about the rhetoric of the Cold War—all of which distinguish his project in important ways from a simple assumption of Western superiority. If Richards was not entirely free from the presuppositions of his culture, it is important nevertheless to make a distinction between his notion of an "empire of the mind" and those of pro-imperial advocates such as Churchill. Without a sensitivity to Richards's particular motivations and intentions, we run the risk of blurring a complex process of cultural interaction by reducing individuals to the social codes that inform them.

This is not to deny that Richards's interpretation of China was governed to a large extent by his critical concerns. In this sense his idea of the East was another kind of "empire of the mind"—a product of his own intellectual interests and preoccupations. Richards's key ideas about the nature of language, interpretation and modernization were developed largely in the Twenties, in the particular context of interwar Cambridge. His sense of the challenges and remedies for a modernizing nation like China took form primarily from his literary ideas and from those values informing the Chinese affections of intellectuals like Goldsworthy Lowes Dickinson and Bertrand Russell. During the Japanese invasion, Richards's optimism about China's future had more to do with his faith in the efficacy of Basic than with the political realities of the war. Similarly, his enthusiasm for the Communist victory in 1950 was as much an expression of his frustration at postwar global developments as it was an endorsement of the changes underway in China. In each case, Richards's picture of China conformed to convictions developed earlier in the course of his pedagogical career. The very fact that he conceived of Basic in global terms, equally applicable to China, Latin America or the United States, underscores his tendency to see world problems in terms of a unified, and to some degree myopic, intellectual scheme.

But to assume that Richards's East was entirely a creation of his critical agenda is to overlook the historical context of his enterprise. Richards arrived in China at a time when many Chinese were seeking solutions to their country's social and economic concerns by appropriating Western theories, institutions and scientific methods. A century of imperial interference, both from the Western nations and increasingly from Japan, had resulted in a generation of Chinese men and women willing to learn from the modern West in the interests of freeing their country from foreign dependence. The existence of a national university like Tsing Hua, where Richards first taught in 1929 and where he made most of his important academic friendships, was both a product of this Westernizing impulse and a gesture of resistance against imperial domination. Given this context, Richards's efforts to teach English were regarded by many as a means of defying the legacy of empire and a step toward Chinese autonomy. This helps to explain the success of the Orthological Institute in the Thirties, the Nationalist government's willingness to adopt Basic in the middle school curriculum, and the general respect that Richards continued to receive in Chinese academic circles throughout his career. Richards's understanding of China was by no means disinterested, but neither was it merely an imposition of his own categories and assumptions upon a silent, passively figured Orient. Rather, his program dovetailed with Chinese interests and purposes at a moment when Western models were being seriously considered as a means to national independence. His belief in the value of English for making Western thought accessible to the Chinese was largely confirmed by the response he met with from those academics, students and government officials he encountered through his work with the Orthological Institute. In short, Richards's notion of China was not so much imagined as negotiated, relying on a complex interplay between Chinese aspirations and Richards's decidedly Cantabridgian ideals at a unique moment in the history of China's relations with the West. Although firmly rooted in the values and assumptions of his culture, Richards's enterprise in China must be seen as part of a wider historical context that includes the interests and designs of the Chinese as well.

Finally, for Richards the "empires of the mind" carried another meaning as well: the primacy of ideas in shaping perception. Since *The Meaning of Meaning*, his 1923 "study of the influence of language upon thought," Richards had argued for the active, constituent role that language plays in determining our picture of reality. He regarded words not as transparent markers of the things they signify, but as the bearers of complex (and often questionable) philosophical propositions. For Richards, the meaning of a word was not to be found by determining its most precise definition, as his teacher G. E. Moore had insisted, but by disclosing the communicative intention it carried through a full consideration of its overall context—be it poem, novel, philosophical statement or political propaganda. The problem, he argued, is not that words are used imprecisely, but that the same words are used to say a variety of things. The first step to eliminating misunderstanding, then, is to determine the manner in which a speaker is using words to communicate his or her ideas. This process of discerning the intended context, aided by techniques such as Multiple Definition, was one that for Richards applied equally to literary and international affairs. Just as the conflict between Poetry and Science disappears when we understand the different emotive and symbolic intentions behind these two distinct uses of language, Richards believed that global conflict could be avoided by a clearer appreciation of the contending parties' objectives.

In part, Richards's confidence in the power of communication was governed by a Benthamite faith in rationality; understanding is ultimately possible across different times and cultures because human motives are relatively stable. But his view of language had a more radical dimension as well. What he believed communication required was not simply a common language but a common *attitude* toward language, one in which words are regarded as instrumental rather than descriptive. Categories of thought such as East and West, or self and other (as in his discussion of *Hsing* in *Mencius on the Mind*) are the result of certain linguistic habits, which over time are mistaken for natural phenomena—the pernicious "Word Magic" familiar from *The Meaning of Meaning*. Richards's critical work was aimed at regaining control of these meanings by revealing language as an instrument of human aims and purposes. One intention of Basic English was to throw speakers back upon a limited vocabulary in which habitual terms and distinctions were not available, thus forcing them to examine the linguistic categories that shape their assumptions about the world. In this respect, Richards's approach to language has strong affinities with that of contemporary historians who subscribe to the "linguistic turn," maintaining that a society's "truths" are the product of a larger constellation of cultural discourses—produced by certain institutional and social patterns—that determine what is classified as knowledge. Richards's work in China was actuated by a similar assertion: namely, that the Chinese would not be able to make use of Western ideas until they grasped the implied contexts that gave them meaning. To teach the English language was therefore to teach the cultural codes underpinning Western philosophy, science and literature. By mastering these systems of knowledge (or "speculative instruments," to use a more Richardsian term), China could stake an equal claim in the burgeoning empires of the mind.

But Richards's program of "linguistic engineering" failed to take into account those factors that limit control over language and thought. Throughout his literary and Basic writings, Richards advocated a rational understanding of how language operates as a way of directing and controlling meaning. Convinced of the malleability of our linguistic and intellectual categories, he neglected the complex of historical, economic, political and institutional factors that give them shape. Here Richards differs radically from scholars of the "linguistic turn," who are much more sensitive to the institutions, power relations and techniques of social control that produce culturally sanctioned ideas and meanings. Richards, who dismissed history as an undergraduate because he "didn't think [it] ought to have happened," was reluctant to acknowledge those social and political realities that interfered with his transnational plans for Basic.[9] As a consequence, he tended to underestimate many of the challenges that Basic faced in China—the continuing dependence upon funding from the Rockefeller Foundation, the lack of adequate institutional support from the Chinese, the severe disruption of the Japanese invasion and the subsequent Communist victory, and the growing demonization of English for ideological purposes during the Cold War.

Although Richards gradually acknowledged the failure of Basic due to political developments outside of his control, he never surrendered his belief in the power of ideas to effect change independently of their specific social, institutional and cultural contexts. But as Churchill's speech at Harvard illustrated, the possibilities for English as a world language were subject to purposes quite different than those Richards himself had envisioned. Through the work of institutions like the British Broadcasting Corporation and the British Council, English was to become an important tool for maintaining Britain's cultural influence in regions of the former empire and elsewhere. Part of Richards's story, then, is a failure to account for the broader network of ambitions and interests that interfered with his more benign conception of an "empire of the mind."

In conclusion, Richards's period in China involves some of the major issues of the late-twentieth century—the relationship between language and power, the impact of culture upon perception, the changed nature of imperial practices in a postcolonial world, and the rise of a transnational global economy whose currency is increasingly information and ideas. Edward Said concludes his recent study, *Culture and Imperialism*, with the following observation:

> [Just] as human beings make their own history, they also make their cultures and ethnic identities. No one can deny the persisting continuities of long traditions, sustained habitations, national languages, and cultural geographies, but there seems no reason except fear and prejudice to keep insisting on their separation and distinctiveness, as if that was all human life was about. . . . It is more rewarding—and more difficult—to think concretely and sympathetically, contrapuntally, about others than only about 'us.' But this also means not trying to rule others, not trying to classify them or put them in hierarchies, above all, not constantly reiterating how 'our' culture or country is number one (or *not* number one, for that matter). For the intellectual there is quite enough of value to do without *that*.[10]

It is a sentiment that Richards would have entirely endorsed. His career exemplifies the qualities of sympathetic engagement and critical acumen that underpin the more theoretical agenda of postcolonial scholars like Said. His ideal, like Said's, was one in which all hierarchies of classifications would be subject to analysis in terms of the human needs and purposes they serve. In trying to put that ideal into practice, Richards grappled with questions of communication, modernization and cultural exchange in a post-imperial context that are still acutely relevant today. Though his answers were sometimes different from our own, his experience in China should be understood as a part of the ongoing interrogation of linguistic, national and ethnic identities that characterizes our shift to an increasingly global perspective. We can only hope that the empires of the future turn out to be as humane as Richards envisioned.

Reference Matter

☙ Notes

The following abbreviations are used in the notes:

RCMC   Richards Collection, Magdalene College, Cambridge
RFA   Rockefeller Foundation Archives, Rockefeller Archive Center, North
         Tarrytown, New York

Chapter 1: Introduction

1. See D. L. LeMahieu *A Culture for Democracy: Mass Communication and the Cultivated Mind in Britain Between the Wars* (Oxford: Clarendon Press, 1988) for a further discussion of these issues.

2. Dudley Young, quoted in Elmer Borklund *Contemporary Literary Critics* (London: St. James Press, 1977), 440.

3. John Paul Russo *I. A. Richards: His Life and Work* (Baltimore: Johns Hopkins, 1989), 397–430.

4. *Selected Letters of I. A. Richards*, ed. John Constable (Oxford: Clarendon Press, 1990).

5. Jonathan D. Spence *The Gate of Heavenly Peace: The Chinese and Their Revolution, 1895–1980* (New York: The Viking Press, 1981) gives an excellent account of these developments.

6. I. A. Richards to Frank Salter, transcribed under diary entry for June 28, 1950. RCMC.

7. Russo *I. A. Richards*, 429.

8. Edward Said *Orientalism* (New York: Vintage Books, 1979), 254.

9. Edward Said *Culture and Imperialism* (New York: Vintage Books, 1993), 11.

10. Ibid., xiii.

11. Said *Orientalism*, 3.

12. Said *Culture and Imperialism*, 15.

13. Ibid., 50.

14. See "By bread alone: Signs of violence in the mid-nineteenth century" in Homi K. Bhabha *The Location of Culture* (London: Routledge, 1994).

15. The recent AHR Forum in *The American Historical Review* 99: 4 (Dec. 1994) provides a useful discussion of Subaltern Studies. See also the article "Subaltern Studies: Deconstructing Historiography" reprinted in Gayatri Spivak *In Other Worlds: Essays in Cultural Politics* (New York: Methuen, 1987).

16. Said *Orientalism*, 3.

17. Said *Culture and Imperialism*, 15.

18. See, for example, "Signs Taken for Wonders: Questions of Ambivalence and Authority under a Tree Outside Delhi, May 1817" in Bhabha *The Location of Culture*, 102.

19. Said *Orientalism*, 11.

20. Jonathan Spence's *The Gates of Heavenly Peace: The Chinese and their Revolution, 1895 to 1980* (New York: The Viking Press, 1981) and John Israel's *Lianda: A Chinese University in War and Revolution* (Stanford: Stanford University Press, 1998) along with his *Student Nationalism in China, 1927–1937* (Stanford: Stanford University Press, 1966) are just a few of the studies which deal with the historical context from Chinese points of view.

21. See Victor Purcell's *Chinese Evergreen* (London: M. Joseph Ltd., 1938), discussed in Chapter 6.

Chapter 2: The Cambridge Background

1. Christopher Isherwood *Lions and Shadows: An Education in the Twenties* (London: Hogarth Press, 1938), 75.

2. See, for instance, discussions of Richards's work in Raymond Williams *Culture and Society, 1780–1950* (New York: Harper and Row, 1958); Terry Eagleton *Literary Criticism: An Introduction* (Oxford: Basil Blackwell, 1983); Pamela McCallum *Literature and Method: Towards a Critique of I. A. Richards, T. S. Eliot and F. R. Leavis* (Dublin: Gill and Macmillan, 1983); D. L. LeMahieu *A Culture for Democracy: Mass Communication and the Cultivated Mind in Britain Between the Wars* (Oxford: Clarendon Press, 1988). The most extensive critique of Richards's work is to be found in W. H. N. Hotoph *Language, Thought and Comprehension: A Case Study of the Writings of I. A. Richards* (London: Routledge and Kegan Paul, 1965).

3. Jonathan Culler "Odd but Optimistic" (a review of John Paul Russo's *I. A. Richards: His Life and Work*), Times Literary Supplement, Mar. 9–15, 1990.

4. John Paul Russo *I. A. Richards*, 22.

5. McCallum *Literature and Method*, 1.

6. Stephen Heath "I. A. Richards, F. R. Leavis and Cambridge English," in *Cambridge Minds*, ed. Richard Mason (Cambridge: Cambridge University Press, 1994), 26.

7. See Eco's Introduction to C. K. Ogden and I. A. Richards *The Meaning of Meaning* (1923; reprinted by Harcourt, Brace Jovanovich, Inc., 1989), ix.

8. Ibid., 10.

9. Ibid., 149.

10. Ibid., 153.

11. "An Interview" in I. A. Richards *Complementarities: Uncollected Essays*, ed. John Paul Russo (Cambridge: Harvard University Press, 1976), 257.

12. I. A. Richards *Principles of Literary Criticism* (New York: Harcourt, Brace and World, 1924), 26.

13. Ibid., 248.

14. Ibid., 78.

15. I. A. Richards *Practical Criticism: A Study of Literary Judgement* (1929; reprinted New York: Harcourt, Brace and Company, 1929), 10.

16. Ibid., 4.

17. I. A. Richards *Principles of Literary Criticism*, 17.

18. Ibid., 57.

19. For a fuller discussion of Sherrington's influence on Richards's work, see Russo *I. A. Richards*, 177–201.

20. Richards *Principles of Literary Criticism*, 98.

21. Ibid., 237–38.

22. I. A. Richards *Science and Poetry* (London: Kegan Paul, Trench, Trubner, 1926), 33.

23. Ibid., 43.

24. Richards *Practical Criticism*, 269.

25. Richards *Complementarities*, 259.

26. T. E. B. Howarth *Cambridge Between Two Wars* (London: Collins, 1978), 20.

27. Richards *Complementarities*, 257.

28. Ibid., 257.

29. For accounts of the development of English studies at Cambridge see E. M. W. Tillyard *The Muse Unchained: An Intimate Account of the Revolution in English Studies at Cambridge* (London: Bowes and Bowes, 1958); Basil Willey *Cambridge and Other Memories, 1920–1953* (London: Chatto and Windus, 1968); Joan Bennett "How It Strikes a Contemporary: the Impact of I. A. Richards's Literary Criticism in Cambridge, England" in *I. A. Richards: Essays in His Honor*, ed. Reuben Brower, Helen Vendler and John Hollander (New York: Oxford University Press, 1973), 45–59.

30. For more on Quiller-Couch, see A. L. Rowse *Quiller-Couch: A Portrait of 'Q'* (London: Methuen, 1988).

31. Quoted in Tillyard *The Muse Unchained*, 40.

32. Ibid., 48.

33. Ibid., 59.

34. Ibid., 88.

35. Quoted in Howarth *Cambridge Between Two Wars*, 70.

36. Richards *Complementarities*, 257.

37. Tillyard *The Muse Unchained*, 21.

38. "I. A. Richards Interviewed by Reuben Brower" in Brower, Vendler, Hollander *I. A. Richards: Essays in His Honor*, 19.

39. Ogden and Richards *The Meaning of Meaning*, 17.

40. Ibid., 29.

41. Richards *Science and Poetry*, 3.

42. Richards *Principles of Literary Criticism*, 57.

43. Richards *Science and Poetry*, 35.

44. Richards *Principles of Literary Criticism*, 36.

45. Ibid., 230.

46. Ibid., 231.

47. Richards *Practical Criticism*, 301.

48. Ibid., 319.

49. Russo *I. A. Richards*, 91.

50. Isherwood *Lions and Shadows*, 75.

51. Richards *Science and Poetry*, 6.

52. Ogden and Richards *The Meaning of Meaning*, 150.

53. Ibid., 125.

54. Ibid., 153.

55. Richards *Principles of Literary Criticism*, 17.

56. Richards *Science and Poetry*, 15–16.

57. Ibid., 49.

58. Ibid., 52.

59. Ibid., 59.

60. Ibid., 56.

61. Ibid., 61.

62. Ibid., 59.

63. Ibid., 82.

64. See E. M. Forster *Goldsworthy Lowes Dickinson* (London: Chatto and Windus, 1934).

65. "Beginnings and Transitions: I. A. Richards Interviewed by Reuben Brower" in Brower, Vendler, Hollander *I. A. Richards: Essays in His Honor*, 31.

66. Quoted in Forster *Goldsworthy Lowes Dickinson*, 148–49.

67. Goldsworthy Lowes Dickinson *Letters from John Chinaman* (1901; reprinted as *Letters from a High Chinese Official* Tucson: Omen Press, 1972), 14.

68. Ibid., 25.

69. Ibid., 15.

70. Ibid., 47.

71. Ibid., 65.

72. Ibid., 68.

73. Ibid., 75.

74. Ibid., 21.

75. Ibid., 42.

76. Ibid., 45.

77. Ibid., 38.

78. Ibid., 78.

79. Jonathan Spence *The Gate of Heavenly Peace: The Chinese and Their Revolution, 1895–1980* (New York: The Viking Press, 1981), 136.

80. Caroline Moorehead *Bertrand Russell: A Life* (London: Sinclair-Stevenson, 1992), 325–26.

81. Quoted in Ray Monk *Bertrand Russell: The Spirit of Solitude, 1872–1921* (New York: The Free Press, 1996), 591.

82. Spence *The Gate of Heavenly Peace*, 179.

83. Bertrand Russell *The Problem of China* (London: George Allen and Unwin, 1922), 10.

84. Ibid., 17.

85. Ibid., 12.

86. Ibid., 17.

87. Ibid., 10.

88. Ibid., 12.

89. Ibid., 198.

90. Ibid., 13.

91. Ibid., 213.

92. Ibid., 31.

93. Ibid., 12.

94. Ibid., 51–52.

95. Ibid., 14.

96. Ibid., 194.

97. Ibid., 13.

98. Ibid., 198.

99. Ibid., 252.

100. Ibid., 250.

Chapter 3: A Moment in Paradise

1. Bertrand Russell *The Problem of China* (London: Allen and Unwin, 1922), 217–18.

2. Richards diary, Jan. 16, 1929. RCMC.

3. Ibid., Nov. 27, 1929.

4. For a fuller discussion of this process, see Jonathan D. Spence *The Gate of Heavenly Peace: The Chinese and Their Revolution, 1895–1980* (New York: The Viking Press, 1981).

5. Jonathan Spence *The Search for Modern China* (New York: W. W. Norton, 1990), 312.

6. Ibid., 231–35.

7. Richards diary, Dec. 9, 1928. RCMC.

8. Christopher Isherwood *Lions and Shadows: An Education in the Twenties* (London: Hogarth Press, 1938), 74.

9. William Empson "The Hammer's Ring," in *I. A. Richards: Essays in His Honor*, ed. Reuben Brower, Helen Vendler and John Hollander (New York: Oxford University Press, 1973), 73.

10. Richards diary, Oct. 16, 1927. RCMC.

11. Ibid., Feb. 8, 1928.

12. Ibid., Oct. 15, 1931.

13. John Paul Russo *I. A. Richards: His Life and Work* (Johns Hopkins University Press: 1989), 89.

14. Richards diary, Dec. 1, 1927. RCMC.

15. I. A. Richards *Practical Criticism: A Study of Literary Judgement* (New York: Harcourt, Brace and Company, 1929), 296.

16. Richards diary, Nov. 13, 1928. RCMC.

17. Russo *I. A. Richards*, 89.

18. Arthur Pollard-Urquhart to I. A. Richards, transcribed under diary entry for Jan. 16, 1929. RCMC.

19. Ibid.

20. Richards diary, Oct. 5, 1926.

21. Dorothea Richards to John Pilley, transcribed under diary entry for May 14, 1927.

22. Richards diary, Sept. 29, 1929.

23. Ibid.

24. Ibid.

25. Richards to Piccoli, undated, transcribed in back of diary volume for 1929.

26. Richards diary, Nov. 13, 1929.

27. Richards to Piccoli, undated, transcribed in back of diary volume for 1929.

28. Richards diary, Sept. 15, 1929.

29. Ibid., Sept. 17, 1929.

30. Ibid., Sept. 20, 1929.

31. Ibid., Sept. 29, 1929.

32. Ibid.

33. Ibid., Oct. 29, 1929.

34. Ibid., Sept. 29, 1929.

35. Ibid., Sept. 16, 1929.

36. Ibid.

37. Ibid., Nov. 14, 1929.

38. Ibid., Sept. 15, 1929.

39. Ibid., Oct. 22, 1929.

40. Ibid., Sept. 22, 1929.

41. Ibid.

42. Ibid., undated, transcribed in back of diary volume for 1929.

43. Keh Kung-chao would later go on to an illustrious career first at the Chinese Ministry of Information, where he served both in Singapore and in London, and later as Minister of Foreign Affairs for the Nationalist Government and adviser to President Chiang Kai-shek in Taiwan.

44. Ibid., Nov. 14, 1929.

45. Ibid., Sept. 15, 1929.

46. Ibid., Sept. 20, 1929.

47. Ibid., Oct. 18, 1929.

48. Richards to William Empson, transcribed under diary entry for Nov. 8, 1929.

49. Richards diary, Nov. 26, 1929.

50. Russo *I. A. Richards*, 406.

51. Richards to Empson, diary entry for Nov. 8, 1929. RCMC.

52. Richards diary, Nov. 30, 1929.

53. Ibid., Sept. 29, 1929.
54. Ibid.
55. Ibid., Nov. 14, 1929.
56. Richards to Empson, diary entry for Nov. 8, 1929.
57. Richards diary, Oct. 11, 1929. RCMC.
58. Ibid., Nov. 30, 1929.
59. Ibid., Sept. 20, 1929.
60. Ibid., Sept. 29, 1929.
61. Ibid., Nov. 14, 1929.
62. Ibid., Nov. 27, 1929.
63. Ibid., Dec. 15, 1929.
64. Ibid., Sept. 19, 1929.
65. Ibid., Oct. 20, 1929.
66. Ibid., Oct. 10, 1929.
67. Ibid., Oct. 23, 1929.
68. Ibid., Nov. 6, 1929.
69. Ibid., Oct. 26, 1929.
70. Richards to F. R. Leavis, transcribed under diary entry for Apr. 16, 1930.
71. Richards diary, Mar. 25, 1930.
72. Ibid., May 7, 1930.
73. Ibid., Apr. 26, 1930.
74. Ibid., June 10, 1930.
75. Ibid., Feb. 27, 1930.
76. Ibid., June 10, 1930.
77. Ibid., Feb. 28, 1930.
78. Ibid., undated and transcribed in back of diary volume for 1930.
79. Richards to T. S. Eliot, transcribed under diary entry for Apr. 23, 1930.
80. Richards diary, undated, transcribed in back of diary volume for 1930.
81. Ibid., May 27, 1930.
82. Ibid.
83. Ibid., Feb. 27, 1930.
84. Richards diary, July 23, 1930.

Chapter 4: Both Sides of the Looking-Glass

1. Notes for remarks at Eliot House, May 12, 1958. RCMC.
2. T. S. Eliot to Richards, Aug. 9, 1930. RCMC.
3. I. A. Richards *Mencius on the Mind: Experiments in Multiple Definition* (London: Kegan Paul, Trench, Trubner, 1932), 9.
4. Ibid.
5. Ibid., xii.
6. Ibid., xi.
7. John Paul Russo *I. A. Richards: His Life and Work* (Baltimore: Johns Hopkins University Press, 1989), 406.
8. Richards *Mencius*, xiii.

9. Ibid., 9.

10. Ibid., xii.

11. Ibid., 1.

12. Ibid., xiv.

13. Edward W. Said *Orientalism* (New York: Vintage Books, 1979), 254.

14. Richards *Mencius*, 1.

15. Ibid., 5.

16. Ibid., 4.

17. See Chapter 2, above.

18. Richards *Mencius*, 7.

19. Ibid., 7.

20. Ibid., 8. Italics mine.

21. Ibid., 82.

22. Ibid., 85.

23. Ibid., 87.

24. Ibid., 92.

25. Ibid., 90.

26. Ibid., 92.

27. See Chapter 2 above.

28. Richards *Mencius*, 91.

29. Ibid., 91.

30. Ibid., 92.

31. Ibid., 93.

32. Ibid., 93.

33. Ibid., 93.

34. Russo *I. A. Richards*, 412.

35. "Beginnings and Transitions: I. A. Richards Interviewed by Reuben Brower" in *I. A. Richards: Essays in His Honor*, ed. Reuben Brower, Helen Vendler and John Hollander (New York: Oxford University Press, 1973), 19.

36. Ibid., 22.

37. Russo *I. A. Richards*, 88.

38. "I. A. Richards Interviewed" in Brower, Vendler, Hollander *I. A. Richards: Essays in His Honor*, 34.

39. C. K. Ogden *Basic English: A General Introduction with Rules and Grammar* (London: Kegan Paul, Trench, Trubner & Co., 1932), 9.

40. Ibid., 9.

41. Ibid., 10.

42. Ibid., 14.

43. Ibid., 9.

44. Russo *I. A. Richards*, 768 (footnote 4)

45. C. K. Ogden *Basic English: International Second Language* (New York: Harcourt, Brace & World, Inc., 1968), 119.

46. Ibid., 123.

47. Russo *I. A. Richards*, 400.

48. Ibid.

49. See, for example, I. A. Richards *English Self-Taught Through Pictures* (New York: Pocket Books, 1949) and *Nations and Peace* (New York: Simon and Shuster, 1947).

50. Russo *I. A. Richards*, 401.

51. Ibid., 362.

52. David H. Stevens to Richards, Sept. 19, 1932. RCMC.

53. Stevens to Richards, Jan. 20, 1933.

54. Ibid.

55. Jonathan D. Spence *The Search for Modern China* (New York: W. W. Norton & Co., 1990), 384.

56. RFA, R.G. 1.1, ser. 601, box 12, folder 129, item: "Report on Visit to China 6/9–30/31 by Selskar M. Gunn," 2.

57. Ibid.

58. Ibid.

59. Ibid.

60. Ibid.

61. Ibid., Jan. 13, 1934, 40.

62. Ibid., 21.

63. Ibid.

64. Ibid., 4.

65. Ibid., 1931 report, 7.

Chapter 5: The Orthological Institute of China, 1936

1. Richards diaries, Dec. 9, 1931. RCMC.

2. Ibid., July 1, 1932.

3. Ibid., Nov. 16, 1932.

4. Ibid., Sept. 8, 1932.

5. Ibid., Oct. 25, 1931.

6. Ibid., Nov. 18, 1932.

7. Ibid., Dec. 18, 1932.

8. Ibid., Dec. 5, 1931.

9. Ibid., Nov. 21, 1932.

10. Richards to Dorothea, Oct. 20, 1935. RCMC. Letters transcribed in the Richards diaries appear under the diary date at which they were entered.

11. I. A. Richards *Basic in Teaching: East and West* (London: Kegan Paul, Trench, Trubner & Co., 1935), 8.

12. Ibid., 16.

13. Ibid., 12.

14. Ibid., 15.

15. Ibid., 16.

16. Ibid., 15.

17. Ibid., 35.

18. Ibid., 70.

19. Ibid., 74.

20. Ibid., 64. Italics mine.

21. Ibid., 24.

22. Ibid., 23.

23. Ibid., 20.

24. Ibid., 25.

25. Ibid., 29.

26. Ibid., 30.

27. Ibid., 31.

28. Ibid., 40.

29. Ibid.

30. Ibid., 41.

31. Ibid., 32.

32. Ibid., 46–47.

33. Ibid., 20.

34. R. D. Jameson to Richards, Nov. 16, 1933. RCMC.

35. Ibid.

36. Ibid. Lin Yutang was also the author of *My Country and My People*, one of the most popular accounts of China in English; between Feb. 1936 and May 1942 it went through ten editions.

37. Ibid.

38. Ibid.

39. Jameson to Richards, Dec. 9, 1934.

40. Ibid.

41. Richards *Basic in Teaching*, 98.

42. Jameson to Richards, Dec. 9, 1934. RCMC.

43. Ibid.

44. Ibid.

45. Jameson to Ogden, Nov. 21, 1933.

46. Ibid.

47. Ibid.

48. Jameson to Richards, Aug. 22, 1934.

49. Gunn to Stevens, Mar. 8, 1935. RFA, R.G. 1.1, ser. 601, box 48, folder 397.

50. R. D. Jameson Note on the Present Position of Basic in China, Gunn to Stevens (attached), Mar. 8, 1935, box 48, folder 397.

51. Ibid.

52. Ibid.

53. Ibid.

54. Grant-in-aid, Jan. 16, 1936. RFA, box 48, folder 397.

55. Grant-in-aid, Feb. 28, 1936. RFA, box 48, folder 397.

56. Richards diaries, Feb. 23, 1936. RCMC.

57. Ibid., May 29, 1936.

58. Ibid., June 13, 1936.

59. Ibid., May 16, 1936.

60. Ibid., June 11, 1936.

61. Ibid., July 14, 1936.

62. Ibid., July 11, 1936.

63. Ibid., July 22, 1936.

64. The address was also Jameson's house. In September the Institute moved to more "commodious and quiet new offices" at 5 Sui An Po Hutung. (Richards diaries, Sept. 29, 1936. RCMC.)

65. In Jameson *Note on the Present Position of Basic in China*. Gunn to Stevens, RFA RG 1.1, ser. 601, box 48, folder 397.

66. Richards to Stevens, May 12, 1936. RFA, Box 48, folder 398.

67. Ibid.

68. Richards diary, July 22, 1936. RCMC.

69. Ibid., June 12, 1936.

70. Richards to Stevens, May 12, 1936. RFA, box 48, folder 398.

71. Richards diary, July 22, 1936. RCMC.

72. Richards to Stevens, July 21, 1936. RFA, box 48, folder 398.

73. Jameson to Grant, May 21, 1936. RFA, box 48, folder 398.

74. Richards to Stevens, July 2, 1936. RFA, box 48, folder 398.

75. Richards to Stevens, July 21, 1936. RFA, box 48, folder 398.

76. Jameson to Grant, May 21, 1936. RFA, box 48, folder 398.

77. Gunn to Stevens (attached), Sept. 28, 1936. RFA, box 48, folder 398.

78. Richards to Stevens, Aug. 17, 1936. RFA, box 48, folder 398.

79. Stevens to Jameson, Oct. 21, 1936. RFA, box 48, folder 398.

80. Jameson and Richards to Stevens, Nov. 20, 1936. RFA, box 48, folder 398.

81. Richards to Stevens, July 21, 1936. RFA, box 48, folder 398. Beginning in July, Tsing Hua placed Jameson on half salary due to his time spent with the Institute.

82. Richards to Stevens, Nov. 18, 1936. RFA, box 48, folder 398.

83. Richards diaries, Oct. 27, 1936. RCMC.

84. Ibid., Nov. 18, 1936.

85. Ibid., Dec. 3, 1936.

86. Ibid., Aug. 9, 1936.

87. Ibid., undated. In Memoranda, 1936.

88. Ibid., Dec. 2, 1936.

89. Ibid.

90. Gunn to Stevens, Dec. 10, 1936. RFA, box 48, folder 398.

91. Ibid.

92. Ministry of Education to Jameson, Dec. 3, 1936. RFA, box 48, folder 398.

93. Ibid.

94. Jameson to Gunn, Dec. 10, 1936. RFA, box 48, folder 398.

95. Ibid.

96. Richards diary, Dec. 20, 1936. RCMC.

97. Ibid., undated. Memoranda for 1936.

98. Ibid., undated. Memoranda for 1936.

99. Richards to Stevens, June 15, 1936. RFA, box 48, folder 398.

Chapter 6: War and the Flight to Kunming, 1937–1945

1. I. A. Richards to D. H. Stevens, Feb. 3, 1937. RFA, RG 1.1, series 601, box 48, folder 399.

2. Ibid.

3. Stevens to J. B. Grant, Feb. 23, 1937. RFA, box 48, folder 399.

4. I. A. Richards to Dorothea Richards, Feb. 27, 1937. RCMC.

5. Richards diary, Apr. 30, 1937. RCMC.

6. Ibid., May 21, 1937.

7. Ibid., May 27, 1937.

8. Ibid.

9. I. A. Richards to Dorothea Richards, Apr. 13, 1937.

10. Richards diary, May 27, 1937.

11. Richards to Stevens, June 3, 1937. RFA, box 48, folder 399.

12. "Charter of Committee on Middle School English Teaching" (attached), T. C. Woo to R. D. Jameson, June 8, 1937. RFA, box 48, folder 399.

13. Richards diary, June 23, 1937. RCMC.

14. Ibid., June 21, 1937.

15. Richards to Derick, Richards diary, June 24, 1937.

16. I. A. Richards to Dorothea Richards, undated.

17. Ibid., June 28, 1937.

18. Ibid., undated [1937].

19. Ibid., June 25, 1937.

20. Jameson to Stevens, June 30, 1937. RFA, box 48, folder 399.

21. Dorothea to Sylvia, Richards diary, June 21, 1937. RCMC.

22. See John Paul Russo *I. A. Richards: His Life and Work* (Baltimore: Johns Hopkins University Press, 1989), 420.

23. Richards diary, July 11, 1937.

24. Dorothea Richards to William Richards, transcribed under diary entry for July 11, 1937. RCMC.

25. Ibid., July 12, 1937.

26. Ibid., Richards to Victor Purcell, transcribed under diary entry for July 16, 1937.

27. Ibid., Dorothea Richards to George Richards, transcribed under diary entry for July 18, 1937.

28. Ibid., Dorothea Richards to Pat F, transcribed under diary entry for July 17, 1937.

29. Ibid., July 21, 1937.

30. Ibid., July 26, 1937.

31. Ibid., July 27, 1937.

32. Ibid., July 28, 1937.

33. Ibid., Dorothea Richards to John Pilley, undated (transcribed in back of diary volume for 1937).

34. Ibid., July 28, 1937. For a further account of Backhouse, see Hugh Trevor-Roper *Hermit of Peking: The Hidden Life of Sir Edmund Backhouse* (Harmondsworth: Penguin Books, 1978).

35. Ibid., Dorothea Richards to John Pilley (in back of diary volume for 1937).

36. Richards to Stevens, Aug. 21, 1937. RFA, box 48, folder 400.

37. Richards diary, Aug. 1, 1937. RCMC.

38. Ibid., Aug. 2, 1937.

39. Richards to Stevens, July 27, 1937. RFA, box 48, folder 400.

40. Richards diary, Aug. 4, 1937. RCMC.

41. Ibid.

42. Ibid., Aug. 2, 1937.

43. Dorothea Richards to John Pilley, undated, in back of diary volume for 1937, Richards diary. RCMC.

44. Dorothea Richards to William Richards, undated (in back of diary volume for 1937).

45. Richards to Stevens, Aug. 21, 1937. RFA, box 48, folder 400.

46. Dorothea Richards to John Pilley, undated (in back of diary volume for 1937).

47. Richards diary, Aug. 12, 1937.

48. Richards to Stevens, Aug. 21, 1937. RFA, box 48, folder 400.

49. Russo *I. A. Richards*, 421.

50. Richards to Stevens, Aug. 21, 1937. RFA, box 48, folder 400.

51. Richards diary, Sept. 10, 1937. RCMC.

52. Ibid., Sept. 4, 1937.

53. Richards to Stevens, Sept. 16, 1937. RFA, box 48, folder 400.

54. Ibid.

55. Richards to Stevens, Sept. 27, 1937. RFA, box 48, folder 400.

56. Ibid.

57. Russo *I. A. Richards*, 425.

58. Ibid.

59. Dorothea Richards to John Pilley, transcribed under diary entry for Sept. 27, 1937. RCMC.

60. Richards diary, Sept. 23, 1937.

61. Ibid.

62. Russo *I. A. Richards*, 425.

63. Victor Purcell *The Memoirs of a Malayan Official* (London: Trubner, Kegan and Paul, 1965), 155.

64. Victor Purcell *Chinese Evergreen* (London: Trubner, Kegan and Paul, 1938), 11.

65. Russo *I. A. Richards*, 429.

66. Richards diary, Sept. 23, 1937.

67. Richards to Stevens, Sept. 27, 1937. RFA, box 48, folder 400.

68. Ibid.

69. Richards diary, Sept. 22, 1937. RCMC.

70. Ibid., Dorothea Richards to John Pilley, Sept. 27, 1937 (transcribed in back of diary volume for 1937).

71. Ibid., Sept. 23, 1937.

72. Russo *I. A. Richards*, 423.

73. Richards to Stevens, Sept. 27, 1937. RFA, box 48, folder 400.

74. Richards diary, Sept. 25, 1937. RCMC.

75. Dorothea Richards to John Pilley, Sept. 27, 1937 (in back of diary volume for 1937).

76. Yunnan-fu was later named Kunming. I follow Richards's practice of using the former term until the Institute officially moved to the capital in 1938.

77. Richards to Stevens, Sept. 27, 1937. RFA, box 48, folder 400.

78. Purcell *Chinese Evergreen*, 76.

79. Dorothea Richards to John Pilley, Nov. 11, 1937 (in back of diary volume for 1937). RCMC.

80. Richards diary, Oct. 11, 1937.

81. Dorothea Richards to Lady Ellerman, transcribed under diary entry for Nov. 1, 1937. RCMC.

82. Richards to David, Jan. 15, 1938 (in back of diary volume for 1937).

83. Winter to Stevens, Oct. 11, 1937. RFA, box 48, folder 400.

84. Jameson to Stevens, Nov. 12, 1937. RFA, box 48, folder 400.

85. Jameson to Stevens, Dec. 3, 1937. RFA, box 48, folder 400.

86. Richards diary, Dec. 23, 1937. RCMC.

87. Richards diary, Jan. 4, 1938 (in back of diary volume for 1937).

88. Dorothea Richards to John Pilley, Jan. 9, 1938 (in back of diary volume for 1937).

89. Ibid.

90. Dorothea Richards to John Pilley, Jan. 13, 1938 (in back of diary volume for 1937).

91. Stevens to Selksar Gunn, Feb. 3, 1938. RFA, box 48, folder 401.

92. Dorothea Richards to John Pilley, Jan. 13, 1938 (in back of diary volume for 1937).

93. I. A. Richards to Dorothea Richards, Feb. 5, 1938.

94. Ibid., Feb. 2, 1938.

95. Richards to Stevens, Feb. 14, 1938. RFA, box 48, folder 401.

96. I. A. Richards to Dorothea Richards, Feb. 9, 1938. RCMC.

97. Ibid., Mar. 8, 1938.

98. Ibid.

99. Russo *I. A. Richards*, 429.

100. I. A. Richards to Dorothea Richards, Feb. 19, 1938. RCMC.

101. Ibid., Feb. 9, 1938.

102. Ibid., Mar. 8, 1938.

103. Ibid., Mar. 16, 1938.

104. Ibid., (n.d.) 1938.

105. See Chapter 2 above.

106. W. H. Auden and Louis MacNeice, "Last Will and Testament," in *Letters from Iceland* (1937; Random House, 1969), 234. Also cited in Russo *I. A. Richards*, footnote 106, 774.

107. I. A. Richards to Dorothea Richards, Mar. 20, 1938. RCMC.

108. Ibid., Apr. 30, 1938. RCMC.

109. Ibid., (n.d.) 1938.

110. Ibid., Feb. 24, 1938.

111. Jameson to Stevens, Mar. 22, 1938. RFA, box 48, folder 401.

112. Ibid., Apr. 17, 1938.

113. Quoted from "Orthological Institute China," 7. RFA, box 48, folder 400.

114. Kung Tae-Chih to Richards, May 19, 1939. Quoted from "Rockefeller Foundation Report, May 19, 1939." RFA, box 48, folder 403.

115. I. A. Richards to Dorothea Richards, Apr. 9, 1938. RCMC.

116. Ibid., May 13, 1938.

117. Ibid., June 16, 1938.

118. Ibid., Dorothea Richards to I. A. Richards, June 9, 1938.

119. Arthur Pollard-Urquhart to Stevens, Sept. 7, 1938. RFA, box 48, folder 402.

120. Pollard-Urquhart "General Report on the Province of Yunnan: the Education and Possibilities of the Future," Apr. 4, 1939. RFA box 48, folder 403.

121. Ibid.

122. Robert Winter to Stevens, Oct. 13, 1938. RFA, box 48, folder 402.

123. Pollard-Urquhart to Stevens, Nov. 1, 1938. RFA, box 48, folder 402.

124. Ibid., Oct. 3, 1938.

125. Ibid., Nov. 1, 1938.

126. Excerpt from diary of J. B. Grant, sent to WAS (?), Nov. 7, 1938. RFA, box 48, folder 402.

127. Winter to Stevens, Dec. 17, 1938. RFA, box 48, folder 402.

128. Pollard-Urquhart to Stevens, Feb. 1, 1939. RFA, box 48, folder 403.

129. Pollard-Urquhart "General Report on the Province of Yunnan," Apr. 4, 1939. RFA, box 48, folder 403.

130. "Rockefeller Foundation Report," May 18, 1939. RFA, box 48, folder 403.

131. Cited in "Rockefeller Foundation Report," May 19, 1939. RFA, box 48, folder 403.

132. Pollard-Urquhart "General Report on the Province of Yunnan," Apr. 4, 1939. RFA, box 48, folder 403.

133. Richards to Stevens, Oct. 23, 1938. RFA, box 48, folder 402.

134. Pollard-Urquhart to Stevens, Feb. 9, 1940. RFA, box 48, folder 404.

135. Ibid.

136. Pollard-Urquhart to Stevens, Aug. 15, 1939. RFA, box 48, folder 403.

137. Richards to Stevens, Mar. 23, 1939. RFA, box 48, folder 403.

138. Pollard-Urquhart to Richards, Jan. 24, 1940. RFA, box 48, folder 404.

139. Pollard-Urquhart to Stevens, Feb. 9, 1940. RFA, box 48, folder 404.

140. Pollard-Urquhart to Stevens, June 23, 1940. RFA, box 48, folder 404.

141. Richards to Stevens, Jan. 31, 1940. RFA, box 48, folder 404.

142. Ibid.

143. Pollard-Urquhart to Stevens, Feb. 9, 1940. RFA, box 48, folder 404.

144. Rockefeller Foundation Report, Mar. 15, 1940. RFA, box 48, folder 397.

145. M. C. Balfour to Stevens, June 14, 1940. RFA, box 48, folder 404.

146. Ibid.

147. Stevens to Richards, Aug. 14, 1940. RFA, box 48, folder 404.

148. Richards to Stevens, Aug. 29, 1940. RFA, box 48. folder 404.

149. Pollard-Urquhart to Stevens, June 23, 1940. RFA, box 48, folder 404.

150. Balfour to Stevens, Sept. 19, 1940. RFA, box 48, folder 404.

151. J. Leighton Stuart to M. C. Balfour, Oct. 14, 1940. RFA, box 48, folder 404.

152. Pollard-Urquhart to Stevens, Oct. 4, 1940. RFA, box 48, folder 404.

153. Ibid.

154. Ibid.

155. Ibid.

156. Richards to Stevens, Oct. 24, 1940. RFA, box 48, folder 404.

157. Richards diary, Oct. 31, 1940. RCMC.

158. Shui Tien-tun to Balfour, Nov. 2, 1940. RFA, box 48, 404.

159. Balfour to Stevens, Dec. 17, 1940. RFA, box 48, folder 404.

160. Richards to Stevens, Dec. 13, 1940. RFA, box 48, folder 404.

161. Winter to Balfour, Nov. 11, 1940. RFA, box 48, folder 404.

162. Excerpt from a Mar. 1941 article, "Dodging Bombs in a Chinese Graveyard." RFA, box 49, folder 406.

163. Ibid.

164. Richards to Marshall, Jan. 8, 1942. RFA, box 49, folder 406.

165. Rockefeller Foundation Report, May 15, 1942. RFA, box 48, folder 397.

166. Richards to Stevens, Sept. 11, 1942. RFA, box 49, folder 406.

167. Marian de la Motte to Secretary of London Office of the Rockefeller Foundation (attached to Hugh Smith to Miss de la Motte, Oct. 8, 1942). RFA, box 49, folder 406.

168. Winter to Stevens, Aug. 10, 1942 (attached to Marshall to Stevens, Oct. 22, 1942), RFA, box 49, folder 406.

169. Ibid.

170. Winter to Richards, Nov. 18, 1942. RFA, box 49, folder 406.

171. Ibid., Winter to Stevens, Nov. 18, 1942.

172. Winter to Richards, Dec. 25, 1942. RFA, box 49, folder 406.

173. Extract from a letter of J. K. Fairbank, Sept. 21, 1943 (attached to Winter to Richards, Apr. 13, 1943). RFA, box 49, folder 407.

174. Winter to Richards, Dec. 25, 1942. RFA, box 49, folder 406.

175. Included in Rockefeller Foundation Report, Feb. 19, 1943. RFA, box 48, folder 397.

176. Ibid.

177. Richards "Orthological Institute: The United States and Chinese Education: by I. A. Richards," Mar. 1942. RFA, box 49, folder 410.

178. Ibid.

179. Excerpt of report from Oct. 30, 1942, included in Rockefeller Foundation Report of June 30, 1943. RFA, box 48, folder 400.

180. Rockefeller Foundation Report, Apr. 6, 1943. RFA, box 48, folder 397.

181. Ibid.

182. Richards to Marshall, June 29, 1943. RFA, box 49, folder 407.

183. Winter to Fairbank, Apr. 11, 1943 (attached to Winter to Richards, Apr. 13, 1943). RFA, box 49, folder 407.

184. William Sloane of American Information Service of the American Embassy to Stevens, Nov. 21, 1943. RFA, box 49, folder 407.

185. Sloane to Stevens, Dec. 4, 1943. RFA, box 49, folder 407.

186. Ibid.

187. Ibid.

188. Ibid.

189. "Rockefeller Foundation Report," Dec. 31, 1952. RFA, box 48, folder 400.

190. Ibid.

191. Winter to Burton, Jan. 25, 1949. RFA, box 50, folder 416.

Chapter 7: Empires of the Future

1. Winston S. Churchill *His Complete Speeches, 1897–1963*, Volume VII: *1943–1949*, ed. Robert Rhodes James (New York: Chelsea House Publishers, 1994), 6824.

2. Ibid., 6825.

3. Ibid., 6826.

4. I. A. Richards to Stephen Gaselee, transcribed under diary entry for Nov. 20, 1943. RCMC.

5. Ibid., Nov. 1, 1943.

6. Ibid., Nov. 23, 1943.

7. William Empson "The Hammer's Ring" in *I. A. Richards: Essays in His Honor*, ed. Reuben Brower, Helen Vendler and John Hollander (New York: Oxford University Press, 1973), 82.

8. Quoted in John Paul Russo *I. A. Richards: His Life and Work* (Baltimore: Johns Hopkins University Press, 1989), 438.

9. Empson "The Hammer's Ring," 82.

10. Russo *I. A. Richards*, 438.

11. Dorothea Richards to William Richards, transcribed under diary entry for Nov. 9, 1943. RCMC.

12. Ibid., undated (in back of diary volume for 1950).

13. I. A. Richards to Gene and Ellen (?), undated, transcribed under Cash Accounts: Apr. in diary volume for 1950.

14. I. A. Richards to Frank Salter, transcribed under diary entry for June 28, 1950.

15. I. A. Richards to D. H. Stevens, transcribed under diary entry for Sept. 17, 1939.

16. For a fuller account of Richards's various activities at Harvard during this time, see Russo *I. A. Richards*, 434–35.

17. I. A. Richards to Frank Salter, transcribed under diary entry for Dec. 5, 1941. RCMC.

18. Richards diary, Dec. 31, 1940.

19. Ibid., July 15, 1940.

20. Ibid., May 18, 1942.

21. I. A. Richards to George Sansom, transcribed under diary entry for Dec. 4, 1942.

22. Richards diary, July 16, 1946.

23. Quoted in Russo *I. A Richards*, 439.

24. See ibid., 435.

25. William Empson to I. A. Richards, July 3, 1949. RCMC.

26. Ibid.

27. I. A. Richards to Maxwell and Elizabeth Foster, transcribed under diary entry for Jan. 11, 1950.

28. Richards diary, Jan. 15, 1950.

29. Ibid., Jan. 14, 1950.

30. Dorothea Richards to William Richards, transcribed under diary entry for Feb. 2, 1950.

31. Dorothea Richards to William Richards, undated (in back of diary volume for 1950).

32. I. A. Richards to James Wood, transcribed under Memoranda in diary volume for 1950.

33. Dorothea Richards to William Richards, undated (in back of diary volume for 1950).

34. Dorothea Richards to Christine Gibson, undated (in back of diary volume for 1950).

35. Dorothea Richards to William Richards, undated (in back of diary volume for 1950).

36. Richards diary, Mar. 20, 1950.

37. Dorothea Richards to Christine Gibson, undated (in back of diary volume for 1950).

38. I. A. Richards to George Richards, undated (in back of diary volume for 1950).

39. Dorothea Richards to Janet, undated (in back of diary volume for 1950).

40. Ibid.

41. Richards diary, Mar. 8, 1950.

42. Ibid.

43. I. A. Richards to George Richards, undated (in back of diary volume for 1950).

44. Richards diary, Mar. 20, 1950.

45. I. A. Richards to George Richards, undated (in back of diary volume for 1950).

46. Richards diary, Apr. 4, 1950.

47. Ibid., Apr. 7, 1950.

48. I. A. Richards to ?, undated, transcribed under "Cash Accounts: April" in diary volume for 1950.

49. Ibid.

50. Ibid.

51. I. A. Richards to the Master of Magdalene College, transcribed under diary entry for June 30, 1950.

52. I. A. Richards to ?, undated, transcribed under "Cash Accounts: April," 1950.

53. I. A. Richards to James Roxburgh, undated, transcribed under "Cash Accounts: April," 1950.

54. Richards diary, Apr. 6, 1950.

55. I. A. Richards to ?, undated, transcribed under "Cash Accounts: April," 1950.

56. Dorothea Richards to William Richards, undated, transcribed under "Cash Accounts: July" in diary volume for 1950.

57. Dorothea Richards to William Richards, undated, transcribed under "Cash Accounts: August" in diary volume for 1950.

58. Richards diary, Apr. 20, 1950.

59. Dorothea Richards to ?, undated, transcribed under "Cash Accounts: September" in diary volume for 1950.

60. Richards diary, May 1, 1950.

61. I. A. Richards to Roxburgh, undated, transcribed in "Cash Accounts: April," 1950.

62. I. A. Richards to ?, undated, transcribed under "Cash Accounts: April," 1950.

63. I. A. Richards to Mac Alpine Woods, undated, transcribed under "Memoranda" in diary volume for 1951.

64. I. A. Richards to Gene and Ellen ?, undated, transcribed in "Cash Accounts: April," 1950.

65. I. A. Richards to Langdon, undated, transcribed under "Cash Accounts: November" in diary volume for 1950.

66. Postcard to ?, undated, transcribed under diary entry for Aug. 3, 1950.

67. I. A. Richards to Gene and Ellen ?, undated, transcribed under "Cash Accounts: April," 1950.

68. I. A. Richards to Mather, undated, transcribed under "Cash Accounts: December" in diary volume for 1950.

69. I. A. Richards to Frank Salter, transcribed under diary entry for June 28, 1950.

70. I. A. Richards to ?, transcribed under "Cash Accounts: April," 1950.

71. I. A. Richards to Christine Gibson, undated, transcribed under "Cash Accounts: August" in diary volume for 1950.

72. I. A. Richards to ?, undated, transcribed under "Cash Accounts: April," 1950.

73. I. A. Richards to Michael Redpath, transcribed under diary entry for July 2, 1950.

74. I. A. Richards to Langdon, undated, transcribed in "Cash Accounts: November," 1950.

75. Richards diary, Apr. 12, 1950.

76. Ibid., May 12, 1950.

77. Ibid.

78. RFA, RG 1.1, Box 50, Folder 415, Aug. 2–7, 1956.

79. Richards diary, June 7, 1950.

80. Ibid.

81. Ibid., June 10, 1950.

82. Ibid., May 25, 1950.

83. Dorothea Richards to William Richards, transcribed under diary entry for June 2, 1950.

84. I. A. Richards to ?, undated, transcribed under "Cash Account: November" in diary volume for 1950.

85. Dorothea Richards to John Pilley and William Richards, undated, transcribed under "Cash Accounts: September" in diary volume for 1950.

86. I. A. Richards to Hughes, transcribed under diary entry for July 5, 1950.

87. Dorothea Richards to John Pilley, transcribed under diary entry for July 14, 1950.

88. Postcard to ?, transcribed under diary entry for Aug. 3, 1950.

89. Ibid.

90. Richards diary, Sept. 5, 1950.

91. Ibid., July 29, 1950.

92. I. A. Richards to E. M. W. Tillyard, transcribed under diary entry for June 30, 1950.

93. Dorothea Richards to William Richards, transcribed under diary entry for Nov. 28, 1950.

94. I. A. Richards to Willink, transcribed under diary entry for Dec. 4, 1950.

95. I. A. Richards to the Master of Magdalene College, transcribed under diary entry for Dec. 5, 1950.

96. Richards diary, Dec. 10, 1950.

97. I. A. Richards to Shears, transcribed under diary entry for Dec. 29, 1950.

98. Richards diary, Dec. 10, 1950.

99. Ibid., Dec. 21, 1950.

100. Dorothea Richards to William Richards, transcribed under diary entry for Oct. 28, 1950.

101. I. A. Richards to P. M. S. Blackett, transcribed under diary entry for Dec. 17, 1951.

102. I. A. Richards, Notes for Speech, Dec. 12, 1950.

103. Ibid.

104. Text of speech delivered at Amherst College, Jan. 10, 1951.

105. Ibid.

106. I. A. Richards to Elizabeth and Maxwell Foster, transcribed under diary entry for Jan. 1, 1951.

107. Russo *I. A. Richards*, 467.

Chapter 8: Conclusion

1. Quoted in John Paul Russo *I. A. Richards: His Life and Work* (Baltimore: Johns Hopkins University Press, 1989), 671.

2. Richards diary, May 6, 1979. RCMC.

3. Ibid., May 19, 1979.

4. Ibid., May 29, 1979.

5. Ibid., June 16, 1979.

6. Quoted in Russo *I. A. Richards*, 672.

7. Edward Said *Orientalism* (New York: Vintage Books, 1979), 3.

8. "An Interview Conducted by B. A. Boucher and J. P. Russo" in I. A. Richards *Complementarities: Uncollected Essays*, ed. John Paul Russo (Cambridge: Harvard University Press, 1976), 268–69.

9. "Beginnings and Transitions: I. A. Richards Interviewed by Reuben Brower" in *I. A. Richards: Essays in His Honor*, ed. Reuben Brower, Helen Vendler and John Hollander (New York: Oxford University Press, 1973), 19.

10. Edward Said *Culture and Imperialism* (New York: Vintage Books, 1994), 336.

Bibliography

Primary Sources

Manuscripts

Richards Collection. Magdalene College, Cambridge University, England.
Rockefeller Foundation Archives. Rockefeller Archive Center, North Tarrytown, New York.

Printed Material

Auden, W. H., and Christopher Isherwood. *Journey to a War*. New York: Ran-
dom House, 1939.
Auden, W. H., and Louis MacNiece. "Last Will and Testament." In *Letters
from Iceland*. 1937; New York: Random House, 1969.
Barnett, Lincoln. "Basic English: A Global Language." *Life*, 18 October 1943.
Beaton, Cecil. *Chinese Diary and Album*. With an Introduction by Jane Car-
michael. Oxford: Oxford University Press, 1991.
Bell, Clive. *Art*. 1914; New York: Capricorn Books, 1958.
Bennett, Joan. "How It Strikes a Contemporary: The Impact of I. A. Richards'
Literary Criticism in Cambridge, England." In *I. A. Richards: Essays in His
Hono*r. Edited by Reuben Brower, Helen Vendler and John Hollander.
New York: Oxford University Press, 1973.
Churchill, Winston S. *His Complete Speeches, 1897–1963*: Volume VII, *1943–49*.
Edited by Robert Rhodes James. New York: Chelsea House Publishers,
1994.
Dickinson, Goldsworthy Lowes. *Appearances: Notes of Travel, East and West*.
London: J. M. Dent and Sons, 1914.
———. *The Autobiography of G. Lowes Dickinson, and Other Unpublished Writ-
ings*. Edited by Dennis Proctor. With a Foreword by Noel Annan. London:
Duckworth, 1973.
———. *An Essay on the Civilisations of India, China and Japan*. Garden City,
New York: Doubleday, Page, 1915.
———. *Letters from John Chinaman*. 1901; reprinted as *Letters from a High Chi-
nese Official*. Tucson: Omen Press, 1972.
———. *A Modern Symposium*. London: J. M. Dent and Sons, 1910.

Eliot, T. S. *Christianity and Culture: The Idea of a Christian Society and Notes Towards the Definition of Culture.* New York: Harcourt, Brace and Company, 1940.

———. "Literature, Science and Dogma." *Dial* 82, 1927.

———. *The Sacred Wood: Essays on Poetry and Criticism.* 1920; London: Methuen, 1960.

———. *The Use of Poetry and the Use of Criticism: Studies in the Relation of Criticism to Poetry in England.* 1933; London: Faber and Faber, 1980.

Empson, William. *Argufying: Essays on Literature and Culture.* Edited by John Haffenden. Iowa City: University of Iowa Press, 1987.

———. "The Hammer's Ring." In *I. A. Richards: Essays in His Honor.* Edited by Reuben Brower, Helen Vendler and John Hollander. New York: Oxford University Press, 1973.

———. *Seven Types of Ambiguity.* 1930; New York: The Noonday Press, 1955.

———. *Some Versions of Pastoral.* 1935; London: The Hogarth Press, 1986.

———. *The Structure of Complex Words.* London: Chatto and Windus, 1951.

Fairbank, John King. *Chinabound: A Fifty-Year Memoir.* New York: Harper and Row, 1982.

———. *China's Response to the West: A Documentary Survey, 1839–1923.* Coauthor Ssu-yu Teng. Cambridge, Mass.: Harvard University Press, 1954.

———. *The United States and China.* Cambridge, Mass.: Harvard University Press, 1949.

Hu Shih. *China's Own Critics: A Selection of Essays.* Coauthor Lin Yu-Tang. Commentaries by Wang Chung-wei. Westport, Conn.: Hyperion Press, 1981.

———. *The Development of the Logical Method in Ancient China.* Introduction by Hyman Kublin. 1922; New York: Paragon Book Reprint Corporation, 1963.

Isherwood, Christopher. *Lions and Shadows: An Education in the Twenties.* London: Hogarth Press, 1938.

Jameson, R. D. *A Comparison of Literatures.* London: Kegan Paul, Trench, Trubner, 1935.

Lin Yu-Tang. *My Country and My People.* London: William Heinemann, 1942.

Moore, G. E. *Principia Ethica.* 1903; Cambridge: Cambridge University Press, 1971.

Ogden, C. K. *Basic English: A General Introduction with Rules and Grammar.* London: Kegan Paul, Trench, Trubner, 1932.

———. *Basic English: International Second Language.* New York: Harcourt, Brace and World, 1968.

———. *The Basic Words: A Detailed Account of Their Uses.* London: Kegan Paul, Trench, Trubner, 1933.

———. *Bentham's Theory of Fictions.* London: Kegan Paul, Trench, Trubner, 1932.

———. *Debabelization, with a Survey of Contemporary Opinion on the Problem of a Universal Language.* London: Kegan Paul, Trench, Trubner, 1931.

———. *Opposition: A Linguistic and Psychological Analysis.* With a New Introduction by I. A. Richards. 1932; Bloomington: Indiana University Press, 1967.

———. *The System of Basic English*. New York: Harcourt, Brace and Company, 1934.

Pound, Ezra. "Debabelization and Ogden." *New English Weekly* 28, February 1935.

Purcell, Victor. *Chinese Evergreen*. London: M. Joseph Ltd., 1938.

———. *The Chinese in Southeast Asia*. London: Oxford University Press, 1951.

———. *The Memoirs of a Malaysian Official*. London: Cassell, 1965.

Richards, I. A. *Basic English and Its Uses*. New York: Norton, 1943.

———. *Basic in Teaching: East and West*. London: Kegan Paul, Trench, Trubner, 1935.

———. *Basic Rules of Reason*. London: Kegan Paul, Trench, Trubner, 1933.

———. "Beginnings and Transitions: I. A. Richards Interviewed by Reuben Brower." In *I. A. Richards: Essays in His Honor*. Edited by Reuben Brower, Helen Vendler and John Hollander. New York: Oxford University Press, 1973.

———. *Coleridge on Imagination*. 1934; Bloomington: Indiana University Press, 1960.

———. *Complementaries: Uncollected Essays*. Edited by John Paul Russo. Cambridge, Mass.: Harvard University Press, 1976.

———. *Design for Escape: World Education Through Modern* Media. New York: Harcourt, Brace and World, 1968.

———. *English Self-Taught Through Pictures*. New York: Pocket Books, 1949.

———. *The Foundations of Aesthetics*. Coauthors C. K. Odgen and James Wood. London: Allen and Unwin, 1922.

———. *Interpretation in Teaching*. New York: Harcourt, Brace, 1938.

———. "An Interview Conducted by B. A. Boucher and J. P. Russo." In *Complementaries: Uncollected Essays*. Edited by John Paul Russo. Cambridge, Mass.: Harvard University Press, 1976.

———. *Learning Basic English: A Practical Handbook for English-Speaking People*. Coauthor Christine M. Gibson. New York: Norton, 1945.

———. *The Meaning of Meaning: A Study of the Influence of Language Upon Thought and of the Science of Symbolism*. Coauthor C. K. Odgen. Introduction by Umberto Eco. 1923; San Diego, New York and London: Harcourt, Brace Jovanovich, 1989.

———. *Mencius on the Mind: Experiments in Multiple Definition*. London: Kegan Paul, Trench, Trubner, 1932.

———. *Nations and Peace*. New York: Simon and Schuster, 1947.

———. *The Philosophy of Rhetoric*. New York: Oxford University Press, 1936.

———. *Poetries: Their Media and Ends*. Edited by Trevor Eaton. The Hague: Mouton, 1974.

———. *Practical Criticism: A Study of Literary Judgement*. 1929; New York: Harcourt, Brace and Company, n.d..

———. *Principles of Literary Criticism*. 1924; New York: Harcourt, Brace and World, n.d..

———. *Science and Poetry*. London: Kegan Paul, Trench, Trubner, 1926.

———. *Selected Letters of I. A. Richards*. Edited by John Constable. Oxford: Clarendon Press, 1990.

———. *So Much Nearer: Essays Towards a World English*. New York: Harcourt, Brace and World, 1968.

———. *Speculative Instruments*. Chicago: University of Chicago Press, 1955.

Russell, Bertrand. *The Problem of China*. London: George Allen and Unwin, 1922.

———. *The Autobiography of Bertrand Russell*. Boston: Little, Brown, 1967.

Sitwell, Osbert. *Escape with Me!: An Oriental Sketchbook by Osbert Sitwell*. New York: Harrison-Hilton Books, 1940.

Tillyard, E. M. W. *The Muse Unchained: An Intimate Account of the Revolution in English Studies at Cambridge*. London: Bowes and Bowes, 1958.

Willey, Basil. *Cambridge and Other Memories, 1920–1953*. London: Chatto and Windus, 1968.

Wittgenstein, Ludwig. *Tractatus Logico-Philosophicus*. Introduction by Bertrand Russell. Translated by C. K. Ogden. London: Kegan Paul, Trench, Trubner, 1922.

Secondary Sources

Ashcroft, Bill, Gareth Griffiths, and Helen Tiffin, eds. *The Post-Colonial Studies Reader*. New York: Routledge, 1995.

Baldick, Chris. *The Social Mission of English Criticism, 1848–1932*. Oxford: Clarendon Press, 1983.

Berthoff, Anne E. "I. A. Richards and the Audit of Meaning." *New Literary History* 14, 1982.

Bhabha, Homi. *The Location of Culture*. London and New York: Routledge, 1994.

Borklund, Elmer. *Contemporary Literary Critics*. London: St. James Press, 1977.

Brower, Reuben, Helen Vendler, and John Hollander, eds. *I. A. Richards: Essays in His Honor*. New York: Oxford University Press, 1973.

Carey, Hugh. *Mansfield Forbes and His Cambridge*. Cambridge: Cambridge University Press, 1984.

Carey, John. *The Intellectuals and the Masses: Pride and Prejudice Among the Literary Intelligentsia, 1880–1939*. London: Faber and Faber, 1992.

Colley, Linda. *Britons: Forging the Nation, 1707–1837*. New Haven: Yale University Press, 1992.

Culler, Jonathan. "Odd but Optimistic," *Times Literary Supplement*, March 9–15, 1990.

Cunningham, Valentine. *British Writers of the Thirties*. New York: Oxford University Press, 1989.

Day, Gary, ed. *The British Cultural Tradition: A Re-evaluation*. London: Macmillan, 1993.

Eagleton, Terry. *Literary Criticism: An Introduction*. Oxford: Basil Blackwell, 1983.

Evans, Paul M. *John Fairbank and the American Understanding of Modern China.* New York: Basil Blackwell, 1988.

Fairbank, John King. *The Great Chinese Revolution: 1800–1985.* New York: Harper & Row, 1986.

Fairbank, John King, and Albert Feuerwerker, eds. *The Cambridge History of China,* vol. 13: *Republican China, 1912–1949,* Part 2. Cambridge: Cambridge University Press, 1986.

Florence, P. Sargant, and J. R. L. Anderson, eds. *C. K. Ogden: A Collective Memoir.* London: Elek Pemberton, 1977.

Forster, E. M. *Goldsworthy Lowes Dickinson.* London: Chatto and Windus, 1934.

Hay, Stephen. *Asian Ideas of East and West: Tagore and His Critics in Japan, China and India.* Cambridge, Mass.: Harvard University Press, 1970.

Hollingsworth, Alan M. "I. A. Richards in China and America." In *R.O.C. & U.S.A. 1911–1981: Collected Papers of an International Conference Held by the American Studies Association of the Republic of China in November 21–23, 1981.* Edited by Tung-hsun Sun and Morris Wei-sin Tien. Taipei: American Studies Association of the Republic of China, 1982.

Hotoph, W. H. N. *Language, Thought and Comprehension: A Case Study of the Writings of I. A. Richards.* London: Routledge and Kegan Paul, 1965.

Howarth, T. E. B. *Cambridge Between Two Wars.* London: Collins, 1978.

Hynes, Samuel. *The Auden Generation: Literature and Politics in England in the 1930s.* London: Bodley Head, 1976.

Israel, John. *Lianda: A Chinese University in War and Revolution.* Stanford: Stanford University Press, 1998.

———. *Student Nationalism in China, 1927–1937.* Stanford: Stanford University Press, 1966.

———. "Southwest Associated University: Preservation as an Ultimate Value," in *Nationalist China During the Sino-Japanese War, 1937–1945.* Edited by Paul K. T. Sih. Hicksville, New York: Exposition Press, 1977.

———. "Lyrical Harmonies in Spring City: Remembering Southwest Associated University: Special Issue in honor of the Fiftieth Anniversary of Southwest Associated University," *Chinese Education,* 21: 2 (Summer 1988).

Kenner, Hugh. *The Pound Era.* Berkeley: University of California Press, 1971.

LeMahieu, D. L. *A Culture for Democracy: Mass Communication and the Cultivated Mind in Britain Between the Wars.* Oxford: Clarendon Press, 1988.

Levin, Harry. *Memories of the Moderns.* New York: New Directions, 1980.

Levy, Paul. *G. E. Moore and the Cambridge Apostles.* New York: Holt, Rinehart and Winston, 1980.

Luckett, Richard, and R. Hyam. "Empson and the Engines of Love: The Governing Body Decision of 1929," *Magdalene College Magazine and Record,* n.s. 35, 1990–91.

Mason, Richard, ed. *Cambridge Minds.* Cambridge: Cambridge University Press, 1994.

McCallum, Pamela. *Literature and Method: Towards a Critique of I. A. Richards, T. S. Eliot and F. R. Leavis.* Dublin: Gill and Macmillan, 1983.

Monk, Ray. *Bertrand Russell: The Spirit of Solitude, 1872–1921*. New York: The Free Press, 1996.

———. *Ludwig Wittgenstein: The Duty of Genius*. New York: The Free Press, 1990.

Moorehead, Caroline. *Bertrand Russell: A Life*. London: Sinclair-Stevenson, 1992.

Needham, John. *The Completest Mode: I. A. Richards and the Continuity of English Criticism*. Edinburgh: Edinburgh University Press, 1982.

Pei-sung Tang. "Chinese Universities on the March," *American Scholar*, 10: 1 (1940–41).

Prakash, Gyan. *After Colonialism: Imperial Histories and Postcolonial Displacements*. Princeton: Princeton University Press, 1995.

Prakash, Gyan, Florencia E. Mallon, and Frederick Cooper. "AHR Forum," *American Historical Review*, 99: 4 (December 1994).

Pratt, Mary Louise. *Imperial Eyes: Travel Writing and Transculturation*. London and New York: Routledge, 1992.

Ross, Heidi. *China Learns English: Language Teaching and Social Change in the People's Republic*. New Haven: Yale University Press, 1993.

Rowse, A. L. *Quiller-Couch: A Portrait of 'Q'*. London: Methuen, 1988.

Russo, John Paul. *I. A. Richards: His Life and Work*. Baltimore: The Johns Hopkins University Press, 1989.

Said, Edward. *Orientalism*. New York: Vintage Books, 1979.

———. *Culture and Imperialism*. New York: Vintage Books, 1994.

Schwab, Raymond. *Oriental Renaissance: Europe's Rediscovery of India and the East, 1680–1880*. Translated by Gene Patterson-Black and Victor Reinking. 1950; New York: Columbia University Press, 1984.

Selected Subaltern Studies. Edited by Ranajit Guha and Gayatri Chakravoty Spivak. New York: Oxford University Press, 1988.

Spence, Jonathan D. *The Gates of Heavenly Peace: The Chinese and Their Revolution, 1895 to 1980*. New York: The Viking Press, 1981.

———. *The Search for Modern China*. New York: W. W. Norton and Co., 1990.

Spivak, Gayatri. *In Other Worlds: Essays in Cultural Politics*. New York: Methuen, 1987.

Stansky, Peter, and William Abrahams. *Journey to the Frontier: Two Roads to the Spanish Civil War*. Stanford: Stanford University Press, 1966.

Tang, James Tuck-Hong. *Britain's Encounter with Revolutionary China, 1949–1954*. New York: St. Martin's Press, 1992.

Thomas, John N. *The Institute of Pacific Relations: Asian Scholars and American Politics*. Seattle: University of Washington Press, 1974.

Trevor-Roper, Hugh. *Hermit of Peking: The Hidden Life of Sir Edmund Backhouse*. Harmondsworth: Penguin Books, 1978.

Tuchman, Barbara. *Stilwell and the American Experience in China, 1911–1945*. New York: Macmillan, 1971.

Watson, George. *The Literary Critics: A Study of English Descriptive Criticism*. 1962; Harmondsworth: Penguin Books, 1973.

White, Theodore H., and Annalee Jocoby. *Thunder Out of China*. New York: William Sloane Associates, 1946.
William Empson: The Critical Achievement. Edited by Christopher Norris and Nigel Mapp. New York: Cambridge University Press, 1993.
William Empson: The Man and His Work. Edited by Roma Gill. London: Routledge and Kegan Paul, 1974.
Williams, Raymond. *Culture and Society, 1780–1950*. New York: Harper and Row, 1958.

Index